Beyond the Storm

To Dee

with best wishes.

William Tilton MD.

Beyond
the Storm

Treating the powerless
and the powerful in
MOBUTU'S Congo/Zaire

William T. Close, M.D.

with

Malonga Miatudila, M.D., M.P.H.

MEADOWLARK SPRINGS PRODUCTIONS, LLC

Published by
Meadowlark Springs Productions, LLC
P.O. Box 4460
Marbleton, Wyoming 83113
www.williamtclosemd.com

**Beyond the Storm: Treating the Powerless and
the Powerful in MOBUTU'S Congo/Zaire**
By William T. Close, M.D.
with Malonga Miatudila, M.D., M.P.H.

Publisher's Cataloging-in-Publication Data
(Prepared by The Donohue Group, Inc.)

Close, William T.
  Beyond the storm : treating the powerless and the powerful in Mobutu's
Congo/Zaire / William T. Close ; with Malonga Miatudila.
    p. : ill. ; cm.
  Includes bibliographical references.
  ISBN-13: 978-0-9703371-4-6
  ISBN-10: 0-9703371-4-0
1. Close, William T. 2. Missionaries, Medical—Biography. 3. Physicians—
Congo (Democratic Republic)—Biography. 4. Congo (Democratic
Republic)—History—1960–1997. 5. Medicine—Congo (Democratic
Republic)—History—20th century. 6. Mobutu Sese Seko, 1930–1997—
Health. I. Miatudila, Malonga. II. Title.
R722.32.C56 C56 2006
610.69

Book design by Christine Nolt
Cirrus Design, Santa Barbara, California

Cover design by Peri Poloni-Gabriel, Knockout Design
www.knockoutbooks.com

Copyedited by Barbara Coster
Cross-t.i Copyediting, Santa Barbara, California

Book production coordinated by
Gail Kearns, www.topressandbeyond.com

Printed in the United States of America

This book is dedicated to
Congolese men and women
who have dared to venture beyond
"It is not my fault" and have persevered
in their care for each other.

Contents

Preface

The Democratic Republic of Congo (DRC) is endowed with so many natural resources that some have called it scandalous. The country also can boast of a young population that is malleable, enthusiastic, affable, and optimistic. From 1965 to 1997, the Congo was ruled by Mobutu Sese Seko, a man with exceptional charisma who aroused adulation in his own people and the practical friendship of leaders from around the world.

In May 1997, when he fled into exile, Mobutu was a man empty of will and passion: a man devoid of hope. His destitute country was among the ten poorest on the planet. How did Mobutu, the toast of Washington and European capitals between 1965 and the early 1970s, degenerate into a dissolute and hopeless pariah?

This book was written to explore this tragic paradox and, hopefully, to vaccinate history against repeating itself. In 1997, Laurent Kabila had just succeeded Mobutu as president of the DRC. He made a triumphant entry into the country's capital, Kinshasa, and was wildly acclaimed as a liberator by the population.

By May 21, 1997, the "liberator" had taken control of the Congo under conditions similar to those adopted by Mobutu in November 1965. The two dictatorships were legitimized and institutionalized. Everything was different, but nothing had changed. For change had occurred only in the players, not in the game or the system. Laurent Kabila had committed the classical error of dictators: he had accepted a toxic dose of power. Indeed, Decree 003 placed in his hands, as the new chief of state, all legislative, executive, and judiciary powers. Once again, new opportunists and flatterers joined the old ones and came out of the woodwork into the presidential court. These sycophants competed among themselves to reinstate a personality cult around "the chief."

Lord Acton issued epic warnings that political power is the most serious threat to liberty. "Power corrupts," he declared, "and absolute power corrupts absolutely." Dr. Close's book provides supplementary proof of the old adage.

Beyond the Storm avoids the common tendency of presenting modern dictators as devils or angels. In this work, Mobutu appears as a man, a human being with qualities and defects, more exactly, a big man in which grand qualities and fatal defects were intermingled.

Mobutu was born and raised among the poorest of the poor, yet, while the power was his, he had every opportunity to improve the lot of his people. As a young man, he expressed a high degree of patriotism. Then around 1975, his attitude and behavior began to change. The havoc caused by the virus of power became increasingly evident. Dr. Close's narrative describes some of the moral transformation that led Mobutu to a sad ending. It presents Mobutu in full as a man who lost a unique opportunity to make his country a better place.

Drawing information from a wide range of sources, the book offers a sensitive, powerful, disquieting account of Mobutu's legacies and sheds new light on the thorny paradoxes of political leaders, especially in developing countries. It pulls apart the tangled truths of national and international politics to help concerned individuals and groups draw useful lessons. This is no journey into the heart of darkness; it is a brave adventure into the human heart. Many readers will be challenged to abandon simplistic clichés, rise from moralism and platitude, and open their minds to new perspectives.

Malonga Miatudila

Chapter 1

Twilight, August 8, 1994, Kinshasa, Zaire

IN THE TWILIGHT, President Mobutu stood at the top of the marble steps with his head cocked and the broad smile I remembered so well. He hugged me when I reached him.

"*Depuis quand?*—Since when?" He answered his own question. "Eighteen years."

He led me past the French doors to the main living room, and we sat at a table with a view of the river. The setting sun painted the sky vivid hues of magenta and scarlet.

Antoine, the butler, gave me a friendly nod and poured pink champagne with ceremonial dignity. The president asked about the family, and I showed him pictures of Tine and our home in the western mountains of Wyoming. He wanted news of the children. We raised our glasses and sipped the wine.

Twilight on the Congo River.

"*Tu as parlé contre moi*—You have spoken against me."

"As in the past, I spoke out of concern for your people and your mother's command when she died."

He looked away.

I had often thought about what to say to him if we had a chance to meet once more. Violence had erupted again in Kinshasa in September 1991 and January 1993. Many claimed that Mobutu had encouraged the mutiny and rioting for his own political reasons. Among those killed in 1993 was Bernard Philippe, the French ambassador. The diplomat was shot in his embassy office, along with an aide who was the telephone operator. France expressed regrets for this "accident," and Philippe's replacement arrived a few months later. France's strange silence about the murder of its ambassador stimulated speculation. Local authorities blamed stray bullets from rampaging, unpaid soldiers, but people who had seen the cadaver knew that Philippe had been shot at close range as he stood at his office window watching the ruckus in the street below. Another version of what happened was that Mobutu's men were in the French embassy awaiting the arrival of Etienne Tshisekedi, the leader of the opposition to Mobutu. The stage had been set for a killing, not of Philippe, but of Tshisekedi. Apparently Tshisekedi had been called on his cell phone by U.S. Ambassador Melissa Wells, who advised him to avoid the embassy and drive straight to her office. Tshisekedi argued, but she insisted and he obeyed. When Tshisekedi failed to appear, Mobutu's men apparently suspected that the French ambassador had leaked their plans, and shot him.

Mobutu stood and stretched the stiffness out of his body. He walked over to a table, opened a metal suitcase, and dialed a number on the satellite telephone. Waiting for the call, he gazed across the abandoned lawns and flower beds and the still, dry fountains to the great river beyond. The setting sun passed behind a line of scarlet clouds and shot blood-red rays into the sky and earthward onto a strip of violent water that announced the rapids. The smell of sun-warmed mud and rotting clumps of hyacinth wafted up from the bank, and the sound of cataracts crashing around Monkey Island reached us like distant drumming wandering in on an evening breeze.

The president sighed and shifted his weight. I watched him and was struck by his obvious depression. During my twelve years with him, I had seen him angry, combative, reflective, often humorously so, but never depressed. He spoke into the phone for a few minutes and then returned.

"Madame Bobi sends you her greetings."

"How is she?"

"*Ça va*—All right," he replied.

Madame Bobi Ladawa. I had taken care of her and helped deliver one of her sons when she was his *deuxième bureau,* his mistress. After the death of Marie-Antoinette, his first wife, Mobutu had solemnly declared that he would remain a widower. But in anticipation of a papal visit to the Congo in 1980, Mobutu and Madame Bobi were married.

The silence between us stretched on.

I said, "Do you remember the times we made rounds at the hospital? I'd come early and we'd drive in my car without bodyguards." He nodded. "I remember when we flew out to the suburbs where one of our teams was vaccinating children against measles. The helicopter landed on a grass patch and everyone clapped and jumped up and down when they saw you." A smile played at the corners of his mouth. "You were happy as *le père de la nation* when you stopped your boat at a village along the river and we held a dispensary on board, especially for the new mothers. They were honored to meet you, and you were generous with them. I have pictures of that."

Depression seemed to have turned off the light in his eyes. I was nattering to a hopeless man. Small talk had never been his cup of tea, nor mine for that matter.

He said, "Kengo told me you came back to renovate the operating rooms and emergency services at the hospital."

"Yes. The people must see evidence that Kengo's government is serious about improving their condition."

"Did he tell you that I brought my hard core up to Gbado one at a time to persuade them not to oppose him?" Mobutu's home-ground palace was in the northwest corner of the country in Gbadolite.

I stressed that if Prime Minister Kengo's government did not succeed in its present reforms because of internal sabotage or the lack of external interest, the future of the country would be severely jeopardized. "Everyone I've talked to, including a few in Washington, feel that this present government is the last chance Zaire has of pulling itself out of chaos."

I suggested that he could still be remembered as a *père de la nation* if he, like President Léopold Sédar Senghor of Senegal, stepped away from the political arena. He glanced at me and said nothing. He was probably too tired to tell me, as he had so often in the past, that I knew nothing about politics.

"I remember when you and I sat with your mother, Mama Yemo, during her last moments. She kept saying to you, '*Il faut aimer ton people*—You must love your people.' You said, 'Yes, I know.' But she kept repeating—" The president stretched out his hand to stop me, and tears rolled down his cheeks.

We sat watching the river, shimmering silver in the twilight. I thought about Mama Yemo's insight and wisdom. Could she have been trying to convince her son that he must listen to the people like the authentic, traditional chiefs? Was she worried that, in the clamor and distortion of power and wealth, the ears of a leader are deaf to the strains of despair in mothers of hungry children and wives of wounded men? Did she see in him a *kapita*, a leader designated and controlled by outsiders who supported and paid him as in colonial times?

I told him about my visit to the hospital. Mama Yemo's statue was still there, and some of the personnel came to work although they had little to work with.

"One of the older midwives recognized me and took my hand between hers. She walks four hours to come to work. She still hopes that things will change for the better. We must keep hope alive in people like her."

"The people still have confidence in me," he said, without conviction.

Gently, I contradicted him. "I'm afraid they don't. They're too hungry and insecure."

After another long silence, we explored the idea of doing a book about the Cold War seen through the eyes of a client state and its chief. He invited me to come

Mobutu and his mother, Mama Yemo.

up to Gbadolite for three or four days so that we could talk and go for walks. He would drive me to villages in his jeep, and we would sit with the elders in the evening and drink palm wine as the people danced, like in the old days. He said Christmas would be a good time, because the music in the chapel was beautiful.

I told him I had seen Dr. Vannotti in Switzerland a few

months ago. "When did you have your last real checkup?"
I asked.

"About a year ago."

"A thorough physical like I used to do?"

He shrugged. "And madame is well?"

"Very well, thank you."

"You will give her my *meilleurs sentiments*."

"Of course."

Mobutu asked me to step over to the French doors. He
pointed to all the people who were waiting to see him, as
usual, on the take. *"Ils sont toujours là*—They are always
there." We walked to the edge of the terrace and embraced.
"The last four and a half years have been the worst of my
life," he said in desperation.

I was surprised by his admission; he never admitted
defeat. But I thought of the mothers who lived beside open
sewers and mounds of rotting garbage in the stinking
slums of the *cité*. They rented their bodies for a few sweat-
soaked zaires to buy food for their families, who ate once
a day if they were lucky. In the east, mothers and children
hid in the forests to escape the gang rapes and murders by
both rebels and soldiers.

At a loss for a neat reply, I said, "I hope I'll be back to
celebrate the renovation of the hospital."

A decade after my last meetings with Mobutu, I think
of him and the two women who held the keys to his
molimo, his soul: Mama Yemo and Marie-Antoinette, his
first wife.

Mama Yemo stuck to traditions. "Joseph" was a tag
given to Mobutu by some white priest at baptism. She
called her son "Zozefu," her version of Joseph, when she
was upset with him to underscore that he was acting like
a foreigner, rather than in a manner true to his African
heritage. But she called him Mobutu when she was making
a request that he could not refuse. She lived in a modest

home in Gemena, a three-hour flight north from the capital, which she avoided, cherishing her independence. Her gentle eyes and strong chin reflected wisdom and dignity.

Marie-Antoinette Mobutu was a short, shy woman but one who knew how to snap out orders. She could be monosyllabic except when surrounded by her special allies, members of her Premier Bureau Club, made up of the prime minister's wife and the wives of some generals. They were allied against the younger women picked up as *deuxièmes bureaux* by their husbands.

(L-R) Mobutu, Tshibambi of protocol, Marie-Antoinette Mobutu, unidentified protocol officer, and Dr. Bill Close.

On some visits abroad, official and unofficial, Tine was part of madame's entourage. During a formal lunch on a private visit to Reims, France's champagne capital, where two of the Mobutu children were in school, our hostess—it may have been the mayor's wife—whispered to Tine, "Is she always this rude?" Tine replied that she was shy. Madame, I'm sure, was bored by the sycophantic chitchat around the table and was focusing on a comic book she held on her lap. I got to know her a little, mainly because I took care of her husband and occasionally her children. She had her own personal doctors, some of whom I knew and some I didn't, especially a marabout from Senegal who received vast sums for his spells and potions. When one of her babies developed measles, I called a colleague in the United States and had some serum flown overnight to the capital. I rushed it out to madame and injected the child, feeling proud of modern science and transport. I pressed a cotton ball on the site of injection. Madame removed my finger, licked one of hers, and placed it over the spot. "Now it will work," she said with a knowing smile.

During part of our acquaintance, she had several yappy, nippy Yorkshire terriers. She was given a German Shepherd, who killed the little dogs. Madame had him fed to Mimi, Mobutu's pet leopard in his private zoo. Mobutu could pat Mimi and rub her ears. Others tried, but were scratched or bitten. When one of his young daughters tried the same thing, Mimi raked her razor sharp claws across the child's face. She was rushed to my clinic, where I repaired the wounds with the care of a plastic surgeon. Up until this point, Mobutu was proud that he was the only one who could approach her. The leopard was his talisman, and he wore a leopardskin hat. After his daughter was injured, Mobutu had an extra railing put up around Mimi's cage so that no one, except him, could approach her.

President Mobutu and Madame Marie-Antoinette in Switzerland.

In 1977, Marie-Antoinette wanted to move to Switzerland. Her husband refused; his addictions to money and power were well established. She must have foreseen his degradation.

Marie-Antoinette's death in a Swiss hospital in 1978 provoked prudent questions. She had apparently suggested again that her husband resign. Allegedly, in a towering rage, Mobutu had brutalized her. Some said that she was pregnant at the time. She was flown to Switzerland in a private jet, saying that some of her children were in school there and needed to see their mother. Rumors spread like poison gas that she was in Switzerland because her husband had beaten her.

Mobutu sent Nlandu Lusalakasa, his press attaché, who was one of the top journalists from the Voice of Zaire, to interview her. "It is said that you fled from Kinshasa because of a problem with your husband," announced the reporter in front of the television camera.

Marie-Antoinette answered, "*Non*. I came because I am a mother and need to take care of my children. One of them broke a bone skiing."

Few people believed the story.

Madame stayed in Switzerland for two months, then Mobutu made her come home and took her to Lubumbashi with him during the first Shaba war between the Katangese gendarmes and the national army in 1977. It was her duty to be seen with him. Her medical condition deteriorated, and she was flown back to Switzerland and died shortly thereafter. I have no privileged medical information and can only vouch that these events were reported to me years later by those I trust.

Mobutu must have been eaten alive with guilt over Marie-Antoinette. Did he, like so many men confident of their machismo, crave the support and approbation of a beloved woman? There is no doubt in my mind that he did. She had known him as a young, poor soldier in the Force Publique and had supported him at his apogee, when people filled stadiums to hear his vision for the country and his command that everyone must roll up their sleeves and work. The population had roared its approval when he attacked corruption in those heady days in the late sixties and early seventies. But Marie-Antoinette knew that those closest to her husband were the most corrupt, including the family of his mistress, headed by the arch crook, Jean-Joseph Litho. In the early 1990s, Mobutu made Dr. Victor Ilanga, a military doctor who had been my assistant, appear before the Congress of the Mouvement Populaire de la Révolution, his party. The president posed the question, "Did I kill my wife?"

Ilanga replied, *"Oh non, Patron."* He could say nothing else. Inwardly, people laughed.

Mama Yemo's last words to her son had been "You must love your people," and the death of Marie-Antoinette, whether or not brought on by his brutality, may well have exacerbated the destruction of Mobutu's self-image and ego. A man who had never doubted his personal, nearly divine, calling to lead his people to noble goals would have been devastated by the loss of esteem from the two women so closely bound to his persona. During the last years of his reign and his life, his course downhill was marked by heavy drinking and a loss of interest in Zaire and its people. He clung to illusions. "They owe me more than I owe them," he declared to the press. In the mid-nineties, those rare ministers who were granted an audience found a man who had no more projects for the country, a man who had deserted his office. He lived on his boat moored out of town next to his Chinese pagoda at Nsele or flew up north to Gbadolite with its Concorde-sized runway carved out of the forest.

Once a woman minister carrying her dossiers found him lounging in a stuffed chair nursing a glass of cognac. He offered her a drink and a chair and stated, "I am here. Whoever wants my throne will have to fight for it. I stay to defy my enemies." The minister left, convinced that her president had become *je-m'en-foutiste*—a man who didn't give a damn. Defiant in defeat, he became ineffective, the ultimate insult.

How did a man with such high hopes and ambitions for his country become an international pariah? How did I, as his doctor, come to observe his rise and fall?

Chapter 2
My Early Exposures

DURING THE SUMMER OF 1932, Miss Elizabet Compte, the Swiss head nurse at the American Hospital in Paris where my father was the managing governor, took my hand and led me to the elevator. She had brown eyes and a comforting smile, and her starched white apron rustled when she walked. My stomach was tight with anticipation as we stepped out onto the surgical floor. I was eight years old. Two doors swung open, and tall figures wearing white hats and long white gowns emerged, smiled at us, and walked down a shining corridor. I caught the whiff of ether and clean linen. Miss Compte eased the door open just enough for me to peek through. Two gowned figures were leaning over a stretcher outside one of the operating rooms. To my relief, she explained that we could not go in because we were not properly dressed.

Staff of American Hospital in Paris. Dad (center) with Miss Compte on his left, 1935.

The surgical gowns, caps, and masks were like mystical robes of high priests, and the rubber gloves suggested exploring fingers capable of delicate maneuvers. But more than anything else, the sound of starched linen and the faint smell of ether stimulated my imagination. Downstairs in my father's office I told his secretary that I would be a surgeon when I grew up, and if I wasn't smart enough to be a surgeon, I'd be a hospital administrator like my dad. She thought that was cute, but I was serious. I wanted, with all my heart, to be part of that mysterious world, to share in the prestige of being called "Doctor," and to wear the distinctive uniform of a surgeon.

From early schooling in France, my twin brother and I were boarders in an English prep school and at Harrow, an English public school. We were called "little frogs" because of our French accents. At the end of 1939, we returned to the United States on the S.S. *Washington* on what would be her last round trip from Bordeaux to pick up stranded Americans. We arrived in New York City, with our English accents, in time to be introduced to hamburgers at the World's Fair for Building the World of Tomorrow.

I graduated from St. Paul's School in Concord, New Hampshire, a year ahead of my class. I wanted the preliminaries over so I could head for Harvard and then to medical school. We had been called "limeys" until our English accents were suppressed and we became, more or less, "Amurican."

In 1943, at the age of eighteen, I left Harvard College at the end of my sophomore year. Like many of my classmates, I wanted to be part of the war effort, and I enlisted in the Army Air Corps Cadets. With my call-up two or three months away, I married Bettine Moore. We'd been secretly engaged at sixteen. The wedding was held on February 6 at the Moore home in Greenwich, Connecticut. We spent our first night at the Ritz in New York, then hopped a train to Chicago and boarded the Chief for the two-day trip to Phoenix and our honeymoon. We hadn't been able to book a compartment on the train and had to settle for two roomettes. Worried about how young we looked, I showed the porter our marriage license and told him that most of the time, we would be using only one of the singles.

Bill and Tine at sixteen.

On arrival in Phoenix, we rented a hacienda in the desert near Scottsdale. The owner, a well-known painter, had defaulted on the payments, and the bank let us have it for $11 a month. We paid for our own water and electricity. We became the caretakers of a beautiful but empty house infested with scorpions and black widow spiders. Cottontails and coveys of quail lived in the cactus garden. We bought a Model A Ford with a chrome condor on the radiator cap, and from the plush seats, fleas transferred onto our first dog, a little black-and-white puppy called Penny. We bought her from a couple who lived across the dirt road from Scottsdale's single general merchandise store.

Tine learned to cook in two wedding presents, a toaster and a waffle iron, until we bought a secondhand stove at the Swaperoo. Eggs and bacon, toast and marmalade, and B&W Baked Beans were staples. We were madly in love.

The air corps' Randolph and Thunderbird Fields were near Phoenix, and I watched Stearmans, the blue-and-yellow two-winged primary trainers, take off and land and AT-6s practice formation flying over the desert. I couldn't wait for the day I too would be an Air Corps Cadet flying like a bird in clear blue skies. Once I bounded out of our marriage bed to gawk at a plane doing acrobatics over the house. When I returned, Tine was in a tight little ball on her side of the bed.

Each day I went to the mailbox anticipating, but dreading, the letter with orders to report for duty. I had enlisted in Connecticut, my home state. Tine had attended Jokake School near Scottsdale and had many friends there, including the president of a local bank who found the honeymoon house for us. When we decided to honeymoon in Arizona, I wrote a short note to the commanding general of the First Army Corps in New England telling him that I was about to be married and requesting that he transfer me to the Texas Gulf Command. The transfer came right through. After I had been in the air corps for a while, it seemed miraculous that such a simple request, for such a simple reason, had been taken care of so promptly. At the time of my enlistment, cadets were allowed to be married, but their wives were not recognized, a social status that could only have been dreamt up by the army.

My call-up came after forty-nine days of honeymoon. On March 28, 1943, Tine's nineteenth birthday, she drove me to the station in Phoenix and I boarded a train to Texas and Sheppard Field. It was the first good-bye of our marriage. Over our sixty-three years together, we have said good-bye so often. As the train pulled out, I folded my arms over my chest and rocked a little to keep the tears from falling.

The train ride to Texas was a long, hot journey into the bleakest, flattest country I had ever seen. The passenger car with cracked plastic seats was shunted onto sidings several times and finally came to rest next to a gray wooden platform at the end of the line. I got out along with a half dozen other young men carrying suitcases. The place was deserted except for a corporal, an unpleasant-looking individual, who sat on the hood of an army truck picking his teeth. The peak of his garrison cap was pulled down over his eyes, and the back of his head and neck were crinkled and sunburned like the parched, scrubby land that stretched to the horizon. His sideburns came down to thin, tight lips, and under a pointed chin his Adam's apple stuck out from the open neck of faded fatigues. I walked up to him.

"Good afternoon," I said. "I'm an aviation cadet. I have orders to report to Sheppard Field for flight training."

He tipped his head back, looked at me for a moment through squinty eyes, and took the toothpick out of his mouth. He curled his upper lip and squirted tobacco juice through two long yellow teeth. The glob of brown spit rolled in the dust between us. After wiping his mouth on the back of his sleeve, he said with slow disgust, "Mister, you ain't even a buck-ass private. Put your fuckin' fancy suitcase and your fuckin' little ass in the back of the fuckin' truck."

Sheppard Field was an enormous Army Air Corps reception center "in the middle of fuckin' nowhere in the fuckin' Texas panhandle." Every other word was "fuckin'." After the initial shock, I realized that "fuckin'" was the ever-present adjective in army talk.

The two-story white wooden barracks assigned to incoming cadet candidates was full of earlier arrivals. I spent my first night in a barracks for those permanently assigned to the base as garbage and maintenance men. I was given a helmet liner and a baseball bat and told to sit on the stairs between the two floors in the building. My job was to prevent the men from stealing from each other. I spent the night crouched on the steps between the floors of snoring men and was terrified every time a man stumped past me on the way to the latrine. I thought of Tine, and Penny, and the cottontails and coveys of quail in the cactus garden of our honeymoon house.

After basic training, we were sent to College Station, the home of Texas A&M, for transition training. Our wives were allowed to be with us, provided they could find places to live by themselves and take care of themselves.

Finally, the day came when we left College Station on a troop train for the cadet center in San Antonio. After two days of intense mental and physical exams, we were classified as pilot, navigator, or bombardier cadets based on the results of those tests. I was selected for pilot training, and Tine moved into the back room of a house in a decrepit part of San Antonio.

At the beginning of our time in San Antonio, Tine and I were able to be together for two hours every other Saturday evening. Later I saw her more often when I became a cadet officer. There had been a competition for wing officers as each class of cadets went into serious preflight training. I won the position of wing adjutant because my voice carried across the giant parade ground farther than the voices of the other contestants.

After preflight, I was transferred to Hicks Field, near Fort Worth, for primary flight training in low-wing open cockpit PT-19s. Tine moved into a cheap room in a dingy hotel. The room had no window, and the furniture was dark brown with black plastic padding. Her father had given her a secondhand typewriter, and she tried to teach herself how to type. She drove out to the field each Saturday afternoon in our gray Nash so we could spend two hours together. Occasionally, I was able to get a pass and meet her in town for supper. Our situation was tough, but at least we were together some of the time. In a war, separation is normal and needs to be expected. Tine could have gone home to her parents in Connecticut, but like some of the other cadet wives, she chose to stay near our training bases.

In order to increase our time together, I joined the drum and bugle corps. The cadets who took on that duty got up half an hour before the rest to dress and play reveille. This gave them the right to two extra hours off each Saturday. A classmate showed me how to hold the drumsticks, and with great zeal I beat my drum for reveille and for retreat, the daily parade to lower the colors at the end of the day. A couple of weeks before the end of my time at Hicks Field, the flu hit the cadet corps. I was the only member of the drum and bugle corps on my feet for retreat. The training officer, Captain "Chickenshit" Williams, handed me a bugle.

"Sir, I don't know how to blow a bugle," I said, standing at attention.

"Mister, if you're in the drum and bugle corps, you know how to play both instruments." He turned on his heel and went to take the parade. The usual shouting of orders and marching up and down took place, then the order came, "Sound retreat." I put the bugle to my lips and, taking a deep breath, blew as hard as I could. The resulting sound was like a long Bronx cheer. The assembled cadets roared with laughter. I was restricted to the field for two weekends and kicked out of the drum and bugle corps.

Basic training near Brady "Deep in the Heart of Texas" was followed by advanced twin-engine training in Waco. Finally, graduation day arrived. Most of us had made it, although one of my classmates was killed doing a low-level loop for the benefit of his parents who had come to Texas to see him fly. We stood at attention on a hot concrete ramp while a Lone Star politician droned on and on about the glories of his state and welcomed us as new Texans now that we had graduated from the Texas Gulf Training Command. There had been a party the night before, and several graduating cadets keeled over in the heat. Finally, we marched up to the rostrum, and our wings and second lieutenant bars were pinned on by a general.

Tine and I and two other couples had rented a large apartment in town during this last phase of our training. After the ceremony, we drove back to the apartment, and while our wives were putting the finishing touches on a celebration dinner, the three of us walked around town returning the salutes of enlisted men and cadets. The novelty wore off quickly.

For the next two months, I was posted to an office job in Garden City, Kansas. Tine and I found a place to live off the base and were starting to enjoy a more relaxed and normal married life, when my orders arrived for overseas duty. I headed for the port of embarkation in New York and she drove back to Connecticut alone. The day before I was due to leave for Europe, I managed to get an overnight pass. I met Tine in New York at her aunt's apartment on the east side. We had a quiet, poignant dinner and spent the night together. In the morning, we said good-bye again. Tina, our first daughter, was conceived on that October night in 1944.

I boarded a troop ship in New York along with hundreds of other pilots and crews. The long days were filled with running poker games as the ship zigzagged across the Atlantic to avoid German submarines. We landed in Scotland, and a troop train took us to a staging area. After a week of waiting and spending the evenings in the local pubs, I climbed aboard a C-47 with a dozen other pilots and, on a cold, wet, November day, flew across the channel to France.

The plane landed on a metal strip somewhere in Normandy, and four of us jumped out to join our new outfits. Our B4 bags and other gear were thrown out to us, and the plane wheeled around and took off into the gray sky. We stood in the rain, surrounded by our bags, for twenty minutes until a jeep roared down the flight line and stopped in front of us. A captain, in helmet and raincoat, jumped out.

"Welcome to the 442nd Troop Carrier Group. My name's Flounlacker," he said, sticking out his hand. "I'm the mess officer and general scutt boy for the 306th Squadron."

"Bill Close," I replied.

"Cook," said the other pilot. We shook hands. The other two pilots introduced themselves.

"Where are we?" I asked.

"The field's called B-24, the control tower is Jampot, and over there is St. André-de-l'Eure," he said, waving in the direction of a village we could just see a mile or so away in the rain. We stuffed our bags into the back of Flounlacker's jeep and set off between rows of camouflaged twin-engine C-47s, the air corps' transport workhorses. Many of the planes had mud splattered on their bellies, but their three-blade propellers were all lined up with one blade pointing straight down to the ground. A crew was working on one of the planes; otherwise no one was in sight. We dropped off the metal strip and squished and slid along toward the village on a gelatinous track of thick mud the color of milk chocolate. We drove into St. André and turned into the grounds of a small manor house, which had become the officers' club. Flounlacker helped us carry our bags up the stoop and into the building through glazed glass front doors and shouted up the stairs, "Here are your new men."

Two officers came out from a room to the left of the entrance hall. One was tall with wisps of hair on the top of his head and the squashed nose and heavy eyebrows of a boxer. He introduced himself as Ringdahl. The other shorter, portly man had a ring of white hair around his bald head.

"Bill McMahon. Welcome to our humble club."

I saw from the wings on their jackets that they were glider pilots. We shook hands and introduced ourselves.

"We heard a rumor that two new power pilots were joining the squadron. We're getting a head start on this evening's party to celebrate your arrival." He raised his glass. "Come in and join us." He had an Ivy League accent.

"Jingleballs," said McMahon, "pour our new friends a toddy. We'll drink to their arrival and to our late lamented comrades they're here to replace." The tall one turned to a collection of bottles behind the bar and poured the drinks. Cook and I took our glasses.

"Cheers," said McMahon, ceremoniously raising his glass.

We raised ours. "Cheers." I took a swallow.

I blew out my breath and fanned my burning tongue. "Jee-sus, what is this?"

"We call it a Fat Fuck," said McMahon proudly. "It's our squadron drink. A third gin, a third vodka, and a third Calvados, courtesy of our local Normandy farmers."

After a while, Cook, who'd become "Cookie," and I were rescued from McMahon and Jingleballs by the squadron operations officer, Major D. J. Erwin. He drove us back out to the flight line and his office in the operations tent, which was next to Flounlacker's mess tent. On the way he told us a little about the 306th, ending with a warning about glider pilots.

"They're crazy," he said, as we slowed to a crawl in the mud. "Most of them are frustrated power pilots who were either too old to go to regular flying school or had some physical disability that kept them out of the cadets. Ringdahl and McMahon are both from New York. Ringdahl was in some sort of import-export business, and

McMahon was a Wall Street lawyer. They're both good glider pilots, drunk or sober. It's a rough job. They're as expendable as the gliders they fly. We lost three in the Normandy landings, and there's only a trickle of new ones coming from the States. The colonel lets them do what they want until a glider mission comes along."

D.J. told me I would be flying copilot for Lieutenant Doug Lippe.

"Doug is a damn good pilot," continued D.J., "but his nerves are shot. He crashed his plane when the glider he was towing across the channel flipped over on its back as they were coming down through an overcast. The glider cut off at the last moment and smashed into the beach. Everyone was killed. Doug just pulled up in time to belly-land in a field. He was saved from capture by the 101st Airborne."

Model of Haunted D Dog.

We walked into the mess tent and I was introduced to troop carrier coffee, which had the consistency of tar paper juice. I learned that the three squadrons that made up the 442nd Troop Carrier Group flew C-47s, twin-engine transports, the workhorses of the Air Corps. Doug's plane was called "D Dog." The squadron's call name was "Haunted." Our aircraft and crew, which included Sergeant Teeling, our crew chief, were proud to be "Haunted D Dog." Lippe volunteered us for every behind-the-lines mission.

Since his crash landing five months ago, Doug had taken to heavy drinking so he could sleep. The flight surgeon, a pediatrician before the war, refused to give him medicine for his nerves until he stopped drinking, but Doug wouldn't stop drinking until he was given medicine. It was a standoff.

Some of the officers were billeted in St. André, but most lived in tents near the flight line. D.J. assigned Cook and me to a tent and showed us where to get wood for the barrel stove we could use to heat water in our helmets for shaving in the morning. He

Doug Lippe and Bill before glider tow mission.

told us there was a bathtub in the officers' club but that it usually ran out of hot water very fast, especially when "the Immaculate Weeks," a pilot with an abnormal fear of dirt, mysophobia, locked himself in the bathroom.

That evening, Cookie and I were officially welcomed to the squadron. There was a roast suckling pig, potatoes, and large amounts of Calvados, procured from farms around St. André in exchange for cigarettes, chocolate, soap, and toothpaste. Dinner over, we gathered around the bar, and after that I don't remember much except the repetitive raucous singing of the Troop Carrier Command (TCC) anthem:

> Mother, take down your service flag.
> Your son's in the TCC.
> He's SOL, but what the hell,
> He's as happy as he can be.

The next morning, McMahon and Ringdahl shook me awake. I'd spent the night on the billiard table. After I splashed cold water on my face, they led me back into the empty bar. My head exploded with every step. The ashtrays were overflowing with cigarette butts; half-empty glasses and empty bottles of champagne were scattered over the tables and on the windowsills. Two inflated condoms decorated the antique chandelier. On the bar, bluebottle flies feasted on bits of rancid cheese, drying sausage, and crusts of bread swimming in a greasy platter. McMahon put an enamel jug of coffee and three tin mugs on the bar, and Ringdahl produced a paper bag with fresh warm croissants from the village bakery. We sat on the stools and had breakfast.

Apparently they had gathered something about my background during the festivities of the previous evening. Over breakfast, McMahon suggested that since I'd been brought up in Paris and was fluent in French, I would make a fine squadron liaison officer. When I asked what that meant, he said I would be responsible for the billeting of officers in St. André and for the entertainment and liquor supply in the club.

"You'd be the . . . ," he thought for a moment, "the Squadron Billeting, Booze, and Morale Officer. And of course we'll be glad to help you."

In spite of the pounding in my head and the queasy nausea in my gut, I was flattered to be considered for so important a job by these two men of the world: immediate acceptance into the brotherhood of bon vivants.

Just after Christmas, our squadron flew missions of resupply and evacuation of the wounded out of Liege when the Germans were shelling that air strip during the Battle of the Bulge. Our efforts had been given impetus by General McAuliffe's one-word answer, "Nuts," to von Runstedt's call for his surrender when he and his paratroopers were surrounded by five German divisions.

The weather was terrible, with all of Europe dripping and freezing in rain and snow, the ceilings almost down to the ground. We flew our wounded and the men with trench foot out over the channel to receiving fields on the English coast. The wounded were strapped onto stretchers that ran in two tiers down the sides of the aircraft. A flight nurse, only recently attached to our squadron, made the men as comfortable as she could.

Forty-four years later, I was invited to give a couple of speeches at Michigan State University in Lansing. My host was Dr. Roy Gerard, head of the department of family practice. As he walked me around the campus to meet various people, I noticed that he was limping.

"What's the matter with your leg?" I asked him.

"Oh, just a wound from the Second World War."

"Where were you?"

"It was during the Battle of the Bulge, when the Germans counterattacked. The half-track I was in took a direct hit. I was the only survivor. I was rushed to a field hospital and flown to England."

"What do you remember about your evacuation?"

"We were lined up on stretchers under tents next to a grass airstrip that ran parallel to a railroad track. I remember a couple of mining tips in the distance."

"And?"

"Three troop carrier C-47s landed and lined up near the tents. The Germans started shelling the strip, and everybody rushed around to get us out of there. My stretcher, along with others, was pushed into one of the planes, and we took off right away. I was scared out of my mind. It was my first plane ride."

"Was there a flight nurse on the plane?"

"Yeah. She strapped me in after takeoff."

"What do you remember about the flight?"

"Not much. We flew very low over water and made a wild landing."

I grabbed his shoulder. "I flew you out. Our plane was the only one with a flight nurse."

We stared at each other, speechless. That evening, he introduced me at a public meeting by telling this story.

Tine and I asked Doug Lippe to be our daughter Tina's godfather. He accepted and often came to Greenwich for visits during the late fifties. Then his visits became less frequent as he went into a long struggle with alcohol and crushing depression. In the fall of 1977, Lippe's sister called Tine to tell us that he had shot himself with his service pistol.

When our squadron moved up to Metz, I transferred to Frankfurt, and later to Berlin, where I became the staff pilot, aide, and interpreter of General Robert Harper, commanding the air division in Berlin. That job was fascinating, if dissolute. I wrote Tine that I was thinking of staying in the air corps, and received a blistering response.

I flew home for discharge in the United States after I had done my three years and accumulated the points

Bill with eight-month-old Tina in 1946.

needed to return to civilian life. Tine and I met in Tucson to be free from involvement with our families for a while. It was there that I saw Tina for the first time, a cute eight-month-old baby sucking on her crib when we first met. Soon we were back in Greenwich living in a small ivy-covered cottage on Tine's family's estate.

Chapter 3

Medical School

LIKE MANY YOUNG MEN who had been in the service, I had no job to come back to and no real training to do anything much on my own. I signed up for a course in shorthand and typing, which I thought would help in whatever came along. I worked a little on the Moore farm, cutting hay and stacking it in the barn. We had a cordwood business one fall as we cleaned up the woods next to the lake.

One day Tine and I were at her aunt's house in Greenwich for lunch. Tine's cousin, Gene Moore, and I were fixing drinks in the pantry. Gene had been a squadron commander in the Air Transport Command that flew the dangerous Hump route in the Burma-China campaign.

Columbia College of Physicians and Surgeons, New York City.

We were talking about our options. He was headed into the family manufacturing business, Manning, Maxwell, and Moore. Tine's grandfather was the Moore of MM&M.

"And what about you?" Gene asked.

"I'm not sure. Maybe a job teaching French in a private school somewhere, or a job flying with the airlines."

"How much flying time do you have?"

"Over eight hundred hours."

"Lots of guys with over three thousand hours are having a hard time getting jobs." Gene paused and glanced at me as he measured out the Scotch. "I thought you'd always wanted to be a surgeon."

I stopped putting ice cubes in the glasses for a moment and looked out the window above the sink. That was true. From an early age, when I was in English schools, I'd looked forward to tagging along with Dad in the halls and rooms of the American Hospital when we were back in Paris for the holidays.

I looked back at Gene. "Yes, I did want to be a surgeon. But after three years away from the books, I really can't go back to school. Anyway, I doubt any good school would take me. My grades at Harvard were terrible. The war came along just in time to keep me from flunking out. And what will we live on if I don't get some kind of a job?"

As we loaded the glasses onto a tray, Gene told me about the GI Bill, which he thought would probably pay for my medical training. Then he looked at me with a grin and said, "You ought to do what you've always wanted to do."

In 1945, three years in the air corps were worth one year of college credit. Many medical schools were accepting students with three years of college. So, armed with my transcript from Harvard with all the C's and my air corps papers, I marched up the steps to Cornell Medical School in New York City. The dean of admissions looked over my unimpressive credentials and laughed.

"There is no way you can get in here with these grades."

I was embarrassed. But if the door was closed to his school, I would go somewhere else and approach my next interview differently. Grades couldn't be the only thing they looked at in their applicants.

Seated in front of the dean of admissions at Columbia College of Physicians and Surgeons in uptown New York, I came right to the point. "I know my grades are lousy and that I only have three years of college credit, but I want to go to P&S, and I will do whatever has to be done to get in and will keep applying until I do get in."

Dean Severinghaus, a small white-haired gentleman, didn't laugh. He looked at my records carefully and told me that I would need to take biochemistry and physics again and pass them with at least B's. I would also need more college credits. He pointed me toward the Columbia night school, where I could make up these deficiencies. I commuted to Columbia every day, slogged through biochemistry and physics, and added French literature, music appreciation, and geology for extra credits.

Armed with my new credits, B's, and two letters of recommendation, I went to see Dr. Severinghaus again. He was a little surprised to see me back, but impressed with my perseverance. I waited and agonized for weeks, and finally the letter of acceptance arrived. At last I was on my way to becoming a surgeon.

Tine and Bill with Tina and Glennie in Greenwich, Connecticut.

The first two years at Columbia College of Physicians and Surgeons were hell. I commuted from Connecticut, where we still lived, into medical school every day, getting up at 4:30 in the morning and driving an hour each way in the secondhand Nash Tine's dad had given us when we'd first gone to Texas during cadet training. We had two daughters by this time. Tina was two and a half and Glennie was one year old. Tine had no car.

Memorizing things like the branches of the carotid artery, the Krebs cycle, and learning the new language of medicine was grueling work. I have never been one of those students who could read a page of text and store it for retrieval at will. I had to sit there and drill the words into my memory. My powers of concentration were rusty. I suppose three years of flying and boozing it up in the air corps had not sharpened my academic keenness.

Now that I was launched into medical school, the hard work and long hours took hold of me and put their stamp on our life as a family. "Girls, be quiet! Go outside if you want to make noise. Your dad is trying to sleep . . . or study . . . or think. No, he doesn't have time now to play . . . or read to you . . . or swing on the ropes in the barn." It went right along with "Drink your milk, wash your hands, and get ready for bed."

Tina remembers trying to be quiet: "But that continued for years. It's a normal part of being a doctor's kid," she now says, with the grace that comes with time and having children of her own. I guess somehow they all grew up in spite of having to be quiet when I was home. Certainly it was impossible to repress Tina's shouts, "Git up, horse," or to silence Glennie's responding whinny as she galloped down the hall as the black stallion.

When I came home in the evenings from New York, I ate quickly with Tine and the kids—if I wasn't too late; hamburger and succotash were staples. More often I got home when the kids were already in bed. After bolting down whatever was on a plate kept warm in the oven, I went into my back room to study. I had a plain table for a desk and some rough bookshelves for my growing family of medical texts and notebooks. A few jars of pickled rat embryos I had obtained from a professor in the anatomy lab, as well as the necromantic smell of formaldehyde, added scientific atmosphere to the dark space. But it was the place where I could study. Tine called it the "inner sanctum."

Each first-year medical student was issued a long, narrow, wooden box filled with bones of a human skeleton. One night, right after Halloween, I had the bones spread out on the carpet of my study trying to fix in my mind their names and their various knobs and hollows as well as their relationship to each other. Something made me look up, and at the door that was ajar, I saw Tina's little round face staring wide-eyed at the broken skeleton on the floor. Glennie was on all fours peeking between her sister's knees. I went "Booo!" and Tina, with Glennie galloping behind her, ran down the hall to the kitchen, yelling, "Bones, bones!" From then on, the mystery of the study was like a magnet to the kids. I would be trying to read and would hear whispers and giggles behind the door. Sometimes I let them come in, and they would stand with their hands behind their backs and look wide-eyed at the rats in the jars and a little three-dimensional picture I had of a pussy willow mouse looking out through grass. Tina remembers that they weren't allowed to touch anything, and, above all, that they were always being told to be quiet.

At the end of the second year at P&S, I was up on the floor where the dean's office was located and ran into Dr. Severinghaus, who was on his way to a meeting. He stopped when he saw me.

"Congratulations to you, Mr. Close," he said, with a big smile on his face.

"Thank you, sir," I replied, a little nonplused. "But what for?"

"You passed! After your first year, I had doubts you would make it. You'll do well. From now on, you'll be doing clinical work with patients. You'll like that."

"I'm still very grateful you let me into P&S," I said.

"Well, you can thank your father-in-law as well."

I laughed and we parted.

Tine's father had given me a copy of his letter of recommendation after he put it in the mail:

> To:
> Dr. Severinghaus, Dean of Admissions,
> Columbia College of Physicians and Surgeons.
> New York City, New York.
>
> Dear Sir:
> My son-in-law, William T. Close, wants to
> become a doctor.
> Personally I have no use for the profession.
> However, his determination is such that I
> imagine he will make a good one.
> > Sincerely,
> > Charles A. Moore

During my sophomore year in medical school, in 1949, our first son, Duncan, was born. He died of a lethal cardiac anomaly that went undetected until the day we were scheduled to bring him home. We were devastated, and our marriage was in trouble. Tine's grieving was lonely and exacerbated by the constant, narrow repetition of her life. I was consumed by work in New York's Roosevelt Hospital, and felt guilty because I spent so little real time with Tine and the girls. I was a hopeless coward when it came to dealing with tears and recriminations. I hid my emotions and was no comfort to Tine.

A year later, in November, our second son, Alexander—"Sandy"—was born. We had sweated out the chances of giving birth to another child with anomalies, and were greatly relieved that Sandy was a very healthy, robust ten-pound baby.

During the first few months of internship at the Roosevelt, I tried to talk to Tine briefly every evening from the pay phones across from the admitting office. I would tell her about things I was doing, and she would tell me about the children and the animals. Tina, Glennie, and Sandy were six, four, and two, and it seemed that one of them always had a runny nose or a sore throat or an ear infection. A distant cousin, a pediatrician named Freddie Close, saw the children when they were really sick.

Tine's days were filled with getting up, letting the dogs out, dressing and feeding the kids, driving the girls to school with Sandy stuffed into a kiddy seat, coming back home, taking Sandy out of the car, putting him in the playpen set up in the middle of the living room so she could feed the dogs, cats, birds, and horses, clean the house, and do the laundry. Then, stuffing Sandy back into the car, she rushed to town to grocery shop and run errands and was back at the school in time to pick up the girls and bring them home. Play with the kids, train the pony, run the dogs, and back to the cottage for baths and another round of feedings. Then she would read from *Little House on the Prairie* or stories about horses and dogs, and, later, when Sandy was older, stories about trucks and trains and finally, put the children to bed. For an hour or so she read or paid the bills or figured the taxes, then dropped off to sleep exhausted, but still on call if any of the kids was sick or had bad dreams. A mother doesn't have every other night off.

Tine's life was repetitive and implacable and made more difficult by a painful back and varicose veins. Her spine had been injured during her early teens after her horse had reared up and fallen backward on top of her in a rock quarry on her parents' estate. Her varicose veins were the result of her pregnancies. On the nights I came home, I was exhausted. I wanted to sleep; Tine wanted to talk. She was a good mother, but she missed having an adult to talk to.

During medical school, I had been home every weekend and most weekday evenings, even though I was holed up in my study. But during internship and residency, I was seldom home. Sometimes, when I had a Saturday and Sunday off, I went with the family to pony shows and helped transport and brush Brownie, the girls' Shetland pony. But mostly, when I was home, I slept. My memory of the children's early years is filled with large empty spaces, for in truth, I was an absentee father.

The days and nights of each thirty-six-hour stretch of duty at the hospital became periods of intense preoccupation with my patients and with my main objective of becoming a surgeon both in the operating room and at the bedside. My singleness of purpose earned me promotions and kudos from my professors and teachers. After a successful operation, I walked on air. I chased responsibility and coveted challenge.

At home, things were different. At first I went home regularly, every other night. Then, as I went on to become a resident, there were evenings when I was too tired to drive home and other occasions when I stayed at the hospital to catch up with charting my patients' condition and progress. And then there were times when I was driven to stick with patients I'd operated on to see them through a critical post-op period. On those nights I didn't go home.

I was elected president of the house staff and organized get-togethers for the nurses and doctors, which were tamer than the squadron evenings in France during the war but were, nevertheless, good parties.

In the summer of 1953, Jessie, our youngest daughter, was born in Greenwich. I was a first assistant resident. I went into the delivery room with Tine. She now had four children under the age of eight at home. Exhausted all the time, she became more and more depressingly bitter, not just with my infrequent visits home, but also with my lack of time for her and the children when I was home.

Looking back at those years, it is clear that duty to my patients, and duty to my community, came before duty to my family. Certainly, as things became more tense and sometimes outright unpleasant at home, it was easier and less traumatic to sacrifice that time with the family for the rather more heroic call of the hospital. I volunteered for duty on holidays, thereby submerging the uncomfortable feelings of guilt at not being at home. Action was still the best protection against feelings. My carapace protected me from remorse and inadequacy, but in its own semipermeable way, it let in the gratitude of patients and the approbation of medical colleagues.

I came home late on a rainy evening and found the trash can blocking the way into the house. The message was clear: empty it before you come in. I kicked it as hard as I could, and the garbage flew all over the flower bed. I stomped into the house. Tine was in the kitchen, standing at the stove as usual. Jessie was on her left hip, and Tine was stirring something in a pot with her free hand. Sandy was in his high chair, and Tina and Glennie were at the kitchen table doing homework. They were laughing as I barged in.

"Thanks a lot for the great welcome by the front door," I said, angrily.

"I thought you wouldn't mind emptying it," Tine said tightly.

"Well, I do mind," I said, taking off my raincoat and hanging it up behind the door.

Tine turned off the flame under the pot and came toward me carrying Jessie. The wooden spoon was still in her hand, and standing straight in my way, she waved it in front of my face.

"Listen, goddammit, you may be a little tin god in the hospital, but here you are nothing. I don't mind you working your butt off for your patients, and I do realize how hard you work. I've always supported you in that and you know it. But even when you're home, you don't give us the time of day, and now you're too high and mighty to empty the garbage. I suppose you expect me to stop cooking dinner, put on my raincoat, go out and empty the garbage, then come in and serve you a cold beer as you relax in front of the TV. Fat chance! We were all having a happy time until you came home. I may not be saving lives and doing fancy operations, but I'm doing the undramatic, unheroic job of raising our children, and if you're going to be such a shit when you come home, then for God's sake stay at the hospital and do your noble work." She spun on her heel and, whirling Jessie around, went back to the stove. I heard one of the girls start to cry. I put my raincoat back on, went out and stood in the partial shelter of the overhang. The light over the door shone into the rain, which had settled into a soaker. I was exhausted, done in, and my ego oozed out of my wet shoes and joined the water in the puddles by the gate. I stood there for a while, my mind a raw blank, staring at my car glistening in the rain.

We'd been married ten years—three of those in the air corps. Our times together had been fleeting during the year and a half when she had lived in sleazy motels and rooming houses near air corps training fields in Texas. Then we were apart during the year and a half I had been overseas, then a year of night school, followed by medical school, and now the hospital. We had four children but never had a "normal" family life. Over the past year or so, laughter had left our home, at least when I was there, and our lives had become increasingly separate.

Tine and I were thirty, Tina was nine, Glennie seven, Sandy four, and Jessie one. I have a picture of all of us standing in front of our cottage in Greenwich. Tine is holding Jess on the flat top of the white fence. Sandy is between our two big collies, the girls are astride their ponies, and I am standing in the back clutching the halter on our mare Stargrain. We look like a happy, well-balanced, suburban family, but we weren't. The tracks Tine and I traveled along had ceased to be parallel. They were clearly diverging.

Family photo in Greenwich, Connecticut, home, 1953.
(L-R) Tina, Tine, Jessie, Sandy, Bill, Glennie (Horses: Nubbins, Stargrain, Brownie; dogs: Ben and Taffy).

During our summer vacation in 1953, the year Jessie was born, we loaded the children and the collies into a Ford van, and pulling a thirty-foot trailer, we drove to Wyoming. Tine and I had fallen in love with the Rocky Mountain country in the movie *My Friend Flicka* and wanted to see it for ourselves. The Sidleys, friends of Tine's family, had a large cattle ranch called the Silver Spur set up against the mountains near Encampment, a small town located between the Medicine Bow National Forest and the Colorado border. They invited us to park our trailer at the back door and plug in.

The Sidleys introduced us to Al Baldwin, the ranch

foreman. Al and his wife, Sally, introduced us to the West. Al knew cows and horses and was a master builder of corrals and barns. He made his own chaps and belts and could fix any machine on the ranch. I went riding with Al almost every day as he worked the cattle and checked fences. The Sidleys were experimenting with crossing Angus cattle with Herefords, and each morning we rode into pastures of rich grass and huge cottonwood trees to check the calves that had been born in the spring when the snow had still been on the ground. After the gray slush of New York and the sooty air from the Con Edison plant near the hospital, Wyoming seemed like a paradise of purity. Al was a good teacher and I even learned to do a little roping.

We drove up to the Continental Divide in the pine forest of Medicine Bow country, had a picnic, and drove over the mountains to Baggs. We dropped in on an ancient white-haired doctor who had practiced there for years. He wore a loose-fitting white jacket with bulging pockets and a black waistcoat with a heavy gold chain across his belly. On top of his rolltop desk were jars of arnica root and other plants whose uses he had learned from the Indians. He told us how he'd been kidnapped by bandits and taken to their hideout to sew up one of the gang who'd been wounded in a knife fight. Just like in the Westerns, they had blindfolded him on his horse so he couldn't see where they were taking him and told him that if the patient died, they would come back into town and kill him. He was the first village doc I'd met. I admired his independence and the way he fit into the town and the rugged mountains.

Late one afternoon, Al and Sally took us to a large empty log house on the ranch where people were gathering for a barn dance. Ranch hands from the Silver Spur and people from the village arrived in their pickups and carried in stacks of sandwiches, jugs of steaming coffee, and chocolate cakes with thick icing and set them on trestle tables across one end of the room. Babies in wool blankets were put on another table while the older children helped bring in the food or chased each other around the folding chairs that lined the walls. The men had on clean western shirts with bright kerchiefs tied around their necks, and the women came in full skirts that swirled as they danced. Everyone wore their fanciest western boots, some made of crocodile or pigskin. Al and Sally introduced us all around. The people were friendly, a little formal, and didn't seem to chatter very much. When the music started, Al interpreted the calls and led us through our first steps. The dancers were serious, and as Tine and I picked up the steps and joined the other couples, we became part of the whole and felt at home.

The Sidleys were warm and generous hosts and often had us join them for supper. Tine and I loved the country and the people, and a determination grew in both of us that we would come back to the Wyoming Rockies and set up a medical practice in a place where a doctor was really needed.

Chapter 4
Enter Missionaries

AFTER THE VACATION, I concentrated on getting all the extra training I would need if I was to practice medicine on my own in the Rocky Mountains. I persuaded the ENT doctors to show me how to snare tonsils and scrape out adenoids. I spent as much time as I could reducing broken bones and dealing with deep wounds from jagged bottles mashed into faces and puncture wounds from ice picks and nails driven through clubs—the daily bread of a New York emergency room.

About a month after our western trip, two Mormon missionaries knocked on the door of the cottage. Their names were Elder Price and Elder Barton—one was tall and skinny, the other short and stout. We were about to sit down to dinner. I asked them to wait a moment and went to the kitchen to ask Tine whether she wanted to invite them for supper.

"Why not," she said. "Maybe we can find out whether it's true that Mormons wear long underwear all year round."

I invited them in. Over supper they told us about Joseph Smith, his visions, the Book of Mormon, and the trek to the Great Salt Lake. They explained that polygamy had been encouraged early on so that more of the amorphous uncommitted babies from the heavenly pool of souls would be born into the Mormon Church. Although we found it hard to accept their theology, it was interesting to meet people who believed so unconditionally in something bigger than themselves. Tine did their laundry and confirmed their choice of underwear.

A few weeks later, at Edgewood School in Greenwich, Tine met Ron Mann, a young Englishman, at a ceremony for alumni killed during the war. Tine was there representing her brother, who had gone down with a torpedoed troop ship in the Mediterranean. She liked Ron and invited him and his American fiancé to come and see us.

Ron was pleasant, had been in the service, and was now a member of a movement called Moral Re-Armament (MRA). He talked to us about the movement's four absolute standards: honesty, purity, unselfishness, and love. He made the point that if people wanted to change the world, they had to change themselves first. He told us stories of how people who had put their lives in order based on the four standards had then brought some changes into their workplaces and homes. Tine and I hadn't thought much about changing the world. We had wanted to do something for people from the time we had first met, but our horizons were limited to home and hospital.

Over the next months, we met more MRA people. We were invited to meals at their estate in Mt. Kisco, New York, called Dellwood, and heard more stories of how changed individuals had apparently catalyzed solutions to problems affecting those around them and were now spreading around the world the gospel that human nature could change. As we became more closely involved with the people in MRA, our families and friends found the whole thing embarrassing, like exposing dirty linen.

The professors at the Roosevelt were alarmed when I told them I wanted to resign before the end of the year and join a world mission with MRA. To throw away my surgical training and run off with a religious group seemed to most of my professors a great waste of time. Two of them invited me to their clubs for "father-son" talks. But as so often happens, this son had become inaccessible to any commonsense arguments to finish out the year. I had seen the light, and there was a world out there waiting to be saved from itself by men and women who had changed themselves.

MRA was a religious and self-styled ideological movement started by Frank Buchman (1878–1961), an American Lutheran minister. Buchman preached that personal change, through the application of the four absolute moral standards, would create a "force" of men and women capable of changing the world. The movement started with personal change but became a highly vocal anticommunist lobby—the Sermon on the Mount versus the Antichrist of communism.

The challenge was heady wine at the beginning. Buchman's philosophy encouraged me to be honest about my sins and immediately jump into a world arena. And yet my career in New York seemed assured: I would become the assistant of one of the senior surgeons at the Roosevelt. But the prospect of starting as junior attending surgeon in the varicose vein clinic and struggling up the long, steep ladder of the hierarchy lacked excitement. In those days, one could expect a real letdown during the transition from an overworked, responsible chief resident in surgery to the low man on the attending surgeons' totem pole waiting for the crumbs to fall from the professors' tables. I had often said to my colleagues at the Roosevelt, "I want to learn as much as I can and operate as much as I can so I can do anything anywhere." I remember distinctly that although I loved surgery, I was as burned out as a bright blue flame that eventually runs out of gas. The prospect of a "world mission" that would change people and nations impelled me to resign from my surgical residency at Roosevelt six months early and commit to MRA full time. Would it have been smarter to finish my residency and take my boards in surgery? Probably, and in fairness to MRA, some of its leaders urged me to follow that course. But "singleness of purpose" and "boundless enthusiasm," labels pinned on me by my teachers in England, joined forces with the glorious feeling of being "called," and plugged my ears to good sense.

My friend and teacher, the prescient professor of surgery Frederick Amendola, after listening to my plans, commented thoughtfully, "Bill, you are on your way to becoming an accomplished surgeon. You love your work in the operating room and with patients. Surgery is your vocation. Don't give it up."

I pointed out that I felt God's charge to carry a message of personal change to individuals and that the future would be brighter if human nature changed. Already I was toying with the jargon and the bait, like a brown trout dozing under the cut bank of a mountain stream. I wanted, with all my heart, to convince this man, for whom I had profound respect, that my convictions were genuine and right. He replied that a skilled and devoted doctor could offer release from pain and suffering and bring hope into the lives of the people he touched—recompense enough. Over coffee, he told me about patients he had cared for over the years, first as a surgeon, then as a physician, then as a friend. After a long pause, as I pondered my station in life, Dr. Amendola concluded, "It takes time to earn peoples' trust, Bill. Only then will they let you look behind the shield that guards every heart. Only with time and trust can you help them choose to be happy, productive human beings."

Dr. Amendola had brought me down to earth with his calm, realistic dedication to our profession. But I had given my word to my moral sponsors, and with the tickets bought and suitcases all but locked, I could not renege on my commitment to them. And yet, I felt wretched in front of this gentle man. I had not sought his advice, just presented him with a fait accompli. In truth, I was not keen on continuing to work in New York and live in Greenwich. I got up to leave and thanked him for his care. On the way to the subway, I was miserable and unhappy. I had to admit that my leap into MRA had been more impetuous than considered. I supposed that the commitment to a moral cause, with God involved, was, at that moment, more of an obligation than the next rung up the professional ladder.

In 1954, Tine and I were invited to Caux, MRA's sumptuous Swiss headquarters, formerly the Caux Palace, above Montreux on Lake Geneva. The day came, soon after that, when I was seated in front of a white-haired Scottish doctor who was ready to hear where in my life I had failed to live according to the four absolute moral standards. I gave him a litany of sins, including my activities as squadron morale-and-booze officer during the war.

My Scottish colleague asked no questions and seemed rather more embarrassed than shocked at my wartime behavior. However, he reassured me that the simple confession was enough to free me from the bonds of sin. He pronounced

MRA headquarters in Caux, Switzerland.

me ready to serve as a purified conduit between God and the world. Tine went through the same procedure with a white-haired woman. Thus, freed from guilt and reborn, we sacrificed our personal ambitions and even our normal sexual drives to a noble cause. We were ready and eager to take on the rebuilding of the world for our children through a change in human nature. We committed our lives to God and MRA. We also committed a sizeable sum of money.

For the next six years, I traveled around the world with MRA plays, attended conferences, and acted on stage as an Italian-speaking communist doctor or a newspaper editor with white gunk on my hair that melted and ran down my face in the heat of Rangoon. I was also the team's physician. Tine was with me some of the time and, at other times, with the children in Switzerland or the United States. When both of us were away, younger women acted as nannies for the kids. Our separation was a disaster for the children, and good-byes were heart-wrenching experiences. Once, when I left Tine and the kids in Switzerland, I became certain to the point of obsession that I would never see them again. I gave each a little hand-carved statuette of a saint that I bought before we drove to the airport. I could have cried my heart out, but didn't.

I learned later, when I took care of missionary families in Africa, that the missionary children were often confused and rebellious when they saw their parents heading out to save the souls of "natives" but had little time for their own children, who were often relegated to missionary hostels supervised by what the kids sometimes called "hostile parents."

A plan to send an MRA team to the Belgian Congo was initiated in May 1960 at a big meeting in Caux. An MRA team had attended meetings in Brussels between Congolese leaders and Belgian officials to work on a smooth transition from colony to independent nation. The Congolese grand chief of the Lulua, Kalamba, was invited to Caux, along with his secretary, Lwakabanga, who wore two hats, a bowler crowned by a black fedora. At the meeting, the chief was persuaded that MRA might be able to play a constructive role in the settlement of the bloody conflicts between the Lulua and Baluba. The chief invited an MRA team to fly immediately to the Congo with the goal of changing the current politicians into men and women committed to MRA's standards. It was no surprise that in this atmosphere of inspired enthusiasm, the money for such an enterprise was raised rapidly, the bulk of it given by my mother-in-law, Betty Moore.

During the meeting, a group was selected for a mission to the Congo six weeks before that country's independence on June 30, 1960. The team consisted of two former Mau Mau from Kenya, a former student leader from Nigeria, a white man and a black man from South Africa, and a French woman who had been a labor leader and a member of the Resistance, accompanied by a former president of her class at Vassar College, who was also an interpreter. The Colwell Brothers, a trio of western singers from California, were probably the most effective "life changers," with their songs in many dialects, including the four national languages of the Congo. The songs celebrated unity and a vision of a happy future and were just plain fun. The main weapon to be used by the team was a film called *Freedom* shot in Nigeria by one of Disney's top cameramen. It showed how corrupt politicians could change themselves and bring unity to a divided country. I was chosen to go along because I spoke French (the official language of the Congo) and carried a well-equipped black medical bag.

After the meeting, Tine and I walked slowly back to our room along the carpeted wooden hallways in the hotel. We opened the French windows that led to a balcony, stepped outside, and sat on metal chairs. Way below, the lake sparkled under the summer sky. I looked at her, but she turned away. I wanted to take her in my arms and hug her and love her, but that was contrary to MRA's ideal of "absolute purity."

Looking back now on our sixty-three years of marriage, that moment, when I surrendered my own best instincts to a code of conduct dictated by others, was the weakest, most ineffectual moment of my life.

"How long do you think you'll be gone?" Tine asked quietly.

"They said six weeks."

She dried her eyes with a soggy ball of Kleenex. "Well, six weeks isn't all that long."

Chapter 5
Bright-eyed Missionary with a Switchblade

EVEN THOUGH I had been accepted as part of a team heading for Conrad's turbulent, dangerous heart of the dark continent under God's guidance, as interpreted by MRA's leaders, a vestige of insecurity pushed me to ride the cogwheel train from Caux down to Montreux to buy some sort of unobtrusive weapon.

After my shopping, I felt like a thief sneaking back to his cell after a short visit to the outside world. Through the rear window of the train I gazed over the treetops at the serene lake sparkling below. As the train wound its way up the mountain, the round turret of Chillon's chateau and the towers of Montreux's prestigious hotels shrank in size and became neat, Swiss-clean toys. The train ratcheted around another bend and stopped at a siding in the steep forest of mountain pine and spruce. The down train ambled by and the conductors waved with dignity. We climbed through Glion and more tight curves in the trees and approached Caux under the looming parapets of MRA's headquarters. Real-world perspectives diminished in me, and MRA's new, changed world filled my life with its importance and commitment.

Nine-inch switchblade, forty-six years later.

To ride the train down to Montreux alone for an unguided mission was a sinful lack of teamwork. Glancing around to make sure nobody was watching, I eased my new nine-inch switchblade, which folded into a cow horn handle, from my pocket. I pushed the little button that snapped the blade into position but quickly closed it and slipped it back into my pocket, feeling stupid and mixed up. The train stopped at Caux and I stepped off. My gut emotion was excitement: a leap into the unknown. My head worried about the chaos and violence reported in the Belgian Congo. My heart ached at the thought of more separation from Tine and the kids, for whatever noble reason.

A glorious sense of adventure was sharpened by my first ride in a jet airliner, the 707. The powerful whine outside the window in the back of the plane added to the thrill as we took off from Brussels at dusk for the eight-hour flight to the Congo.

In the early morning of May 4, 1960, the cabin lights came on and the hostess announced that in an hour we would be landing in the capital of the Belgian Congo, Léopoldville. Coffee and a crumbly roll were served with slivers of cheese and meat. I stepped into the rear bathroom to wash up, and as I tucked my shirt into my pants, I felt the bone handle of my switchblade. They say fools walk in where angels fear to tread. I guess I had some faith in our mission, buoyed by the hope that where God guided, He provided. Yet, having read a good bit of Joseph Conrad's *Heart of Darkness*, I was filled with exhilaration spiced, as always, with the sting of fear.

I was first in line to get off the plane. When the door opened, I was surprised by the blast of hot air that smelled like tar. I walked down the steps toward a crowd of smiling, expectant faces. Some seemed official, others eager to lead us through customs. A senior Belgian official, Mr. Maton, who had been to Caux, had provided two minibuses. Most of the team climbed into the first bus and headed into town, where we had reservations at the Memling

Hotel. Maton and I stayed behind and helped negotiate our films, books, and projectors out of customs. After a suitable time for talk, Maton stuffed a roll of money into the agent's hand, and our equipment was loaded onto a cart. On the way to the minibus, a gaggle of shouting kids surrounded us and grabbed for our bags. Maton yelled at them and they ran off laughing.

The ride into town was long, hot, and dusty, with the smell of exhaust, concrete, and rotting vegetation. We drove past roadside stalls selling manioc, corn, and sun-cured fish. Approaching the outskirts of the capital, we slowed to a crawl in the traffic of trucks and buses crammed with people jouncing in rhythm to the potholes and constant blare of horns. Other passengers were festooned on the outside of the vehicles waving to the pedestrians and happy for any handhold on the chassis. Ticket takers, leaning from the open doors, banged on the side of the bus to attract passengers. We skirted riverside factories and warehouses, dodging people walking beside the road or on bicycles. The masses of Congolese striding along the roadside on their way to work seemed a sign of the people's energy. Some of the women balanced stacks of bread or manioc or enamel tubs filled with bottles of Fanta or Coke on their heads. They were dressed in colorful wraparounds and walked with an easy gait. Most had a sleeping infant wrapped snugly to their backs with another length of cloth. A few ancient women, bent at the waist, staggered along toting heavy loads of sticks and logs in slings that ran across their foreheads. The men, walking smartly to work, wore white shirts and trousers. We passed a shipyard where the clang of hammers on steel accompanied sparks from welders, and from a palm oil factory, a sweet tropical fragrance hung in the air. A swing to the left and then straight on to Boulevard Albert, where the statue of former King Albert of Belgium gazed benevolently from under his pith helmet down

Léopoldville's main avenue. The contrast between the shacks and rutted streets of the native quarters and the multistoried modern buildings along the boulevard was striking.

Léopoldville with Congo River in background.

Later I learned that the Belgians, especially those whose lives and fortunes were intimately tied to the Congo, were content and comfortable with their pacified colony. I learned quickly that most of the Congo's Belgians thought that if only *la métropole*—the mother country—would let the *colons* run the Congo, then the Ten-Year Plan, born after World War II, would continue to provide work and stability for the *indigènes* (the natives). River and rail transportation were advanced, and basic health care, including the control of major pandemics such as sleeping sickness (trypanosomiasis), were rightful bragging points for the Belgians. In 1955, during King Baudouin's first royal visit to the Congo, Governor General Pétillon presented him with millions of happy natives appreciative of Belgian's colonizing efforts. The Congo was a model of tranquility, and in the eyes of the Belgians, there was no way that Le Congo Belge should become involved in the independence movements agitating the colonies of Britain and France. At least this was the opinion in Belgium . . . until Sunday, January 4, 1959. On that day, violence exploded in Léopoldville, much to the surprise of Belgians in Brussels.

The inhabitants of Léopoldville screamed *"Dipanda, dipanda*—Independence, independence."

"What?" asked the Belgians in Europe. *"Mais c'est quoi, ça?*—What's that all about?"

In a speech that became etched in stone, King Baudouin of Belgian declared that he shared the natives' thirst for independence and that the response to the demand for independence must not be delayed or rushed, a moderate position that irritated both Belgian and Congolese extremists.

After a week in Léopoldville, arranging lodging and logistics, I joined the rest of the team in Luluabourg, a city in the middle of the country in the territory under our host, the Luluas' Grand Chief Kalamba. The early morning was cool and seemed peaceful after a skirmish between the Congolese troops and the Belgian colonials the day before. Sitting out on the porch of the hotel, I watched the arrival of a fresh dawn. Palm trees and distant hills were silhouetted against a pink and yellow sky. As the sun climbed out of the horizon, groups of young women carrying loads on their heads walked by, their bodies straight and strong. As they walked, they called out full-throated greetings, and their laughter and high-pitched voices were a relief in the streets where fear of more violence kept the Europeans close to the shadows.

In the theaters where *Freedom* was shown and some of the team spoke of a unity that would come from change, the crowds shouted with glee and clapped their hands. I saw such a crowd for the first time from the projection booth. Soldiers stood against the walls with their rifles, the police were at the doors, and during many parts of the film the crowd erupted to a point where I asked the projectionist if a riot was under way. He laughed and said, "No, they're just enjoying the cinema."

We had no idea of what we were getting into. Most Europeans predicted the normal tensions of independence but assured us that any disorder would be controlled by the Belgian-officered native military, the Force Publique.

Chapter 6
Independence Breaks Out

ON JUNE 30, 1960, the Belgian Congo was declared an independent and sovereign nation, the Democratic Republic of Congo, by King Baudouin. The evening before, a bystander had charged the open car in which the king was seated and snatched his saber. The unexpectedness of the act and the shaky control of the crowds had provoked a flurry of anxiety down Léopoldville's central Boulevard Albert.

Independence Day started with a solemn *Te Deum* in the cathedral a stone's throw from a statue and monument to King Albert. After the mass, the foreign and national dignitaries made their way to the Congolese parliament's national palace on the other side of town. I followed a crowd of guests into the hall and found myself just to the right of the podium along with other standing-room-only observers. In the distance, ceremonial cannon fire saluted the occasion and King Baudouin rose to speak.

King Baudouin and President Kasa Vubu arriving for independence ceremonies.

The tone and content of his speech were paternalistic: "The independence of the Congo is the crowning of the work conceived by the genius of King Léopold II undertaken by him with firm courage, and continued by Belgium with perseverance." He spoke of the achievement of the colonial pioneers "who deserve admiration from us and acknowledgment from you. It is your job, gentlemen, to show that we were right in trusting you."

In the plaza adjacent to the parliament, spade-bearded King Léopold II, former owner and tyrant of the Congo, sat astride his bronze horse gazing with pride and self-assurance above the crowds.

At the time, even as an amateur observer with my European upbringing and adventuresome image of *les Colonies*, I was shocked by the king's attitude. It was hard for me to imagine King Baudouin speaking with

Statue of King Léopold II.

such lofty condescension. The man I met a few years later, when Mobutu was a guest in the king's Brussels palace and the royal hunting lodge in the Ardennes, struck me as a man whose reality was matched by grace and humility. I understood that the king, whatever his personal views, was a mere mouthpiece for the particular Belgian government in power. Who, I wondered, wrote the king's speech? Was he a bureaucrat in the African section of the government determined to vindicate the eighty years of exploitation of the Congolese by Léopold II and his acolytes, or was he a Brussels-based colonial civil servant involved in his country's service to the *indigènes* but insensitive to the effects the king's self-righteousness would have on *les noirs*—the blacks? Baudouin's speech was greeted by polite clapping among the whites and an embarrassed silence from the Congolese. Joseph Kasa Vubu, the newly elected president of the Congo, responded in his high-pitched voice with bland gratitude. It was later reported that he had cut the last five paragraphs of his speech, which bordered on the sycophantic.

Patrice Lumumba, the Congo's first and only elected prime minister, was not scheduled to speak. Earlier, Thomas Kanza, a confidant and member of the new cabinet, insisted that the speech Lumumba had prepared would threaten his life, and he urged him not to read it. Lumumba ignored the advice, strode to the lectern, and grabbed the microphone. King Baudouin, turning toward President Kasa Vubu, asked, "What is going on? Lumumba is not on the program."

Kanza, officially the Congo's first Belgian university graduate and a member of Lumumba's government, reported in his book *Conflict in the Congo* that on June 30 at 8:30 A.M., Lumumba had summoned him to his private residence and handed him the typed speech he had been working on most of the night with the encouragement of Jean Van Lierde, a Belgian radical pacifist and champion of the Third World. Kanza's reaction was that Lumumba's speech would be excellent if given in a stadium filled with people, but this was not the occasion for it. The prime minister countered by telling him that he *must* speak because President Kasa Vubu had humiliated him and the Congolese people by showing his speech to the Belgians but *not* to Lumumba or anyone in his new government. Lumumba asked Kanza to soften any passages he thought too radical.

Kanza continued: "When we arrived at the parliament, I met Prime Minister Gaston Eyskens and Minister of Foreign Affairs Pierre Wigny. I said to them, 'Mr. Ministers, I think that it is in our interest to delay even for an hour the session for the proclamation of independence to give you the time to negotiate with Prime Minister Lumumba because he is determined to speak.'"

The Belgian ministers were so sure that Lumumba would not speak that they did not accept Kanza's suggestion. During King Baudouin's speech and even during Kasa Vubu's speech, Lumumba continued editing his manuscript. Kanza's eyes met those of Eyskens and Wigny, who now seemed to think that his warning might come to pass.

Lumumba launched into a passionate diatribe against the slavery, oppression, and cruelty of the Belgian colonial era.

> Our wounds are too fresh and too smarting for us who have known ironies, insults, and blows which we had to undergo morning, noon, and night because we were Negroes. We have seen our lands spoiled in the name of laws which only recognized the right of the strongest. We have known laws which differed according to whether they dealt with a black man or a white. We have known the atrocious sufferings of those who were imprisoned for their political opinions or religious beliefs and of those exiled in their own country. Their fate was worse than death itself. Who will forget the rifle fire from which so many of our brothers perished, or the jails into which were brutally thrown those who did not want to submit to a regime of injustice, oppression, and exploitation which were the means the colonialists employed to dominate us?

The audience was stunned, but crowds outside who had listened to the speeches over loudspeakers could be heard shouting and cheering their approval of Lumumba's attack. I was standing near the podium and noticed the prominent veins on Baudouin's temple and forehead as he struggled for control. Immediately after Lumumba's speech, the king and his entourage retired to a side room. He had been insulted and was ready to drive straight out to the airport and fly home. The guests moved slowly out to the terrace, and a U-shaped table was prepared for the banquet. Groups gathered, according to their station and nationality, to express their views. "The Belgians had it coming" or "Why are you surprised; we told you it wouldn't work" crowed the cynics or realists, depending on one's point of view.

I followed the crowd and noticed a tall, thin officer with heavy-rimmed glasses typing away on an Olivetti balanced on a windowsill. The officer was Mobutu. Acting as Lumumba's secretary and confidant, he had gathered reactions to the speech and passed them on to the prime minister. Now he was drafting a toast to be given by Lumumba at the banquet. What he wrote was conciliatory, but did little to ease the atmosphere. The ceremonies were delayed for an hour until the king and President Kasa Vubu came out of the room, made a quick visit to the Pioneers' Cemetery, and returned to the official luncheon for five hundred guests under open tents on the lawn overlooking the river.

Lumumba's violent reaction to Baudouin's patronizing speech and especially to Kasa Vubu's response set the stage for disaster.

At dawn on July 1, 1960, the Congo's first day of independence, all was quiet in the capital city. Some optimists thought that the Belgians' fear of a catastrophe had been exaggerated. Others were nervous. Rumors of discontent in the army camps spread as some of the Belgian military families met in stores and the markets. The soldiers had been on constant duty glued to their assignments to preserve order while their Congolese civilian brothers celebrated their new independence. The soldiers' dreams of equality and better treatment fed by fairy-tale images of greater leisure, the white man's cars and houses, and even their women, were shattered on July 4, 1960. That day, General Emile Janssens, the bantam rooster Belgian commander of the twenty-five-thousand-strong Force Publique, decided to address a group of Congolese non-commissioned officers at Camp Léopold (now Camp N'kokolo of Kinshasa). After a short introduction, he took a piece of chalk and wrote on the blackboard *"Avant Indépendance = Après Indépendance*—Before Independence = After Independence." The message seemed clear: independence was for all the Congolese except for the soldiers; for them nothing would change, including their rank. Before independence, the Belgians had failed to train a single Congolese officer; that was a terrible mistake.

On July 4, after the long holiday for the festivities, work resumed except for the state-run transportation company employees who continued their preindependence strike for better wages. Upriver, in Coquilhatville, the capital of Equateur Province, strikers became rioters and attacked the houses of the new Congolese authorities. The Force Publique fired on the crowd, killing sixteen. In Léopoldville, downriver in Thysville, and in many other towns, the troops repeated their demands that the army cadres be Africanized and that General Janssens be kicked out. That evening, Lumumba announced to Janssens that he, Lumumba, as minister of defense as well as prime minister, would launch a general promotion of the troops in the morning. Janssens objected. In Thysville, the troops had plundered the armory, and the white officers and their families huddled in their houses with thirty "reliable" Congolese troops. Léopoldville and Thysville were under the control of mutineers.

On July 6, Lumumba and Janssens were shouted out of Camp Léopold by troops disgusted with Lumumba's announcement that the officer corps would remain

Belgian. Confusion and fear increased. Belgian troops, including a company of commandos stashed away in the city, remained inactive. Congolese civilians feared their own Force Publique soldiers. The army feared repercussions from the whites, and the whites feared the black troops. Belgian Prime Minister Eyskens considered the events normal, insignificant convulsions in a young country. But he was in Brussels.

In an attempt to appease the mutineers, Lumumba fired Janssens, who sought refuge in the Belgian embassy and, disguised as a corporal, fled across the river to Brazzaville, the capital of the former French Congo, escorted by Belgian troops. He flew to Brussels a few days later and railed against Belgian politicians.

Madame Andrée Blouin, half French and half Central African Republican, led violent propaganda broadcasts on the national radio in the name of Lumumba and his second in command, Antoine Gizenga. Her broadcasts were chilling, high-pitched, and imperative, ordering the population to set up roadblocks to intercept whites fleeing with the country's gold. Insults and threats hurled at the Belgians fanned the army's mutiny, and fear became panic among the whites. Justin Bomboko, newly appointed minister of foreign affairs, and Joseph Mobutu worked overtime to placate the Belgians and to deal with the mutineers, but they only represented two voices against a howling mob of terrified expatriates.

The president of the Cercle Hippique, Pepo Eskenazi, was called to the riding club, because soldiers who had looted private homes and raped several European women were staggering around obviously drunk, with helmets askew, dragging their guns and scaring the staff. Pepo heard the leader of the group speak Swahili. To the soldier's surprise, Pepo said in Swahili that he was a "brother" from Katanga and had spent many years there. He discovered that the man was a Muluba and spoke to him in Kiluba, asking him what he was doing so far from his village. The soldier replied that "God" would soon help him return to his own region where he would not feel like a wandering sheep with no officer in command. He knew that the behavior of the mutineers would provoke a violent backlash from the whites, and he was scared. Pepo talked the mutineers out of harming the club or its seventy horses. The next day, helmets, weapons, and parts of uniforms were found strewn all over the club's property, abandoned by troops wanting out of the military.

During the nights of July 7 and 8, victims of violence and rape arrived in the city, and more panic spread among the whites and the Congolese troops. A Russian plane landed at the airport, and a jeep filled with Congolese military police careened around the army base blaring over a loudspeaker, "The Russians are here." Some of the mutineers climbed into trucks and headed for the airport. Others rampaged through town searching European houses for guns.

My MRA colleagues and I, now back in Léopoldville, kept indoors in our apartment listening to the radio, hoping for hints of good news or at least bad news that was less troubling. We had been in the country for six weeks basking in feelings of "good work" until all hell broke loose. I was frightened because the whole situation was out of control and anything could happen. If the screaming radio toned down its pitch, a little relief would slip in to temper our fear. It was one of those situations in which an emotional roller coaster was slowed even by fantasy hopes. The psychological armor of competent leadership and contingency plans was missing. It was like standing naked in a thunderstorm with no place to hide, no place to go.

A Belgian businessman living next door rushed in to announce that more families, mostly women and children, were being evacuated. Soldiers and houseboys, who had been the guarantors of security for European families, had turned against their *patrons*. Our neighbor had no intention of leaving and was critical of the Europeans, especially the doctors, who were running away. Apparently only one old surgeon remained in the fifteen-hundred-bed native hospital. That caught my attention, and I told him that first thing in the morning, I'd see if I could help. He suggested that we fill our vehicle with gasoline to be able to move fast if necessary.

I drove our secondhand Volkswagen bus a few blocks to top off the tank, just to be safe. The Flemish garage owner greeted me waving a large-bore hunting rifle. He was a short, barrel-chested man with a cigar butt protruding from an imperial mustache. His bare torso gleamed with smudged sweat above his greasy shorts.

He sneered, *"Vous foutez le camp comme les autres?*—You're bugging out like the others?"

"Pas encore—Not yet," I replied.

He filled the tank with one hand and waved his gun with the other. "Those *macaques*—monkeys—won't get my station. I'll kill them before they kill me." We heard shouting in the distance, and he pointed downtown with his gun. "A bunch of *idiots* from Thysville demanding protection from the Belgian embassy. The *foutu* embassy is as empty as their heads."

I paid him and drove toward the noise. I was scared, but anxious to see for myself what was going on. In the Place Braconnier, a noisy, frightened mob of Europeans had gathered in front of the Regina Hotel and the as-yet-unoccupied new Belgian embassy. Reports of murder and rape passed from one group of refugees to the next, growing in detail and volume and feeding the panic. Wives and children of planters and provincial administrators flooded into the city on their way out of Africa. A great many of the white functionaries, technicians, and shop owners, as well as doctors and teachers, fled the country.

A truck crammed with mutineers drove by, and the shouts from the crowd turned to shrieks of terror and protest and demands for protection and evacuation. In the midst of the human storm, a Jeep with three military police and a short, chubby Congolese drove up. The civilian was Justin Bomboko, who reminded me of a well-rounded, cherubic choirboy. With impressive bravery, he stood in the Jeep and pleaded for people to return home. The disturbances would be controlled, he assured them. He was shouted down and insulted for his act of courage.

At 3:00 A.M., the ferries and barges between Léopold-ville and Brazzaville were put into service, and three thousand people, abandoning their cars and possessions on the docks, crossed over to the French Congo. More would have followed, but this route to escape was blocked by the mutineers. In the melee, some Congolese chased after their employers and officers to try and persuade them to stay. The sudden, massive exodus of whites threw Léopoldville into even greater confusion.

Chapter 7

Dawn before the Storm

THE HOWLING OF DOGS, abandoned by fleeing whites, aroused me from a light sleep. Slipping out of bed, I stepped onto the narrow balcony of our apartment. Boulevard Albert was lifeless, unnatural, ominous without the shuffle and chatter of crowds walking with a will to work and dodging cabbies riding their horns. The dogs' misery pulled at my heart. Whites who had not fled to Brazzaville cowered behind shutters, fearing more violence. A solitary night bird repeated its mournful call.

A barefoot man wielding a broom of sticks in broad rhythmic strokes swept refuse floating in turgid water along the gutter. Suddenly a jeep swerved onto the avenue and sped past. Two soldiers held a blindfolded white man, his hands tied behind his back. The jeep careened around another corner toward the military camp. Again, an eerie pall of fear surrounded me. The cité was seething, with independence now less than a week old. Distant stutters of automatic weapons and shouts echoed along the narrow streets. A rattletrap car wove uncertainly down the boulevard. It stopped and six women stepped out, lifted their long wraparound skirts, squatted and peed. They climbed back in, and with a puff of smoke, the vehicle lurched toward the center of town. The puddles left behind coalesced and trickled into the freshly swept gutter.

I got dressed and tiptoed out so as not to awaken the others in the apartment. I crossed the boulevard on a run and jogged down a side street toward the hospital known as Hôpital des Congolais. As I approached the corner, I heard a ruckus and stepped into the shadow of a doorway. Two drunken soldiers dragged a man behind them, one pulling on a leg and the other on an arm so that the miserable victim hopped behind them pleading for mercy.

At the top of the picture is the beginning of the *cité* Africaine. At the bottom is the beginning of the European city. Between these two is the no-man's-land that includes the zoo, the botanical garden, and the fifteen-hundred-bed hospital for the natives that became Mama Yemo Hospital.

I ran the two remaining blocks to the hospital. Approaching the front entrance, I heard shouts and screams and the thud of night sticks on bodies. I pushed my way through the crowd in front of the grill, shouting, "*Je suis un docteur, docteur, docteur*—I'm a doctor." A policeman in a sweat-stained gray uniform opened the grill just enough for me to squeeze through.

People with bloody rags on their heads and limbs sat passively next to a wall, waiting to be seen. Half a dozen wounded lay on stretchers lined up in front of the emergency room. A Congolese in a blood-stained smock stuck his head out of the door, people shouted and waved, and the nearest patient was wheeled in. I ran and squeezed myself in behind the stretcher and closed the door.

Four male nurses washed, debrided, and stitched the wounded in four bays furnished with simple metal operating tables and instrument stands. Everything was wet and bloody, and filthy dressings were scattered over the floor. The noise outside was muted. The place stank of bodies and the sweetish smell of fresh blood.

"*Salle d'operation?*—Where is the operating room?" I asked. One of the nurses looked up and pointed to a door. I walked into a long ward with beds along each wall. Congolese with legs and arms in casts, bandaged heads, and thick dressings covering chests or abdomens filled the twenty beds. Most of the Congolese soldiers were wearing one part or another of their olive-drab uniforms. Conversation stopped as I entered.

"*Salle d'operation?*" One of the men pointed to a door at the far end of the room. "*Merci,*" I said.

"*Sale* Flamand—Dirty Fleming," a man barked as I walked past his bed. I stopped and looked at him.

"Américain," I said, pointing at my chest. He glared back at me. In that moment, I realized that it made no difference to him. In his eyes, all whites were the same, just as the whites would say about the Africans, "They all look alike."

I walked out of the far end of the ward, along a short covered walkway, opened the screen door in the middle of a long veranda, and stepped into the operating room pavilion. Several patients on gurneys were lined up against the wall between two operating rooms. A Belgian nursing sister came out of the OR to the left.

"*Vous cherchez quelqu'un*—You are looking for someone?" she asked brusquely.

"*Oui, ma soeur. Je suis un chirugien* Américain. *Je*

voudrais vous aider, si possible—I'm an American surgeon. I'd like to help if possible."

"Where did you learn to speak French?"

"I was brought up in Paris."

"Une seconde." She strode back into the operating room.

Looking through the mosquito screens on the veranda, I could see the outside of the pavilion I had walked through. Off to the right, other low, yellow brick pavilions surrounded by covered porches were connected to a central walkway by narrow concrete walkways. The grass between the buildings was freshly cut and uncluttered. I could hear the clamor of people around the emergency room.

"Docteur?" I turned and saw a slight, thin man in a surgical gown and hat, his mask pulled down to his neck. Behind him was a Congolese similarly dressed. He peeled off his right glove and we shook hands.

"Pirquin," he said.

"Close," I replied. "Can I give you a hand?"

"Can you take X-rays?"

"No. But I can learn if you show me."

"Come with me." He pulled off his other glove and his bloody gown and tossed them to the Congolese. He led the way through the screen door onto the walkway and into the trauma ward. The wounded followed us with their eyes. Pirquin opened the door into a room off the ward that housed a simple X-ray machine and tanks of developing fluids.

"Here's a chart that gives you the settings for various X-rays. If the picture is too dark, give it more volts. If the contrast is not clear enough, give it more amps. But try and get it right the first time; we may have a hard time getting film if this chaos continues." He showed me how to develop and fix the film in the baths.

"The patients on stretchers outside the operating

rooms have fractures or wounds of their extremities. X-ray them and bring me the results. Should be easy enough for you, even the Congolese can do it."

We walked back through the sullen patients. Pirquin strode ahead with his chin out. The ward could have been empty for all the recognition he gave the men in bed. Hate and bitterness were palpable. I was embarrassed and frightened. I'd never been in such an atmosphere before. Back in surgery, the sister was waiting.

Pirquin introduced me. "This is Dr. Close. He'll take X-rays."

"Good. Your next patient is ready," declared the sister.

"See you later, Close," said the surgeon as he walked into the OR.

I turned to the sister. "What is your name?"

"I am la Mère Germaine. La Mère Marie Germaine, in charge of the operating rooms." She turned and, as if calling a dog to heel, shouted, "Samuel. Samuel, *ici!*"

A Congolese appeared from one of the rooms and approached reluctantly.

"Samuel is my assistant," announced the sister. "Samuel, this is Dr. Close, an American. He will x-ray the patients who need it."

I stuck out my hand, but he didn't take it.

"Américain?"

"Yes."

"I listen to Radio Moscow every morning."

"Oh," I said, surprised. "Well, maybe you can help me wheel these patients to the X-ray room." He pulled a stretcher to the door and pushed it out. I followed.

During the morning, Samuel and I worked together. He stood by with a long-suffering look on his face as I carefully adjusted and checked the controls on the X-ray console.

"Do you know how to do this?" I asked.

"Of course."

"Then why don't you do it? We could go faster."

"It is not my job."

"What is your job?"

"I am the operating room chief."

"I thought the sister—"

Sam snapped, "That was before independence. The new hospital director will come tomorrow to order the sister to give me the keys to the instrument and medicine cabinets. The Belgians are finished here."

"Is a Congolese surgeon going to replace Dr. Pirquin?" I asked.

"We have no Congolese surgeons. None have been trained."

After taking the X-rays, I helped Pirquin reduce and cast the fractures that hadn't needed surgery. Some patients required IV pentothal, which was administered by Samuel. We worked in silence. Only the sister barked out orders to the Congolese OR crew, whom she called "boys." It bothered me that an adult man would be called a boy. It was a leftover from colonialism: a "boy" is a generic lower-class servant—a degree below "waiter." Pirquin worked rapidly and skillfully. His thin face, deeply furrowed on either side of an aquiline nose, was set in tight-lipped severity. I guessed his age to be mid-sixties. Under bushy gray eyebrows, his red-rimmed eyes were hard behind his thick, frameless bifocals. He was exhausted, but he molded and smoothed plaster over broken limbs with care and artistry.

"Hold the foot carefully while the plaster hardens, and don't dig in with your fingers; it will make pressure points."

I felt like telling him I was good with plaster, but didn't. As I sat there waiting for the plaster to harden, I watched the others going about their duties.

Felix, Eugene, and the venerable Tata Pierre made up

the rest of the OR crew. Each of them came up to me and introduced himself, offering a hand with dignity, the left hand supporting the elbow as a sign of respect. We shook hands and they smiled. Felix and Eugene assisted in the OR, and Tata Pierre worked the antique steam sterilizer that hissed and gurgled in a corner of the instrument room. Makila, a diminutive Congolese with a shallow forehead and deep-set eyes, dragged a soggy mop around the OR. He glanced at me as he mopped the plaster off the tiled floor around the stretchers.

From time to time, another patient was wheeled in and put at the end of the line on the veranda. Sister Germaine greeted each newcomer with "Not another! When will it finish?" Grabbing the stretcher and waving the ER boy out of the door, she examined the patient and attended to what preliminary washing, dressing, and splinting were needed. She worked efficiently with her hands, but her tongue lashed out if the patient moved or complained.

"K'oningana te, zoba—Don't move, idiot!"

Most of the patients were silent, a few moaned softly. They seemed resigned to whatever fate the sister had in store for them.

The sister was a small woman, somewhere in her late thirties or early forties. It is not easy to judge age in a nun. The long skirt of her uniform, cut above the ankle, swayed as she moved. She tied her white apron snugly around her waist, giving her bust some prominence. A tight wimple framed her face and chin, and a starched headpiece, which rose up from the wimple, carried a broad veil over the top of her head and down to the back of her shoulders. Her green eyes had no smile lines at the corners. Between her eyebrows a furrow ran straight up into the cloth that hid her forehead. Her nostrils flared when she gave an order. Wisps of blond hair escaped from the wimple at her temples, and her lower lip was full and petulant. Samuel moved sullenly and made no effort to hide his hatred for this woman. Felix and the others obeyed promptly, apparently used to her gruff tone.

The shouting around the ER had died down. Pirquin and I were wrapping plaster around the leg of a man with a fractured tibia. Felix handed us rolls of plaster he dipped in a bucket of water. In the distance we heard a siren. I looked at Pirquin; he shrugged his shoulders. All of a sudden there was an explosion on the tin roof over our heads, followed by a series of lesser discharges. We dove to the floor. A green coconut rolled off the roof and landed next to the palm tree that stood at the entrance of the building. Felix laughed as Pirquin and I got up.

The sister yelled, "Felix, *tika*—Felix, shut up."

We finished the cast and were washing the plaster off our hands when two ward boys came running down the walkway pushing a gurney. A Congolese soldier, clutching a bloody towel covering his belly, was screaming in pain. As he was wheeled into the veranda, loops of intestine slithered out from under his hands.

In an instant the soldier was carried to the operating table. The sister replaced the towel with an abdominal pad, which Felix held firmly in place. Samuel strapped the patient's arm to a board and started an IV. Pirquin walked over to the sink to scrub up. He motioned to me with his head to follow suit and ordered Samuel to induce the patient with pentothal, then use gas, oxygen, and ether.

The man had been slashed across the abdomen with a machete, opening up a gash of six inches into his peritoneal cavity. The sister swabbed iodine and alcohol onto the abdominal wall, then she and I placed a drape with a hole in the center over the patient as Felix let go of the pad and stepped away from the table. As Samuel added ether to the gas and oxygen, the soldier coughed, and his intestines escaped over the drape. Pirquin and I quickly covered them with wet abdominal pads. He clamped some bleeders in the omentum and I tied them off. He carefully examined every inch of bowel. It had escaped injury. With me pulling on the sides of the wound, Pirquin pushed the intestines back into the abdomen. We washed out the peritoneal cavity with saline, dumped some penicillin and streptomycin powder into the wound, and closed with through-and-through sutures of heavy stainless steel, leaving a soft rubber drain sticking out from the side. The operation had taken less than forty minutes. In spite of the tension and fear that gripped all of us, Pirquin never lost his concentration or thoroughness. We walked out to the veranda to set the fractures still waiting to be reduced.

It was 8:00 P.M. by the time we finished. Pirquin gave me a ride back to the apartment.

"Will you be there in the morning?" he asked.

"Yes, if you want me to be."

"I do." We shook hands and he drove off. I walked back to the MRA apartment. Mark and Martha, two of my MRA colleagues, were in the living room waiting for me.

"We saved some dinner for you," said Martha. "Have a seat on the couch and I'll bring it in."

Mark asked, "Where have you been? What have you been doing?"

"I've been at the hospital, operating all day," I replied. "I guess I should have left you a note. I'm sorry if you were worried."

"We missed you. We've had meetings with some youth leaders who've started going over the four standards."

"Exciting," I remarked.

Martha set a plate of food and a glass of orange juice on the coffee table in front of me. "Were you helping the Belgian surgeon our neighbor told us about?"

"Yes. You wouldn't believe the trauma that poured in all day. We had soldiers who'd been shot, machete wounds, a kid stabbed in the chest, and lots of fractures."

"Well, I'm glad you could help out," Mark said.

"Tomorrow we have two important meetings and we need you to translate."

"You must be kidding. You want me to attend a meeting when there's so much I can do at the hospital? I told Pirquin I'd be there in the morning."

I finished the food, thanked Martha, and carried the plate to the kitchen.

Mark walked in behind me. "We need to have guidance about what you do."

"I've had guidance and I know what I have to do. Now I need to hit the sack. Good night."

I turned off the light and turned on my Zenith radio. Troops had mutinied in the port town of Matadi . . . Joseph-Désiré Mobutu had been appointed chief of staff with the rank of colonel . . . The Force Publique would now be called the Armée Nationale Congolaise . . . Mobutu, addressing the troops in Lingala, the official language of the army, announced that they should elect their officers, designate which white officers were acceptable, and restore order in the camps. Colonel Henniquiau followed in French, urging Belgian officers to stay if they were requested to do so and to leave if they were not. The three thousand Europeans in Luluabourg, in the center of the country, were not reassured. Neither was I.

Hot air, mosquitoes, and the excitement of the day kept me awake on a damp sheet and soggy pillow until the cool predawn air brought relief and, like a feather touch of comfort, let me sleep for a couple of hours.

On July 8, at 4:00 A.M., the British embassy ordered the evacuation of nonessential personnel because of the growing panic and anarchy throughout the city. At 7:00 A.M., the French embassy followed suit.

More than seventy Americans had taken refuge in the U.S. embassy, which was surrounded by mutinous troops. At one point the soldiers stormed the gate, and

Ambassador Clare Timberlake, in a show of sangfroid, limped out to them—he was suffering from an attack of phlebitis—and thanked them for coming to protect the embassy. The situation was defused.

News from beyond the hospital reached us through those who came in for treatment and in the evenings over the radio. The nurses in the OR arrived with the people's bulletins passed on through *radio trottoir*—sidewalk radio—news gleaned during their long walks to work.

The mutiny spread to Elisabethville, the capital of the mineral-rich Katanga Province, and on July 11, after Belgian troops had dealt with the mutineers, Katanga announced its independence from the rest of the Congo. Sixty percent of the national income came from the mines of Katanga. This was the beginning of the long and bloody saga involving Moïse Tshombe, president, and Godefroid Munongo, minister of interior, of the Katangese government.

On July 13, Belgian troops occupied Ndjili, Léopoldville's international airport, to ensure that Europeans could continue their flight from the country. Troops were dug in along the road into the city all the way to Boulevard Albert. Some of the Belgian women who had stayed handed out chocolates to the soldiers. Others, awaiting evacuation at the airport, spit on President Kasa Vubu and Prime Minister Lumumba, who had just landed after a trip to the interior in an effort to prevent further spread of chaos.

Our six weeks in the Congo had come and gone. I was glad that Tine and the kids were in Switzerland at Caux during this period of frightening insecurity. We communicated frequently by letter and telex. In August, I wrote to Tine explaining why we should stay longer. The MRA broadcasts and meetings were providing positive, hopeful alternatives to the violent propaganda on the radio. We needed to continue that fight, and I should continue to help out at the hospital. Tine and the kids were supportive. Often, when the mails were uncertain, I sent letters with people who were flying back to Europe. The telex machines in the post office were available only in fits and starts. I asked Tine to have the Caux telex monitored at 8:00 A.M. each day to receive and confirm our messages. Tine and I exchanged many letters about the children. Should they stay at Caux or be home in Greenwich? Their schooling was a priority. Our decision was that the kids would go to school in Caux, at least for the time being, and I would stay in the Congo, more particularly, in the OR.

Chapter 8
Trauma of Independence

I WALKED in the next morning at eight. Dr. Pirquin was already at work on a Belgian whose head and shoulders were drenched in blood from a scalp wound. The man's wife was sitting in a corner with her arm in a splint. She was crying softly, with her face buried in Sister Germaine's apron.

I stood in the doorway and heard the woman sob, "It was our own houseboy. And after all we have done for him."

"What do you expect?" snapped the sister. "They're all animals, *macaques*." She was oblivious of Eugene, who was helping Pirquin. She looked up, saw me, and said, "There are some blacks you can look at on the veranda. I told Samuel to help you in the other operating room."

Three patients sat on a bench next to the screen door. One was cradling his swollen jaw in his hands. I opened my mouth and made a biting motion. He tried to do the same thing slowly, but winced with pain. His upper and lower teeth were way out of line. I'd never fixed a broken jaw. I'd have to wait for Pirquin. The next patient had a soggy dressing over his face and mouth. I pulled his hand away gently and saw a jagged laceration of his cheek and lips. His eye was swollen shut and purple. The third patient's hands supported a strangulated hernia in his groin. He lay in his vomit. Samuel was at my side.

"We'd better do this one first," I said, pulling the hernia patient's stretcher toward the operating room next to Pirquin's room.

"I'll give him a spinal," said Samuel.

"Fine. I'll change clothes and be right back."

The operation went well. Samuel was an able assistant. The hernia contained a loop of gangrenous bowel that had been forced into the sac and had died when its blood supply was squeezed off. I cut out the dead bowel, sewed healthy ends together, and repaired the hernia.

As we were closing, three more white people were brought into Pirquin's room. From what I could make out through the screaming and sobbing, they'd been mauled by a mob near the parliament building. The operating room boys were stricken and embarrassed, and the sister issued orders in panic-pitched shouts. My adrenals switched to rapid fire. A moment later, a stretcher was pushed into my room with a Congolese soldier crying out with pain from a wound that had opened up his right thigh. The stretcher was soaked with blood. Three other soldiers in full combat gear, waving their automatic rifles, accompanied the wounded man.

"Shot by a Belgian paratrooper," growled one of the soldiers.

Samuel and one of the men lifted the hernia patient off the table, put him on a stretcher, and parked him on the veranda. The soldiers heaved the wounded man onto the table. He howled with pain. Samuel slit the tunic sleeve, pushed in a needle, and started an IV. I injected pentothal into the tubing. The patient relaxed and slept. Sam put an airway in his mouth and kept him down with oxygen and a little nitrous oxide.

The bullet had penetrated the inner part of his thigh about halfway down to the knee. The wound of exit was a gaping hole the size of my fist on the lateral aspect of his thigh. Dark venous blood oozed from shredded muscle, and jets of bright red blood spurted from arteries. I stuffed gauze pads into the wound and pulled over the same basin of soapy water I had used to rinse my gloves off during the previous operation. After washing off the skin next to the wound, I draped towels and went to work. I clamped and tied the bleeders and explored the wound with my fingers. Bone spicules had been blasted off the femur, but the bone itself was not fractured across the shaft. I tied off more bleeders, pulled out as many of the bone fragments as I could feel, cut out dead muscle, and sewed together what was left to reestablish the normal anatomy of the muscle groups as much as possible.

We had run out of catgut. I asked Samuel if he'd go next door and get some from Pirquin's room, but he refused—mumbling invectives about the sister and whites as a whole. I left the table and headed for the door to the veranda. Two soldiers blocked my way. "You can't leave. If you don't save our man, I'll kill you," said the bigger man.

Samuel told them I needed to get more sutures to close the wound. They let me pass into the next room. The sister gave me the sutures.

Pirquin asked, "Do you have a spare tank of nitrous in your room?"

"I think so."

"Could you bring it in? The sister doesn't want to go next door."

"That's ridiculous," I snapped. "For God's sake, why not?"

The sister replied tightly, *"Ils me font peur*—They scare me."

"They're scared of *you*," I said. "I'll bring the tank in when I'm through."

I went back to my patient. The soldiers glowered, their helmets almost hiding their eyes and their guns at the ready.

"Samuel, tell them to get out."

"It won't do any good. They'll go when you're through with their brother."

After cutting away the skin adjacent to the wound of entry, I ran several flat rubber tubes across the whole thigh to drain both sides.

"Samuel, I was thinking about you this morning," I said, as I placed sutures in the wound margins.

"You were? What were you thinking?" he asked, without looking up.

"I was thinking," I said slowly, "that it's probably the attitude of superiority and arrogance in us whites that's made you bitter. I'm sorry about that, but some of us are trying to put it right."

He stared at me for a long moment, then said, "This is the first time I ever heard a white man admit he could be wrong."

After wheeling the soldier into the trauma ward, we took care of the patients on the veranda. Pirquin showed me how to use an external appliance to secure the fragments of the man's broken jaw. More casualties came in. Some we lost, like the man whose head was all but severed from his neck by a machete. Some died from simple blood loss—the blood bank was empty.

Night had fallen and the curfew silenced the city. Pirquin showered, and the sister and the aides cleaned up and prepared sterile packs of instruments and drapes for the morning. I stepped outside and sat on a bench by the door. A gentle night breeze rattled the fronds of the palm tree and cooled the sweat in my OR greens. I thought of all the Saturday nights in the emergency room at the Roosevelt. The blood here was the same color; the pain and fear no different. The violence in New York sprang from turf wars among Puerto Rican and white gangs, as in *West Side Story*. Here the violence was also racial and tribal. But the hatred and bitterness we were living through seemed more emotional and less calculated than at home. Maybe our "civilization" was only a thin veneer of police control partially isolating us from the savage part of ourselves.

The screen door opened behind me and slammed shut. Samuel approached and knelt down in front of me. He started to wipe the blood and plaster off my shoes.

"Sam, you don't need to do that," I said, pulling away my feet. He stood up and walked into the OR. I followed him, but he was out the back door before I could catch up. Pirquin came out of the dressing room. *"A demain*—See you tomorrow."

"A demain," I replied.

I showered, and by the time I was through, everyone had left. I let myself out of the hospital through the back door behind the OR that the nuns used and walked briskly down the street, staying in the shadow of the wall that surrounded the hospital. As I approached the avenue where our apartment house stood, I heard a car racing toward me. I tucked myself behind a flame tree. A Jeep roared past. I ran the rest of the way, bounded up the stairs, and pounded on the door of our apartment. One of the MRA team let me in.

"Where have you been? We've been worried about you."

"At the hospital. Mark knew." I went to my room and, too tired to eat, was asleep as soon as I hit the mattress.

In the operating room, our workload increased as other surgical services in the city ceased functioning because of clashes among the personnel. As Samuel and I operated on patients together, we talked about our families and about human nature and the trouble it sometimes generated when our judgments were clouded by hatred and pride. Sam brought his wife and his son, Hi-Fi, to meet me. I introduced Sam and his family to some of my MRA colleagues. But in spite of the fact that Sam and I were working well together, the hostility between him and la Mère Germaine continued. She snapped orders at him, which he either pretended not to hear or obeyed in

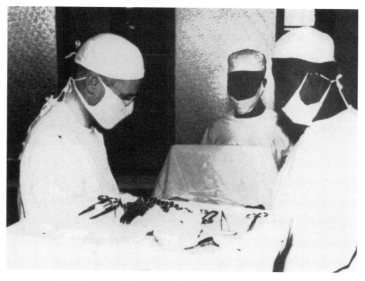

Bill, Sam, and Eugene in OR, Hôpital des Congolais.

slow motion. Pirquin had retreated into a shell of gloom. Then one morning, as I was talking to the sister about the day's schedule, Sam joined us.

"What is it, Samuel?" I asked.

He ignored my question and turned to the sister. "Over the past few days I have thought a lot. I have hated you and other Belgians for the way you have treated me and my people. I know we cannot go on this way, and I would like to ask your forgiveness for my bitterness. I need your help to be different."

The sister stared at him wide-eyed, her face as white as her veil. She turned away and walked out of the operating room. She stayed away all day. The next morning she didn't show up. I walked across the street to the convent and asked to see the Mother Superior. She came out of her office and greeted me.

"I came to find out if Sister Germaine is all right. We really need her in the operating room," I said.

"The sister spent most of the night in the chapel on her knees," said the Mother Superior. "I don't think you need to worry. She will come over a little later." I thanked her and returned to work.

In mid-afternoon, Sister Germaine walked into the operating pavilion veranda and called Samuel. I was there casting a fracture. He came out of the instrument room.

"Samuel, I am the one who needs forgiveness," she said, her voice barely audible. "I have bitterly resented the way your people have treated us after all we have done for you. I've been terrified of being beaten or raped like some of the other white women. I have betrayed my vows. I am the one who needs forgiveness and your help."

Sam was stunned. He walked out but returned in a little while. The three of us sat down and talked about how to best manage our growing workload. Now that Sam and Sister Germaine had dealt with fear and bitterness, planning would be possible. As a result, the individuals in the OR became a team, and they were a good bunch. Every day and some of the nights we operated.

Sam maintained anesthesia with nitrous oxide, oxygen, and open drop ether. The other members of the team were Eugene, Pierre, and Makila.

Eugene had been an OR assistant for many years. He lived way out in Ndjili, the community near the airport, and bicycled twenty-five kilometers to work, starting out at 4:30 A.M. He and his wife had eight children and their own house.

At the height of the violent radio broadcasts by Madame Blouin for Lumumba, we were operating on a patient under spinal anesthesia for appendicitis. As happens sometimes, the patient started to retch. Sam told him to take deep breaths, a panacea for almost anything from vomiting to vertigo. Pierre walked in and, with great ceremony, pulled a stool up to the head of the table. In a voice shaking with revolutionary zeal, he addressed the patient: "My dear compatriot, there is no need to worry, it is me, your prime minister, who is talking to you."

Everyone laughed, and the patient didn't vomit. I warned him to be careful. A pro-Lumumbist might hear him and he'd be in trouble. Pierre shrugged, patted the patient's head, and returned to his instrument room.

I was sitting at the desk, jotting patient data in the register, and heard, "Good morrrrrning, Doctor. Owarya." Some reporters came to the OR after a violent episode in the streets, like flies to dead meat.

"Balls," I mumbled. "Another American press guy on the prowl for a body count." I stood up and met Pierre coming around the corner with a wide grin. He laughed and said that he needed hot potatoes in his mouth to imitate American reporters properly.

Makila, which means "blood" in Lingala, was ever present when we were operating or wrapping plaster around broken limbs. He was monosyllabic, unflappable, short, and muscular, with a foreshortened forehead like a pygmy. He could heft a patient twice his size on and off a stretcher. When he wasn't dragging the bloody mop, which was as long as he was tall, around the operating rooms, he sat on a crate in the instrument room with his head thrown back, snoring like the trombone in Mahler's Third Symphony. He had paroxysms of coughing. We tried to check his sputum for tuberculosis, but the lab was down. He smoked like a chimney, but the floors were clean. Occasionally I had him push the anesthesia balloon in rhythm with his own breathing.

The OR building was bungalow style with two operating rooms, a plaster room, sterilizing room, dressing rooms, and an office. It stood in a two city-block compound, which, with many other pavilions, made up the total hospital of fifteen hundred beds. The pavilions were connected by brick and concrete walks covered by tin roofs so that in the rainy season one could get around without being drenched. People hoping to be seen were like permanent fixtures outside the OR building. They came for surgical consultations or from the dispensaries—or they walked in on their own. There were as many as forty to be seen after the morning operating schedule. A variety of complaints and illnesses was the rule: numerous abscesses, osteomyelitis (bone infections), and infected wounds; many black eyes, lumps on heads, contusions and abrasions from *matata*—the violence—sometimes started in a barroom fight over a woman. Some patients were tragic, like the three elderly men badly beaten because someone accused them of being pro-Lumumba. Some were unusual, like the two young women who had bitten each other's lips during a fight over the same boyfriend. Then there were the soldiers who came from the interior with infected wounds to be treated or with bullets to be removed. Many children were brought in late in their illnesses by worried parents. Often these little tykes were the most stoic of patients.

We saw enormous numbers of patients with protruding hernias in their groins. I never learned the reason for the plethora of hernia patients in the Congo. Sometimes a man would come in, hoping he had a hernia. He would cough and bear down hard in an attempt to produce an acceptable bulge in his groin. When no bulge was evident, it was hard to tell him *motete te*—no hernia. So many people were unemployed and just looking for a place to rest on a mattress and sheet and eat twice a day. We did hernias on Tuesday, generally up to a dozen in a morning. When we were flooded with emergency patients, elective surgery went by the board.

The children were like children in too many places—rascals caught up in adult violence. Seven-year-old Lambert broke his humerus. After his surgery, he stood with his nose glued to the mosquito screening, watching us work in the operating room. He stood there by the hour asking about the patient, what we were doing, and how much longer it would take. I asked him one day if he wanted to be a doctor. With a grin he shrugged his good shoulder and went scampering off. Twelve-year-old Raphael was brought in as a prisoner. His crime was the manufacture of weapons; his problem, a homemade bullet in his hand, which was easy to remove. I didn't know whether he would continue making guns or not. He looked as angelic as a choirboy, a useful facade. Alphonse was playing in a field with some of his friends when they heard a shot. He was looking up with his mouth open ready to catch a ball, and a spent bullet dropped into his mouth. He never cried or tried to pull away even though his lower jaw was torn up. A real *soda ya mpiko*—strong soldier—according to his father.

Other children were not so fortunate. A six-month-old infant with a hard, distended abdomen was rushed in by her parents. Exploration showed an intussusception in which one segment of bowel accordions into itself, causing obstruction. Sadly, the baby had been given some native medicine and died eight hours after the operation. Another child was brought in by her mother after a week of peritonitis from a ruptured appendix. The father was a steamboat pilot on the river. When he came to the hospital, he attacked the mother for not bringing the child in sooner. When the child died, he ran out of the hospital with the small body slung over his shoulder.

One night, after a long stretch of operating, I crawled into the sack late. The telephone rang at 2:00 A.M. It was the night *mère*—the mother of the night. Like most of the nuns, she was a nurse. Senior nursing sisters were called "*mère*"—"mother."

"There is an elephant in the maternity," she announced with clipped authority.

"Come on, Mother, you must be joking," I said, as I would to any normal nurse.

"I do not joke," she said severely, "especially in the middle of the night. Will you please come? Our little mothers are very frightened."

I almost said, *Call the obstetrician, damn it, that's his division. This little doctor is exhausted.* But I didn't.

Sure enough, a baby elephant, attracted by the smell of fresh bread destined for the "little mothers'" breakfast, had pushed open the gate between the hospital and the zoo and was popping rolls into his mouth. We chased him back to the zoo, which was adjacent to the maternity pavilion.

Sister Marie Euphrasie was a senior nursing sister for the surgical pavilion P6. On one side were post-op children, and on the other, men in their sixties and beyond. Women surgical patients were in P8. We had two hundred beds in my division.

Sister Euphrasie was in her late fifties and had been in the Congo since 1926 and in surgery at the general hospital for eleven years without a single break. Unlike Sister Germaine, Euphrasie had a multitude of minute smile lines at the corners of her mouth and eyes. She was a large woman with stiff hips, swollen ankles, and hypertension. She was an angel to her patients.

Once a week, I did suprapubic prostatectomies, scooping huge prostates from the bottom of patients' bladders. We threaded large catheters into the bladders, pushed water into the balloons, and to secure some control of the bleeding, the sister tied one end of a string to the catheter and the other to a weight thrown over the foot rail of the bed. We had no blood bank, but the balloon under pressure worked well, although sometimes the morning found some of the smaller men curled up in a ball at the foot of their bed, pulled down by the weight. That form of primitive hemostasis was her idea and it worked well.

I had written to our oldest daughter, Tina, about the kids in the surgical ward, many of whom were victims of the violence in town. She sent them a big box of bubble gum. Between operations I showed the kids how to blow bubbles, then handed out two pieces to each child. I walked back to the OR and was working on a patient with a twisted colon when suddenly Sister Euphrasie stormed in, waving her hands toward heaven and accusing me of spreading indiscipline among her children. She shouted that the children were covered with rubber and so were their beds. I told her that I would come and help clean it up. She replied, "Never mind. You've helped enough already!"

After the operation, I crept back to P6 and peeked in. Everything was almost back to normal. The kids were sitting at attention in their beds doing their best to suppress their giggles as the sister fussed with their bedsheets and grumbled away.

In the men's ward of P6, the sister used the bed in a private room for patients with tetanus or rabies. Her batting average for tetanus patients was high. The rabies patients died horribly. To me, Sister Marie Euphrasie represented the tough, hard-working saints sprinkled among the sick and dying, dispensing care with gentleness and authority.

Families played important roles in the care of a patient. As I was examining a man with signs and symptoms of a bowel obstruction, a head popped out from under the bed, blinked its eyes, yawned, and answered a question for the patient. It was his wife. When a patient was admitted to the hospital, it was customary for the family to come too. With the children, the mothers came to help in their care. This was necessary, since there were so few nurses. The opposite of this situation was less practical. When a woman was admitted, the father occasionally delivered all the kids to her bedside so she could continue to take care of them. This was hard on the mother and doubly hard on the overworked sisters, who ended up fending for the patient and her children.

One morning I was doing consultations after the schedule. Twenty to thirty people were gathered at the door waiting to be seen. Five boys elbowed their way through the crowd, stepped up to the table and, plunking down five mangos, said in unison, *"Pour vous, monsieur le docteur."* They turned and walked out. Everyone cheered, and I had to wipe my eyes and blow my nose before I nodded for the next patients to step up: two men with their heads bandaged.

"Sango nini—What's up?" I asked.

"My name is Constantin," said one of them, "and he said his name was Constantin. He thought I was lying, and I thought he was lying, so we fought. His name is Constantin, and so is mine. Neither of us is to blame."

"Who is to blame?" I asked.

"The mothers," they answered.

I asked Eugene to change their dressings.

Chapter 9
An Old Surgeon's Exit

THE DAY CAME AT THE END of August when Pirquin had to leave. A Belgian police commissioner, who had been severely wounded during a confrontation with the army, was not doing well and had asked Pirquin to escort him back to Europe. Before he left, Pirquin invited me for an evening horseback ride. The Cercle Hippique was in Binza, a residential suburb on a hill overlooking the city and the river.

We started at five, trotting up and down hills through tall grasses leading to the river. At first the mosquitoes weren't bad, but after crossing a stream that emptied into a marsh, they became fierce. Half an hour later we crested high ground and looked out over the Congo River. To our right, the rapids started below the Stanley Pool. Across the water on the Brazzaville side, flattened tops of giant trees were silhouetted against a crimson sky. A breeze softened the pounding heat of the day. Parrots, chattering and squawking, flew northward in their disorganized way, flapping toward their night perches upriver on M'Bamu Island. High above, hundreds of fruit bats sailed slowly south. The horses played with their bits and pawed the ground, impatient to get back to their stables and grain. We held them still and watched a full moon emerge from the forest on the distant bank. Below us, the river split around Monkey Island, hurling itself against massive boulders. Colors faded into shades of gray, and boiling spume shimmered silver.

Carefully, I followed Pirquin down a steep incline into

a palm grove bathed in moonlight. Some of the trees had been trimmed; in others, palm nuts in clusters the size of beer kegs hung below the fronds. Short grasses carpeted the ground between the rows of trees. I caught up with him, and we rode into the grove side by side.

I remarked, "This is a peaceful place."

The surgeon looked straight ahead, astride his Arabian stallion like a Prussian riding master. "Last night two men were killed in the village we're coming to. The natives have destroyed the tranquility since independence." In a clipped, bitter tone, he added, "They will ruin all we've done in this country." He rode away, then stopped and turned to me. "The liberals in Brussels are just as guilty. Some of us have spent a lifetime forging the best medical system in Africa. We brought discipline and order to the Congo. Rabble-rousers like Lumumba were locked up, and the natives made to work. They're a lazy bunch, you know."

"I don't know," I said. "This is my first time in Africa."

"You Americans are *des enfants naïfs*. Your ideals are filled with illusions." He gave a short humorless laugh. "You think if everyone is free to do as they please, the world will turn rose-colored."

I resisted the temptation to argue. "I'm sure we have much to learn."

Pirquin reined in his horse, and I followed suit; we faced each other. Moonlight reflected off his glasses, and his mouth was a thin line under a hawkish nose. A night bird called, and tree frogs croaked like wooden rattles. He continued with clipped intensity.

"Brussels precipitated independence. The Congo was costing too much, and the bureaucrats panicked when riots erupted last year. We *colons* knew the natives weren't ready to govern themselves."

"And no one listened to you?" I asked.

"Of course not. We told them it would take another

ten years, at least, to train *les indigènes* adequately." He leaned forward in the saddle. "Listen, *confrère*. We've taught most of them to read, but there's still only a handful of university graduates. Now that they are on their own, they'll hack each other to pieces as they did before we colonized them. *Nom de Dieu,* just look at the massacres going on right now between the Balubas and the Luluas." He stopped, uncomfortable perhaps with so many words. "We'd better keep going," he said, spurring his horse into a trot. I followed, and after a little while he slowed to a walk.

He waved toward a fishing village just visible in the moonlight. "There's where the bodies were found by the police this morning."

"Why were the men killed?" I asked, feeling my gut tighten.

"Who knows? Family problems, a drunken fight over a woman, a vendetta—you can't tell with them. The point is that before independence, fear of the authorities tamed their bestiality."

Pirogues on Congo River.

The village curved around a sandy cove off the main channel of the river, whose roar now drowned out the night noises. Pirogues were drawn up on the beach with throwing nets resting in their shallow bows. A dozen mud-and-wattle houses thatched with palm fronds nestled under broad-leaved trees. Thin gray ribbons of smoke rose from cooking fires to be lost in the dark foliage of mango trees. The smell of rotting vegetation and firewood filled the air, and people, squatting or sitting on low stools around fires, were dimly lit by the flames.

Children ran toward us, jumping up and down, yelling "*Mpunda*—horse—*mpunda, mpunda.*" Several of the older ones came to pat our mounts as we stopped.

"*Mbote*," I said to the fishermen.

"*Mbote, mondele*—Hello, white man," they answered dully. A driftwood log cracked under a cooking pot and shot sparks into a column of smoke. I saw the glint of a machete as a man stood up, stared, then backed into the shadows. The brooding hostility was only partly relieved by the innocent delight of the youngsters.

"*Keba, bana*—Watch out, children," Pirquin ordered. They scampered away, and we rode past the huts and the silent people. Leaving the village behind was a relief. Pirquin sat ramrod stiff, walking his stallion slowly and deliberately. We climbed a hill, and the horses broke into a trot as the lights of the riding club came into view.

We dismounted at the clubhouse. Congolese grooms led our horses away. Pirquin and I walked up the steps and into the bar. He was greeted with handshakes and a respectful *"Docteur."* He introduced me as *mon confrère* Américain. The gray-haired Congolese barman filled two beer mugs from a frosty bottle of Primus, the local beer. Pirquin nodded his thanks. We clicked glasses and drank.

"I heard you were leaving," said one of the men nearby.

"Yes, I'm flying out tomorrow with Van der Pic, the police *commissaire*. He was seriously wounded in last night's clash with the army."

"Will you be able to get some rest? How long will you be away?"

"Who knows?" Pirquin looked into his mug, then turned away and walked out onto the porch. I followed.

"I wouldn't go if it weren't for the *commissaire*," he said defensively.

"I am sure of that. You belong here."

It took time for me to realize that, in spite of a long professional career as a surgeon to the Congolese people, Pirquin and we other expatriates in Africa would never be African. With rare exceptions, the ancestral heritage of whites in Africa would remain anchored in Europe with its various cultural differences. Over the last forty years, it seems to me, there are few signs that the condescension of most whites toward darker races has decreased. Pirquin, like other colonials, would return to his country of origin and live without the house boys and chauffeurs, and without the sense of effortless superiority characteristic of so many whites in Africa. But with all that, I would miss Pirquin's skill and patience as a teacher of surgery. I wasn't sure how I was going to run a huge surgical service without him.

Pirquin took a long drink, then sat on the step. I joined him.

After a moment he said, "I'm glad you came to the hospital to help me. I hate to leave you alone on the service, but the sister knows what to do."

"And Samuel," I added.

"And Samuel," he repeated. "But you'll have to watch him. He has Arab blood. He's smart like a fox."

The man who had spoken to Pirquin walked out from the bar and put another bottle of Primus on the step between us. "*Bon voyage, docteur,*" he said, and left.

Pirquin carefully poured beer down the side of my mug and handed it to me. He filled his with equal care and, turning to me, raised it—"*Chin*"—without a smile.

"*Chin*," I replied.

The cold beer tasted good. Laughter came from inside the clubhouse, but the old man's somber mood added darkness to the night.

Shafts of yellow light from the box stalls off to our left stabbed into the night. The sound of hooves stamping and the chattering of men's voices floated up the steps as the grooms hosed down their horses. In the clubhouse, people were saying *bonne nuit* and heading for their cars. We sat together, Pirquin staring ahead, occasionally sipping beer. Behind us all was still except for the clinking of glasses as the bartender tidied up. A single bulb glowed over the door to the bar. In the distance, where dark sky met horizon, a band of gray lay over the center of the city.

Pirquin emptied his mug and turned to me. In the dim light his eyes looked infinitely weary and sad. He waved toward the stable where a groom rubbed down his stallion, Lynx.

"It's like a knife in my belly to think I may never see my horse again." He stood and motioned me to follow him. We walked down the steps to the stable. Lynx was almost dry after his bath, his halter rope looped over the hitching rail in front of his stall.

"*Un moment*," he said to the groom, who stopped his work, moved to the horse's head, and held him steady on a long lead. The stallion looked down at the doctor, his ears forward, nostrils dilating in expectation.

"*Salut*, Lynx," commanded Pirquin. The horse lifted his right foreleg and held it up until the doctor touched the hoof. He laid his hand on the animal's majestic neck, then spun around and walked back to the clubhouse. Once again we sat on the steps. After a while he turned to me, his tears bright in the starlight. "You must ride him after I go."

Pirquin stood and quickly turned toward the parking lot. I followed him to his car. He got in, started the engine, and looked up at me.

"This was my life, but it is finished. Good night, Close. *Adieu*."

He drove away rapidly.

After Pirquin left, there were only three doctors for the hospital: I was in surgery; Paul Beheyt, a Belgian internist, covered medicine for the fifteen hundred beds; and an Egyptian Copt, Bill Morgan, did OB/GYN. He and the midwives averaged 120 deliveries a day. Sister Germaine became my OR nurse, and Sam, my assistant. During the next year we averaged 350 operations a month.

I wrote frequently to Peter Howard, who had become the leader of MRA after the death of Frank Buchman in 1961. I respected his views about the world and human nature. He had been one of Beaverbrook's top journalists in London and played rugby for England. I remember clearly traveling to Twickenham Stadium with other members of the Summerfields school's rugby team to watch England play. A tall wing ran as hard as he could, with a pronounced limp, down the sidelines to make a try. That man was Peter Howard. Years later, when he started having back pain, a result of a shortened and atrophied leg from polio, I built up the shoe on his short leg and relieved much of this pain.

In answer to one of my letters, Peter wrote:

> You are obsessed with the need of that hospital. I know it is a great human need. But, if you were obsessed with the desperate need of nations for the training and faith that you could give them, the thing would assume a new perspective. You must, can, and will cut with that hospital.

To hell with them. I would write back and resign from MRA. But my answer to him was typical of a man who craved approval but refused to bow to the dictates of others. I leaned heavily on the fact that I was now the only surgeon. I could not and would not leave the hospital or the sisters unless an adequate replacement could be found. I was relieved, in a so-you-see fashion, that finding a replacement would be nearly impossible. I wrote about returning to God's guidance to get them off my back. I knew in my heart and gut that I was doing what God had intended me to do on this planet.

Chapter 10

The Prince and the Prisoner

LATE ONE NIGHT, I was operating on a wounded soldier when a noise from the screened-off terrace made me look up. A man wearing a drip-dry gray suit, a drip-dry gray tie, and a drip-dry shirt with a crumpled collar stood at the door of the operating room. He was a big man, showing a middle-aged spread. His round head was balding, and the wisps of hair on the top were in disarray. Sweat poured down his face, and the collar and armpits of his jacket were soggy and dark. He was obviously agitated and in a hurry.

"Are you the American doctor Bill Close?" he asked in heavily accented, educated English.

"Yes."

"My name is Stéphane d'Arenberg. I am a Belgian doctor. I must talk with you. Are you almost through?" He took a handkerchief from his pocket and mopped his face and the top of his head.

"Almost," I said. "What's the problem?"

"I cannot speak in front of them," he said, looking in the direction of the soldier on the table and Makila, who was almost asleep but faithfully squeezing the balloon of the anesthesia machine.

"The patient is asleep and Makila doesn't speak English—he hardly understands French. Go ahead, what can I do for you?" My hope was that he would tell me what he had to, then go. I was exhausted and craved home and bed.

D'Arenberg stepped into the operating room and,

staying by the door, told me that he had just been to Luzumu on the outskirts of Léopoldville. Luzumu was a prison with a reputation of cruelty unequaled by any of the others in the city. Rhinoceros-hide whips, the *"chicottes"* of the colonial period, chains, manacles, and other torture instruments were on display at the entrance for the benefit of inmates and visitors. Colonel Mobutu had arrested some of the more violent men around Lumumba and thrown them into Luzumu. D'Arenberg's mission was to see whether any Europeans were there as well. He found none, but he had been cornered in one of the cells by a half dozen brutes loyal to Lumumba who had threatened to cut his throat if he didn't take a "certain prisoner" out with him "for medical treatment." D'Arenberg had consented. After a discussion with the prison guards, who were loyal to Mobutu, and the passage of a little *"matabish"* for beer and cigarettes, the "certain prisoner" was freed from the wires that bound his wrists to his ankles and thrown into the back of d'Arenberg's car. On the way into town, the doctor learned that the man riding away from Luzumu on his back seat was Fataki, one of Lumumba's henchmen—reputedly a master of torture and slow death. D'Arenberg knew he would be in serious trouble if Mobutu found out that Fataki had been released. His immediate concern was not only to deal with Fataki's "medical" problems but also to hold him securely for the night.

"Where is he now?" I asked, putting the last sutures in the soldier's wound.

"I put him on the X-ray table in your trauma ward. He's complaining of back pain, which is quite likely after being trussed up like a chicken for God knows how long. I thought you could treat him and keep him overnight with a police guard."

"The police took off to fight the army," I said. "We don't have any guards. As a matter of fact, we don't have any X-ray film." I pulled off my bloody gloves and soggy gown and looked at him. He smiled, shrugged, and turned his palms up to heaven in the Gallic way that says silently and so eloquently, *"Eh bien, qu'est-ce que vous voulez? C'est comme ça*—Well, what do you expect? That's the way it is." I laughed and went over to him.

"Glad to meet you, Doctor," I said, as we shook hands. He followed me to the X-ray room. On the table was Fataki, lying on his side with his knees up to his chin.

"Here's the doctor. He will take care of you," said d'Arenberg. Fataki showed me his wrists and ankles where wires had cut into the skin. Although his own men had mistreated him, he had done much worse to others. I examined him. Aside from some bruises on his back and the wounds around his ankles and wrists, he had no other obvious injuries. I went through the motions of taking X-rays with empty cassettes and, after spending a few moments in the darkroom, returned to the X-ray table. Fataki was waiting expectantly. I told him that his back needed to be immobilized to relieve his pain, and that the best way to do that would be to put him in a cast. He nodded. I pulled over the plaster cart and went to work. D'Arenberg took off his jacket, rolled up his sleeves, and helped. The next thing Fataki knew he was in a body cast—a plaster shell that went from his belly button to his knees with a hole cut out for toilet functions. I wrapped plaster around part of a broomstick and fixed it to the cast between his knees to help carry him. As the whole thing hardened, he realized that he was trapped. He was fatalistic about this turn of events as we loaded him back into d'Arenberg's car for the trip back to Luzumu.

I'm not sure what happened to Fataki. I heard rumors that his own people tied him up again and threw him into the river.

Two days later, I was examining patients on the

veranda. D'Arenberg banged on the screen door and walked in.

"I am so glad to find you again," he said, breathlessly.

I led him into the office. Sister Germaine had told me that d'Arenberg was a prince of the royal blood related to King Baudouin as well as a public heath doctor. He sat in front of the desk, pulled out a handkerchief, and wiped his face and the top of his head.

"What's up? What can I do for you?"

My dear, *mon cher confrère*, I must ask of you another favor. I have covered the dispensary of the first paracommando battalion, the best of what remains of the army. Also, Colonel Mobutu, the chief of staff, lives in the camp. But I must return to Belgium immediately. I could drive you to meet Major Tshatshi, the battalion commander, now and it will be settled."

"You want me to take care of the paratroopers and the colonel right away?"

"Yes. I have no other choice."

"Give me a minute and I'll be right with you," I replied.

Before introducing me to Major Tshatshi, Stéphane told me in a conspiratorial whisper, "Speak French, not English. He might be suspicious of an American."

The meeting was short and amiable. I returned in the evening for a longer talk with the major in his home. It took some argument at the entrance of the camp before I was let in. Whites were suspect, and apparently the MPs at the gate had not been told of my new duties.

I said, *"Ngai monganga ya bapara*—I am the doctor for the paras," which reassured them. An MP climbed in and escorted me to the major's house. He indicated that I should stay in the car until he checked to see if I was expected. After a few minutes he returned, opened the door, and led me into the house.

He pointed to a chair in the living room and said,

"*Zela*—Wait."

Eight Congolese men and women sat silently in a circle, comfortably ensconced in deep armchairs and a plush sofa. They stared at me. I had learned quickly that, as in Europe, one was expected to shake hands with everyone and say, "*Mbote*—Good day." I made the rounds and sat in the designated chair, hoping that I would not have to wait for all of them to be seen first. No one spoke. They continued to stare, some at me, some out of the window, and two men gazed with apparent indifference at a Flemish print of a buxom nude coyly peeking out from behind a bowl of ripe fruit. The heavy, elaborate gold frame hung above a dark carved sideboard. What was now a paratrooper camp had been the housing complex for junior colonial functionaries, but the house in which Colonel Mobutu lived had belonged to a Belgian bank.

I offered comments about the heat and the weather, and asked those sitting near me about their families—the usual stuff. The replies were monosyllabic. It was clear that they didn't want to talk. I thought they must be waiting to see the major about some tragedy.

After a while Major Tshatshi strode into the room. "*Mbote, docteur,*" he said, shaking my hand. He turned to the others in the room. "*Monganga wa biso*—Our doctor." He pointed to me, smiling. They acknowledged this with serious nods. "*Viens, docteur,*" he said. I followed him into his office. He pointed me to a chair and sat behind the desk.

"Nice to see you again," I said. "But before we start, can you tell me what has happened?"

"Nothing has happened that I know of. Why do you ask?"

"In the living room there are eight people sitting around in a circle, not talking. Not saying anything at all. Has someone died?"

The major laughed. "No one has died. Everything is

going well. I am glad you can come and take care of the dispensary."

"Thank you, Major." I persisted: "Why are the people sitting in a silent circle?"

He smiled. "Maybe they have nothing to say."

Thus started a happy and busy relationship with the major and his troopers that lasted for several years and included working with an Israeli military doctor to prepare the battalion for jump training in Israel. I was able to do most of the medical care of the troops in the evenings after surgery at the hospital.

Chapter 11

First Encounters with Colonel Mobutu

I CHECKED the para camp dispensary daily after the OR schedule, usually by stopping in, sometimes by phone. One evening it took me only ten minutes to deal with four troopers. Three needed penicillin shots for gonorrhea and one a splint for a broken finger. I climbed into my Volkswagen Beetle and headed home to the house in town that had been lent to MRA. After a full day of surgery, I was drawn to my sack like a dormouse to his nest. Driving home along the low wall that separated the army chief of staff's house from the rest of the military camp, I noticed that Colonel Mobutu's Mercedes was heading toward the open gate. On a hunch, I pulled up next to the entrance and got out. Colonel John Sinclair, the British military attaché, had told me that Colonel Mobutu was the hope of the army and that he was one of a few who could get things done. As the car approached, I waved the driver to a stop. The colonel rolled down the back window and looked at me with a raised eyebrow.

"*Oui?*"

"*Bonsoir, mon colonel.* I'm a surgeon at the Hôpital des Congolais, and I wondered if you could do something about the violence in town so we can catch up in the operating room."

He raised both eyebrows, maybe surprised at my directness or naiveté, but replied, "*Oui. C'est possible,*" and drove off.

That was my first brief encounter with Colonel

Joseph-Désiré Mobutu. To this day, I don't know what he did, but not long after that, the influx of trauma into the hospital seemed to decrease—probably only a lull between eruptions.

A couple of weeks later, Mobutu's senior bodyguard, Lieutenant Donatien Mahele Bokungu, came to the operating room and told me that the colonel wanted me to see his great-aunt in his home. Mobutu greeted me at the door, thanked me for coming, and said that *la mama* had a fishbone in her throat. We stepped into the living room where the old lady was sitting cross-legged on the floor, her mouth wide open, pointing a gnarled finger down her gullet. I knelt down next to her, took a flashlight and throat stick out of my bag, and could see the tip of the bone peeking above the crest of her tongue. Grateful for the stroke of luck, I pulled it out with a clamp. The colonel thanked me. I shook hands with the grinning, happy mama and left.

A few days later, Lieutenant Mahele arrived at the hospital with the message that the colonel wanted me to circumcise his newborn son. Although my surgical professors at Columbia's College of Physicians and Surgeons and at New York's Roosevelt Hospital had been among the best in the United States, I had neither seen nor performed a circumcision, a procedure usually left to the rabbis, at least in New York. I scurried around to find some tiny mosquito clamps and fine sutures. A Gomko clamp, a sort of semiautomatic circumciser, was nowhere to be found. I learned from Sam and Eugene that a circumcision must be done with proper guarantees that the victim's penis remain unblemished and completely functional. The removal of too little foreskin would be as unacceptable as removing too much. Above all, postcircumcision bleeding was considered the mark of a novice and a complication to be avoided at all cost. Although I was doing major surgery every day, this procedure scared the hell out of me.

After quieting the infant with a ball of powdered sugar wrapped in gauze and soaked in cognac, I went to work cutting away the foreskin. I tied off every tiny bleeder I could see and probably some that didn't exist. The cut ends of the ties bristling around the tip of his penis reminded me of an infant porcupine. Mobutu picked up the infant and cradled him in his arms. I stayed long enough to ensure that not a drop of blood would be lost and that the child would pee with the gusto of Brussels' famous statue of a boy pissing. The colonel was impressed, and I was greatly relieved.

Soon I was summoned again. This time to see another great-aunt in her home. Lieutenant Mahele would show me where she lived. After a bumpy drive into the heart of the *cité*, we pulled up to a concrete blockhouse surrounded by a fenced yard of packed dirt. Half a dozen people sat around a charcoal fire. Mahele told them I was the doctor sent by Colonel Mobutu. I shook hands all around and was ushered into the house, down a narrow corridor, and into a small room where a dozen people crowded around a canvas cot on which lay an ancient, skeletal woman almost completely covered by mothballs. Again, I made the rounds shaking hands, then squatted next to the patient. Her crescendo-diminuendo breathing indicated that she did not have long to live. I examined her briefly, then stood up and announced the obvious, "She is not suffering." I shook hands again and left.

On the way back to the colonel, I asked Mahele, "What about the mothballs? Is that a usual custom?"

"When necessary. It suppresses the smells of a dying body."

Standing in front of Mobutu, I reported, "I saw your aunt. I'm afraid she's dying."

"I know that. The family was with her?"

"Yes. The room was packed with people."

"How long did you stay?"

"Oh, I suppose five or ten minutes."

"Please return to the house and sit with her longer. It will comfort the family."

I returned to the house and learned the value of an *acte de présence,* where, doctor or not, you sat with the family watching the approach of death. Those keeping vigil welcomed me warmly. Such an act had not been part of the medical armamentarium taught in medical school.

(L-R) Nendaka, head of security, standing behind the British ambassador, who is shaking hands with Mobutu. Between them is Colonel John Sinclair in his Black Watch Glengarry cap. Far right is Albert Ndele, bank governor.

The first time I saw Mobutu in action was in response to a call I received from John Sinclair, the British military attaché and a colonel in the Black Watch. I first met John in his home when his wife, Pat, had called me remove a lima bean his young daughter, Janie, had pushed into her ear canal. The British embassy had no doctor of their own. I'd been able to tease out the bean with forceps and irrigation. John and Pat offered me a drink, and we started a friendship that lasted for many years. Pat was a no-nonsense lady, a breath of fresh air in the diplomatic corps. She said to me later, "You're a good doctor. Why do you mess around with MRA, whose reputation is of intimate intrusion into people's souls?" I told her that I was my own independent man.

John was a soldier through and through. He had been captured during the Allied retreat at Dunkirk and spent most of the war as a prisoner in Germany. He and I cooperated in training exercises with some of the paratrooper officers. I refereed boxing matches, which involved staying out of the way of flying fists; I measured javelin tosses and played goalkeeper in soccer matches played with heavy leather medicine balls. John helped them through military drills made more realistic by the blank cartridge ammo and smoke bombs he provided. When he wanted to see what was going on in a restricted military camp, John would march up in his full Black Watch dress uniform with swagger stick, sporran, and kilt, throw a salute, and walk in as the guards snapped to attention and presented arms.

On the telephone, John's voice was a bugle sounding a charge. "There's a mutiny at the police barracks. Mobutu is on his way there. I'll pick you up."

We arrived at the police camp in the middle of town as Mobutu was walking through the front gates. Several hundred gray-uniformed men stood resolutely in a semicircle fifty yards away, pointing their rifles at him. They looked tired and surly; a few in the front row had assumed aggressive postures and looked defiant. John and I, with three paratroopers who had been in the colonel's Jeep, started through the gates behind Mobutu. He glanced over his shoulder.

"Where are you going? Stay back," he ordered. We did, and watched from the entrance.

Mobutu halted in front of the police. Slowly and deliberately he scrutinized the men. Then, standing at attention with his shoulders back and fists clenched, he commanded, *"Déposez vos armes*—Drop your weapons."

A low murmur came from the men. No one moved. Their weapons were leveled at the colonel. I held my breath. Two men in the front row dropped the butts of their rifles, released the barrels, and the guns clattered to the ground. In seconds, the crashing of weapons echoed in the camp. The handful of defiant men in the front row stepped forward and saluted. The mutiny was over.

Mobutu commanded attention. Early on I was struck by his easy charm and his natural thoughtfulness. He introduced me as *le docteur* or Docteur Cloooose. He loved his family, treating them with respect and affection, with the occasional toss and catch and cheek squeeze for the youngest. He stood tall and straight-backed and would cock his head and smile when he met you or asked a question like *"Et comment va madame*—And how is madame?"* At the beginning he really wanted to know; later, *comment va madame* became his code for "I don't want to talk about it." His voice was as clear as it was strong and often passionate. With backers, and certainly his doctor, he could banter and laugh; he was a master at imitating stuffy diplomats. Although gentle with a sick child, he had little patience with fools. I learned later that his tolerance of people on the take, especially members of his family, was normal in African society. A successful and powerful leader was expected to provide for his relatives. His wealth was admired by his family as long as their trickle-down share was adequate. As the leader's power and wealth grew, so did the numbers and demands of his expanding extended family. The survival of his identity depended upon his being an intimate and valued member of the clan. He could not, without losing his identity, turn them away. This pressure and duty to tradition was above and beyond all other pressures and would sometimes drive a sociological novice like me around the bend.

At thirty-one years of age, his authority came from

fearlessness and attention to details, which he filed away in his mental vault. He was a voracious reader. Machiavelli's *The Prince* had an honored place on his bedside table along with heavy volumes with soporific titles dealing with economics, geopolitics, and history. Napoléon and de Gaulle were his historical mentors.

Chapter 12
Mobutu's Early Experiences

MOBUTU BELONGED to the Ngbandi, a non-Bantu people that had moved south from the Sudan—not today's Sudan, but a vast region stretching north of the Congo basin and equatorial forests to the southern borders of the Arab Maghreb. The group settled in the far north of the Congo on the northern and southern banks of the Ubangi River, a major tributary of the Congo River. The Ngbandi, a large, well-organized ethnic group of warriors, pushed the Mbuja, the Ngbaka, and other Bantus out of the savannah into the dense isolation of the equatorial forest. The Ngbandi resisted Belgian colonization. Unlike their rivals, the Ngbaka and Mbuja, the Ngbandi were slow to attend Belgian schools and work for the colonists. As a result, they profited less from the colonial occupation than most of the Bantus.

Mobutu was born in Lisala on October 14, 1930. Congolese often name individuals according to their ancestral heritage—their pedigree, so to speak. But Marie-Madeleine Yemo chose for her son a Ngbandi name, Mobutu, which means "soil" or "sand," for she was as low as sand. Indeed, she was destitute in 1930. A few days after his birth, Mobutu was taken to a Catholic church, where a Flemish Scheutist priest baptized him and gave him the Christian name of Joseph-Désiré.

In 1972, under the banner of "authenticity," Mobutu dropped the Joseph-Désiré and added Sese Seko Koko Ngbendu Wazabanga. Various interpretations have been offered for Mobutu's new identity. One translation of this name is "the all-powerful warrior who, because of his endurance and inflexible will to win, will go from conquest to conquest, leaving fire in his wake." According to another claim, this high-sounding version translated as "the rooster that lets no hen pass by." The truth is different. Sese Seko means "eternal." Mobutu wanted to make a clear statement: he was there forever. The Ngbandi terms *kuku, ngbendu,* and *wazabanga* respectively mean "hot pepper," "green," and "it stings." *Kuku ngbendu wazabanga* is a Ngbandi proverb that could be translated "Even if it is not ripe, hot pepper stings." Mobutu resorted to a naming tradition that is deeply rooted in Central Africa.

An individual's personal history and that of his or her ancestors might be used with proverbs, short and deep like Japanese haikus, to define that individual. If a child meets a man along the path, he will say, *"Mbote, Tata—*Hello, father," in respect. The man will not say, "Hello, my son," but will respond with his chosen proverb such as, "Little by little the banana grows."

An older man meeting another might greet him with a proverb that is part of his condition and identity—"The heart of an old man is like a coffin"—thus provoking thought. A conversation can be initiated when they meet and continued with remarks over their shoulders as they separate. Another man may define a tribal chief by saying, "The mouth of our chief smells like shit." This means that to be effective, a chief must listen much and talk little. Since the chief keeps his mouth closed most of the time, his breath smells bad. Symbolism is part of everyday life for many people in Africa. In most villages, elders spend time sitting under a ficus or another venerated tree discussing symbols and interpretations. Nicknames for white people are settled after discussions of their character and what they represent. A Belgian priest I knew in the north was given the nickname of Libela—"forever"—because his forceful teachings were deemed permanent—"forever and ever. Amen."

Bula Matari—Crusher of Rocks—was a nickname given to Henry Morton Stanley when he blasted a road through the Crystal Mountains from Vivi (near Matadi) to Léopoldville. Over the years, Bula Matari came to mean "the state," the crusher of Congolese people, so well documented in *Heart of Darkness* and *King Léopold's Ghost*. Because of the persistent antagonism between a crusher state and the people, Congolese officials, from the head of state to a soldier, are expected to be tough on the people but, at the same time, rob the state to profit their own families and friends. Mobutu was caught in the same contradiction. The more powerful he became, the more the family demanded, and the tougher he became. He even appointed a chief of *la maison civile* to deal with family demands.

Mobutu's stepfather, Albéric Gbemany, was a highly prized cook for the Catholic mission in Molegbe. He married a young woman from Gbadolite in the territory of Banzyville. Her name was Marie-Madeleine Yemo. Together they had one daughter and three sons. A visiting Belgian magistrate managed to steal Gbemany away from the bishop. The heavy-hearted cook was transferred to Lisala, a port city on the Congo River. While in Lisala, Gbemany received news that Yemo, his wife, had given birth to their fourth child, a cretin. Cretinism, caused by iodine insufficiency, was common in the northern Ubangi at that time. Years later, Mobutu would take on the care of this stepbrother.

In Gbadolite, following a death in her family, Marie-Madeleine was among other women who stayed with the bereaved until the end of the mourning period. Men came with their wives and left a couple of days after the interment. The women remained sitting or lying "on the sand" (that is, on the floor) waiting for their husbands to return and "lift them." With the lifting of his wife, a man also left a gift for the family of the deceased.

Unlike other married women, Marie-Madeleine remained on the sand. Gbemany and his relatives "forgot" to come and raise her. This was a deep and painful insult, and she was subjected to humiliating looks from the other women whose husbands arrived to free them from the constraints of mourning. Marie-Madeleine, abandoned by her husband, was now free from any bonds to him. She left Gbadolite and moved to "a village of the whites" in Lisala.

Before independence, native men aged eighteen and above could easily leave their villages and move to a village of the white men where jobs were abundant and attractive in the colonial administration, hospitals, factories, plantations, or small shops run by Greeks or Portuguese. There was a high demand even for the illiterate *indigenes* to work as cooks, housekeepers, or *sentinelles*—watchmen. After some time, most men had saved enough money to start a family and have a bride sent to them by their parents following an arranged marriage. Single women were discouraged from moving to a white man's village where unmarried young women had very limited job opportunities. Those who dared to make such a move were called *femmes libres*—free women—and were required by the colonial health services to undergo a monthly medical examination for sexually transmitted diseases, even if they were not prostitutes. In the early 1930s, Marie-Madeleine opted to become such a free woman. She moved to various cities, including Lisala, Businga, and Gemena. Wherever she stayed, men found her attractive, and she had more children but never married again. When she gave birth to a son on October 14, 1930, she named him Mobutu to remind him and others of their humble origins. Mama Yemo was never able to tell Mobutu the name of his biological father. This identity crisis caused Mobutu, and later his children, shame, distress, and insecurity throughout their lives. When he abandoned his Christian name, Joseph-Désiré, Mobutu chose a name in open, firm rejection of the dust-to-dust, down-and-out, and as-low-as-sand meaning of "Mobutu."

In Lisala, Mobutu attended primary school with the priests from Scheut, a Flemish town, and Maurice Kassongo, an accomplished athlete and writer, taught him and eventually became his mentor. Mobutu was at the top of his class, but his indiscipline matched his intelligence. In 1938, Mama Yemo moved back to Gbadolite, the village of her forefathers. Mobutu was eight years old. In an act of respect to his ancestors on the maternal side, the boy removed his shoes and city clothes and was apprenticed to his grandfather and great uncle. They worked the fields, hunted, and fished together.

Mobutu wanted no more schooling, until the missionaries organized a football team. He became the goalkeeper and resumed his studies. Again, he was first in his class but was kicked out for disobedience. He snuck onto a boat heading downriver from Libenge to Coquilhatville, where he was taken on by the Frères des Ecoles chrétiennes—Brothers of Christian Schools. His discipline was tested at the end of the school year. The *frère-directeur* announced that students were forbidden to go to the capital during their vacation because the city was full of danger: girls and beer. Mobutu disregarded the order, and for three weeks he lived the high life in Léopoldville. Upon returning to school, he learned that a classmate, Laurent Eketebi, had squealed on him. The director accused Mobutu of being a bad Christian and kicked him out. He was immediately picked up by the police and marched over to the military authorities in Coquilhatville. The law was strictly enforced: any young man expelled from school was automatically drafted into the Force Publique for seven years. The date was February

13, 1950. The young recruit was nineteen years old.

Because of his excellent knowledge of French, he quickly became the secretary-accountant to the commander of the special company. Eight months later he was sent to the École Centrale in Luluabourg for two years' training in accounting and secretarial duties. He was number two in his class. Number one was a shy but methodical classmate, Honoré Kulufa, who eventually became General Mobutu's secretary. Another classmate, Pakassa, would try to kill Mobutu ten years later.

During his early training in the Force Publique, Mobutu was a practical joker and hid in the bush to avoid chores and read European newspapers passed on to him by some of the Belgian officers. He drove his Congolese superior, Sergeant Major Bobozo, to distraction. At the time, Bobozo was the highest ranking "native" in the Force Publique. He would later become commander in chief of the army under Mobutu. I became Bobozo's doctor. He was a pleasant, sometimes jovial patient. Once, he called me at 2:00 A.M. to say that he needed more blood pressure pills. I reminded him that I had given him all the pills he needed a few days ago. "I know," he replied, "but the cockroaches ate them." Under Bobozo's supervision, Mobutu completed his studies and, with glowing recommendations, was sent to army headquarters in Léopoldville and assigned to the principal secretary of G2, the unit dealing with intelligence, mobilization, and operations. Mobutu's competence and hard work were particularly appreciated by Colonel Marlière, a Belgian G2 officer who had fought, against all odds, for the Africanization of the Force Publique. Mobutu was promoted to sergeant on April 1, 1954.

Adding to his success in army headquarters, his fifteen-year-old fiancée from Banzyville, Marie-Antoinette, gave birth to their first son. Colonel Marlière was the child's godfather.

The young sergeant's passions were reading and writing, his military duties, Marie-Antoinette, and the baby. In a small house in the camp, Mobutu wrote articles under the name J. Debanzy, for he was from the territory of Banzyville through his mother. Regulations did not permit soldiers to write articles for the press, especially *L'Avenir*, the only paper to accept contributions from Congolese. *L'Avenir* became *Actualités africaines*, with Maurice Kassongo, Mobutu's mentor, as editor-in-chief of the weekly. At the end of 1956, Mobutu had served his time in the military. He chose not to reenlist. He left the army and became a journalist responsible for the editorial pages of both *L'Avenir* and *Actualités africaines*. His pay was one Congolese franc per line.

In 1957, Patrice Lumumba, then a leading politician in eastern Congo, was arrested in Stanleyville for embezzlement and transferred to Léopoldville. He was visited frequently by Kassongo, who brought him *Actualités africaines*. Lumumba was impressed with Mobutu's articles that covered extensively the riots in Léopoldville in 1959 and the preparations for the Brussels Round Table. At the insistence of Albert Kalonji and Joseph Kasa Vubu, Lumumba was released from prison to attend the round table conference. Mobutu was present as Lumumba's secretary, a position that was made official in July of 1960, a few days after independence, when Lumumba became prime minister. Shortly thereafter, with the approval of the troops and Bobozo, Mobutu was appointed chief of staff of the Armée Nationale Congolaise (ANC), formerly the Force Publique, with a rank of colonel.

Even today, questions about Mobutu's biological family remain unanswered. The Ngbandi trace their descent through paternal lines. Ngbandi children have full rights in their father's village; in their mother's village they are, at best, guests. Mobutu built his first palace in Gbadolite, his mother's village. He was thus expected by the population to act like a guest: "Make yourself at home but realize that this is not your home." After a while, Mobutu started parading around like a marshal who owned the place, fueling resentment among the traditional landowners of Gbadolite. The more he demanded recognition of his status and power, the less he behaved like a guest. The local chiefs, who were paid off by the president, remained silent, but the people let him know their indignation over his behavior. He became thoroughly disgusted when they misused the houses he had built for them. The marshal finally got the message: "You have no rights here. If you don't like it in your mother's village, then go somewhere else." Had Mobutu known his father or his father's village, he would have built his palace there. Mobutu decided to move his more personal palace to Kawele, where Litho obtained for him some of the rights of a privileged friend.

Litho came from the territory of Banzyville (Mobayi-Mbongo or Southern Mobayi), more specifically from Kawele, a village a few miles from Gbadolite. He was educated at Centre Agronomique de l'Universite Louvain au Congo (CADULAC), in Kisantu, Bas-Congo, as an agricultural assistant. He received his diploma in the 1940s and was employed by the Belgian Congo's public administration. Sometime before the Congo became independent, he was posted to Stanleyville. It was from there that Mobutu, who had become responsible for the army, had him return to Léopoldville to become the minister of agriculture. Later, he would be appointed minister of finance in Mobutu's government.

When Zairianization (nationalization) was imposed on the country by Mobutu, Litho would be granted all the assets of Sarma Congo, an enormous food and produce importer, as well as several other foreign-owned companies. In every position he held, his management produced a calamity, but no one could touch him. Litho married an Italian-Congolese mulatto from Bosobolo who had twin sisters, Kosia and Bobi Ladawa. Kosia became Litho's most recent consort. After Marie-Antoinette's death, Mobutu married Madame Bobi Ladawa but added Kosia and her older sister, Litho's first wife, to the coterie of his public mistresses.

Chapter 13

Imbroglio

ON SEPTEMBER 5, 1960, less than three months after independence, the national radio carried declarations by President Kasa Vubu that Prime Minister Lumumba was fired. The president had the right to do this. The reason given was the massacres by the ANC in the Kasai followed by a rout of the army. An hour later, Lumumba fired Kasa Vubu for treason. The prime minister had no legal right for this action. Each announced to the country and the world that the other was out, *fini*. The country was virtually leaderless.

Apprehension became chaos when a demonstration exploded into violence, bringing scores of wounded to the hospital: a child clubbed to death, another stabbed in the chest, and adults slashed by machetes. Fear, once more, pervaded the city. Police, their eyes narrowed and glaring fiercely from under plastic helmets, stalked victims. Rifle butts became clubs. Soldiers barged into the OR frequently when we operated on one of their brothers. We glanced over our shoulders as we worked. Anti-Lumumba forces broadcast their propaganda from across the river in Brazzaville warning the Congolese that Lumumba wanted to sell their women to the Russians.

One night, in the street outside the hospital, a civilian tried to disarm a Congolese soldier who himself was holding another civilian by the shirt. Most of the troubles at that time were between the Congolese themselves, especially between different political or ethnic groups. White people were seldom bothered. I approached a Ghanaian soldier on duty at the entrance of our apartment house and asked him how he was getting along with the Congolese soldiers. "Bloody savages, Suh. Don't speak the Queen's English." I thanked him for being there and he snapped to attention. "Suh!"

Having the national radio off the air calmed things down considerably. Ghanaian troops guarded the radio station to keep Kasa Vubu's and Lumumba's propagandists out. Rumors, spread by *radio trottoir,* fueled fear and confusion. Tension grew. Which side would make the first move on the radio station?

The Ghanaian U.N. troops were dug in around the buildings when Lumumba arrived with two truckloads of loyal soldiers and threatened to shoot his way in. Colonel Aferi, the Sandhurst-trained officer commanding the Ghanaian troops in the Congo, marched up to the lead vehicle, pointed to the line of blue helmets and weapons just visible above a trench, and shook his head. Enraged, Lumumba demanded an attack. The story we got was that Mobutu, who was leading the Lumumba troops, recognized his men's dangerous exposure and ordered them to turn back. This episode may have provoked the final break between Mobutu and Lumumba. These events were reported to us by Colonel Aferi himself, who arrived, a little late, for a long-standing lunch date right after the confrontation. I understood why politicians and coup plotters go for radio stations like mad dogs go for the throat. Those who control the flow of news and propaganda control the population.

Had it not been for the people maimed or killed in the streets and bars by the recurrent fighting, the situation would have been an opéra bouffe. I remember discussions with embassy people and others in the hospital that led to the conclusion that no "normal" solutions to some of the acute problems of the day were possible. It was conceded that only an unexpected African solution would work.

A company of U.N. Ghanaians guarding Lumumba's residence were themselves surrounded by anti-Lumumba Congolese soldiers, whose orders were to prevent the Ghana-men from smuggling the "deposed" prime minister out of the capital so he could proceed to his northeastern stronghold in Stanleyville. In the midst of this stalemate, Lieutenant-Colonel N'kokolo, a trusted colleague of Mobutu and commander of the military camp in Léopoldville, attempted to arrest Lumumba but was shot and killed by the Ghanaians as he approached the front door. The men in charge of Ghana's mission in the Congo, Gin and Welbeck, were pro-Lumumba, the latter in Ghana's President Nkrumah's cabinet.

Colonel Mobutu, army chief of staff, backed by his senior generals and the paracommando battalion, stepped into the imbroglio between Kasa Vubu and Lumumba. He fired them both, along with Ileo, Kasa Vubu's choice for prime minister. That done, he closed the embassies of the

Soviet Union and Czechoslovakia and created a college of commissioners general using some of the few Congolese university graduates available at the time. It seemed possible that these young technocrats might be able to crank up the machinery of government and get it going again. Mobutu gave Kasa Vubu the authority

Congo Prime Minister Patrice Lumumba captured in the middle of the country while trying to flee to Stanleyville, December 1960.

to name the commander in chief of the army. In return, the ex-president appointed Mobutu to that position.

Lumumba escaped from Léopoldville during the night of November 27, 1960. He was arrested near Lodi on the right bank of the Sankuru River on his way to join his partisans in Stanleyville. On January 17, 1961, Lumumba and two other government officials intimately associated with Lumumba, Joseph Okito and Maurice Mpolo, were flown to Elisabethville, the capital of Tshombe's Katanga Province. The torture, which started in the airplane, continued after they landed. Lumumba and his fellow sufferers were executed by a firing squad officered by a Belgian in the presence of Tshombe, Munongo, and other high officials of the Katanga. When the news of the brutal assassinations flashed around the world on February 13, mobs in Cairo ransacked the Belgian embassy. In Paris, African students demonstrated against the presence of Belgian troops in the Congo. Personally, I was shocked by the reports of horrible beatings that Lumumba and his friends suffered after they'd been captured. It seemed obvious to me that the country would sink into more violence.

From his headquarters in Stanleyville, Antoine Gizenga pronounced himself president of the Congo. For many in Léopoldville and in Western capitals, Gizenga was considered a communist, but he had only spent some two weeks behind the Iron Curtain at the time. He certainly had his eccentricities and surrounded himself with hefty female bodyguards, formidable in their uniforms. Each was armed with an impressive toy pistol. Gizenga marched his rebel Simbas (Swahili for "lions") south to capture the garden city of Bukavu, with its beautiful *presqu'îles* (peninsulas) pushing into Lake Kivu. Mobutu's troops failed in their attempt to recapture that city.

Gizenga organized Lumumba's militants to sow panic among the whites who had become hostages of the Stanleyville regime. Faced with this threat, Mobutu and his commissioners worked toward a collaboration between Léopoldville and Elisabethville. Mobutu flew to Katanga to pressure Tshombe to join the fight against Gizenga. Kasa Vubu sent proposals for reconciliation. Tshombe said yes, but didn't mean it.

Early in January, the U.S. ambassador, Ed Gullion, and Larry Devlin, introduced as a political officer, came to dinner with their wives. Dave Beal, one of the MRA team members who had stayed, cooked a meal of filet, mashed potatoes, beans, corn muffins, and pineapple upside-down cake. Dave dropped the mashed potatoes on the floor, but they were quickly retrieved and none the worse for it. Over coffee, we showed our guests the Congo army film *On peut compter sur nous—You Can Count on Us*—made with a 16-millimeter movie camera by Beal and Paul-Emile Dentan. With an introduction by Mobutu, the film showed a "bad" paratrooper being bribed by a politician, another giving away military secrets when drunk, and the third being seduced in a bar by a lady of the night needing treatment for gonorrhea. The film then showed a parade and maneuvers and three "good" paratroopers, who marched into the scene emphatically saying no to all forms of corruption and seduction. The film was simplicity itself but became an extraordinary success, measured by the demands for its projection in military units of various sizes all over the country.

Most of the MRA team had left, but Paul-Emile Dentan and Eric Junod from Switzerland and David stayed to carry on our work on the National Radio and with film showings for the army. The pressure for me to return to the fold remained in occasional letters, more questioning than imperative. They wanted me out of medicine, and instead, sharing stories about changing human nature and showing MRA films. I chose to continue my involvement with Congolese leaders and the people through medicine and surgery.

At the end of March 1961, I was invited by the paratroopers to attend a celebration marking Mobutu's return to the capital after a trip to the interior. He spoke from a boxing ring. A couple of paratroopers waved me forward to a chair they had saved next to the ring. A Belgian technician and I were the only whites there. Speaking forcefully to the troops, Mobutu said:

> In September 1960, I put myself in the position of being an arbiter between the politicians. I, as well as you, were wrong. Now what must we do? The answer is up to the ANC. In answer to the first question, What do you think of disarmament? I say that there will not be and will never be any disarmament. When I met the commanding general of the U.N. forces in Equateur [this was Mobutu's home province], I was categorical on this question. For me disarmament means the same thing as giving up. Only a Congolese cadaver will give up his gun. I repeated what the chief of state said to the army. "Every soldier must defend the honor of the republic, the honor of the Armée Nationale Congolaise, and his weapon."

Chapter 14

Tata Felix

IN OUR MRA HOUSE, provided by the army, we were having nervous nights after two break-ins. I resisted the idea of a guard until we were burglarized for the third time. Thieves cut out a pane of glass from a living room window, let themselves in, and crept upstairs into our bedroom. Tine, who was over on a short visit, had her camera and purse stolen; they took my medical bag and Zenith shortwave radio. Between our beds they left a rock, probably to use on our heads had we awakened. After that, the three men took turns guarding the house at night with an assortment of ropes, clubs, and a blank cartridge pistol to try and discourage further attempts.

A week after Tine flew back to Switzerland to join the kids, a black car cruised past our house. A rock smashed through a window with a note attached: "*Nous réservons pour vous une fin spéciale*—We reserve for you a special ending." I drove to the paratrooper camp and asked Major Tshatshi to recommend a man we could hire as a night watchman.

The next morning, a paratrooper sergeant arrived with Tata Felix, a tall, thin Mongala warrior from the north. His bearing was military, and the tribal markings on his cheeks and forehead gave him a distinguished, fearsome look. The sergeant called him "Tata"—a respected older man. The sergeant explained that Tata Felix had been with the Belgian Colonial Brigade in Burma during the First World War. He carried a sharp spear, and his medals dangled from the pocket of a faded khaki tunic.

We quickly agreed that he would come at sundown, and we would give him a regular wage plus a mug of strong tea with milk and four spoons of sugar and a half baguette. That was his choice. If he wanted anything else, he would bring it. His watch post would be on our porch in a broken-down armchair with a pillow to compensate for the springs that had pushed through the webbing.

He returned the same evening, banged on the door, saluted, and stood waiting for his ration. After leaning his spear against the wall, he took the mug, carefully, like a chalice, and placed it on the low wall that separated the terrace from the garden. Pulling a bag of peanuts from his pocket, he sat down and, dipping the bread into the mug, gummed down his food. Ants and cockroaches came to investigate the peanut shells, and Tata Felix crushed them under his calloused heel.

During the following months we had peaceful nights. I don't know whether the old soldier made a deal with the men who had earlier menaced us or whether his reputation was such that they kept away. I was glad for the reprieve, but it worried me that he slept all night curled up in the rump-sprung chair.

Once, at 2 A.M., when I was called to the hospital, I woke him up.

"How can you guard the house if you sleep all night?"

He opened one eye and mumbled, *"Ngai awa, moyibi te*—I am here. Thieves no." He tucked himself deeper into his nest as I drove out of the yard.

Early one morning, as I was finishing breakfast, Tata Felix banged on the door. I opened it, he saluted and barked, *"Yaka o ndako ya ngai. Yaka kotala mwasi wa ngai*—You come to my house. See my wife." Lingala, the army vernacular, has some four hundred words and few courtesies.

I pointed at my watch and shook my head. "No time

before hospital."

He turned on his heel and walked down the steps to the car. He opened the back door, leaned his spear against the seat, and climbed into the passenger seat in front.

"Hey, get out of here, damn it. I don't have time now," I shouted.

He didn't budge—just sat looking straight ahead. Damn. No use. I stomped back into the house, grabbed my bag and half-finished cup of coffee, and walked around to the driver's side. Tata leaned over and opened my door. "Thanks a lot," I said, thoroughly annoyed. Quicker to go than to argue. I pulled out of the drive, made two quick left turns, and headed onto the main boulevard.

The morning traffic was light. The old man smelled of musty dust and charcoal fires. I glanced at him; his eyes were fixed on the road. I opened the window and let the fresh morning air come in. A thunderstorm had crashed through the city during the night. In a few hours it would be sweltering.

In the *cité,* we bounced along narrow dirt roads dodging mud holes and piles of garbage. Goats munching refuse eyed us as we passed them, and squawking chickens scattered. Dusty, pot-bellied children wiped snot from their runny noses and waved shyly from the doors of their hovels. We splashed through an open sewer and stopped in front of a house made of concrete blocks and a tin roof. Children appeared from nowhere and surrounded the car. Tata Felix retrieved his spear and shooed the kids away like so many mosquitoes. He opened the wooden door and I walked in with my black bag.

The room was dimly lit and ventilated through hollow bricks that separated the walls from the tin roof. Translucent little geckos scampered along the beams, aroused by the change in light. In the center of the room, on a dirt floor swept smooth and clean, stood an ancient wooden table and two straight-backed chairs. Next to a wall, a bed of planks was set on blocks, and there, on a thin mat, an old woman lay on her side, her knees pulled up to her chin like a fetus. She was covered with a bright African cloth. I left my bag on the table and approached her.

"*Mbote*, Mama." No answer. I put my hand on her shoulder, squeezed it lightly, and repeated, "*Mbote*, Mama." No response. She was comatose. I glanced at Tata Felix. He looked down at his feet and said nothing.

I stepped back to the table, opened my bag and took out a stethoscope and blood pressure cuff. The old woman's pulse was slow and steady, but her pressure was high. I listened to her heart and lungs. Gently, I tried to extend her limbs and roll her onto her back so I could palpate her abdomen and check her eyes. I couldn't straighten her out. Amazingly, she had no bedsores. It seemed to me she must have had a stroke.

As I stuffed my things back in the bag, I thought I must do something for this old woman. I wanted Tata Felix to think of me as a good doctor.

Many Africans feel they've not been treated properly unless they get a shot, preferably a painful one. I drew up some vitamin B complex, at least a harmless placebo. I pulled back the cloth and wiped off her hip with an alcohol sponge. As the needle went in, she moved a little to avoid the pain and let out a groan. "Ohooooo!"

"*Osali ye nini?*" shouted Tata Felix. "What did you do to her?"

"*Napesi ye ntonga*—I gave her a shot."

"*Mpo ya nini*—What for?" He was angry.

I was stunned—embarrassed—and went on the attack. "Why did you insist I come?"

He walked over to his wife and put his hand on her head. "I wanted our children to know that a *monganga* had come to see their mother." He shook his head slowly. "*Mpo na nini osali ye mpasi*—Why did you hurt her?"

I closed my bag and stepped to the door, then turned toward the couple. They had retreated into a world of their own. I left, closing the door gently behind me, wondering whether I would ever learn the art of medicine.

Chapter 15

The Mango Kid

I WALKED INTO THE OFFICE between the OR and the sterilizer room to add a patient's name and what we had done to him to the register, a simple bound notebook with one line per patient: name, gender, age, diagnosis, operation, disposition. No informed consent, insurance data, payment schedules, and confidentiality forms to fill out, thank God. We did the best we could using rudimentary equipment. There was no fussing around, but rather, after a quick pre-op check, the patient was given a spinal or put to sleep and we went to work. The volume and variety of surgery we tackled was a challenge. If we didn't do it, no one would. The patients seldom complained, because it was so hard for them to get any care. In some services, if they did complain, they were thrown out. If your life depends on swallowing shit, you swallow shit. The patients expected us to do our job as best we could, and occasionally said *melesi*—thank you.

We were one of the few surgical services operating, and one major concern was supplies. We used every millimeter of suture material, and gauze pads were retrieved from buckets, washed, and used again. Our patients were as worried as we were about security and who was in charge. Their reaction was to suffer in silence curled up on gurneys. Fear kept them quiet, but did little for their pain. My reaction to the whole bloody mess was to work all out and hope that some semblance of order would be returned to the streets and the slums. I spent no time trying to figure out where the patient on the table was from, what he did, what side he was on, or whether he was a "good guy" or a "bad guy." None of that would have made a difference. A bleeding and broken man needed surgical repair just as a starving child needs food.

Pierre came to tell me that another patient had been brought in. I stood up, stretched, and followed him out to where a boy lay on a gurney. Apparently he had been plucking mangoes in one of the trees that lined the road to the residential commune of Binza. The branch snapped and he had fallen. A crowd had quickly gathered, and a police officer, passing by in his Jeep, picked him up and brought him to the hospital. The policeman knew nothing about the boy's background, so we assumed he was one of many children who attached themselves loosely to families living in the slums. These waifs foraged in garbage cans or begged for leftovers and, during the mango season, lived off the fruit they sold by the roadside. Unlike many wizened children with swollen bellies from chronic protein deficiency, this boy looked healthy. Sister Germaine came in and grumbled about a dirty *gamin*—urchin—on a clean sheet.

The boy was drowsy and groaned as he moved his head from side to side. His blood pressure and pulse were normal. He winced when I touched a swelling above his right ear. His pupils reacted equally to light and were centered. Although there was a little blood in his nose, he had no blood or liquid behind his eardrums. His neck and limbs checked out well, and he raised his arms and legs and stuck out his tongue when I asked him to. All his reflexes were normal.

We had no way of getting more specific about his head injury except by watching him carefully. He certainly had a concussion, but whether he was bleeding inside his skull we might not know for a while. I sat at the head of the table with his head cradled in my palms. Poor little tyke. He had red sand in his short black hair and eyebrows. His chest rose and fell gently as he breathed. No problem there. His lungs were clear, his tummy soft and flat. Bulging from the right pocket of his khaki shorts was the tip of a green mango.

I sat and watched. The sister brought a basin of soapy water to clean him up. She started with the dried blood and dirt in his nose. Then, with a finger poked into a cloth, she washed his ears, carefully removing the grit from the little caves and crevices in his ear flaps. She cleaned the inner angles of his eyes with wet cotton, then took off his shorts and washed and dried the rest of his body. When she was through, I asked her to put his pants back on—I was worried that his mango would disappear.

We looked down at him. "Good-looking little boy," she said. "Let's call him Patrice."

Every fifteen minutes I checked his vitals and level of consciousness. They were steady. He remained drowsy but obeyed commands when aroused. His pupils showed no changes.

Patients who had lined up outside the door for surgical consultations were told to return the following morning. Some who had come from far away sat on benches outside or slept next to a bundle of personal effects under the palm and mango trees near the building. They lay on the grass, keeping the covered walkways free for the constant traffic of patients and sisters.

I continued at the head of the table, my arms resting on a pillow. The child's soft, steady breathing made me sleepy. My thoughts wandered back to other kids and trauma patients we'd dealt with. I thought about the infant who had been rushed in a few days ago with stab wounds in the chest and abdomen. The baby was a victim of a wild fight in a bar. The person holding him had used him as a shield. I had just concluded that he was dead when the father, screaming hysterically, rushed into the operating room and snatched the little body away. Carrying it high over his head, he barged through the crowd around the hospital entrance and ran out into the street.

I raised my head . . . must have dozed off. Something was different. I looked at the boy: his head was turned to the right, his breathing slow and deep. His right pupil was dilated. Both eyes stared fully to the right and slightly up. I could not arouse him, but his right arm and leg moved sluggishly when I pinched them. His left side was flaccid and did not respond at all to painful stimuli. I ran my thumbnail up the soles of his feet. On the left his great toe pulled back like a hitchhiker's thumb. I called out to the OR boys. Makila shuffled in, dragging his mop.

"Get the sister, quickly." He dropped the mop handle and scurried out. Moments later Sister Germaine came running in, followed by Pierre.

"I think this kid's just localized his injury. Check his pressure."

She pumped up the sleeve. "Hundred and fifty over a hundred." Then. "Pulse only forty-eight."

"The pressure in his head is going up." I closed my eyes. Only once before had I faced this situation, as a resident at the Roosevelt. A neurosurgeon had talked me through the procedure. This kid must have just bled into his subdural or epidural space. Which one? At this point, did it matter? The only thing that might save him was a burr hole through the skull to relieve the pressure on his brain. But where do I drill the hole? "The eyes gaze toward the lesion" sounded somewhere in my memory. "Go in where a line from the eyebrow meets a line coming up from the ear."

"Do we have a trephine—something to make a burr hole?"

"I don't think so." She hurried into the instrument room and returned, shaking her head.

"Run over to the carpentry shop and get a brace and bit. Maybe that'll work," I said. She sailed out of the veranda door, white skirts and veil flying.

By the time she returned with the tools, Pierre and I had shaved hair off the area to be opened and washed it with soap and water. A local anesthetic in the skin was all he'd need; everything below was insensitive to pain. The boy's respirations remained deep and slow. I put an airway in his mouth, then incised the scalp down to the skull with one stroke. We controlled the bleeding with finger pressure on the lips of the wound. The brace and bit, which the sister had wiped off with alcohol, worked well, and I was quickly through the outer plate. Then we advanced slowly, the sister washing away the shavings and soft fragments of cortical bone with squirts of saline from a bulb syringe. A little more, then just a little more, and the bottom of the hole turned blue. With a bone snip, I carefully enlarged the hole, then with the tip of a scalpel, picked away the final layer to expose the dura, the tough fibrous membrane covering the brain; it bulged into the hole. I nicked it and dark blood spurted. Within seconds, the boy's eyes were centered, his pupils equal in size. He awoke and struggled to sit. After that, we kept him in P1, where "miscellaneous" children with chronic diseases and a few kids with no place to go were housed.

After Patrice had recovered from his primitive craniotomy, he would stand outside the veranda and watch me operate. When he arrived at his station each morning, he greeted me with "*Mbote, monganga.*" I replied, "*Mbote, mwana kitoko*—Hello, handsome child." Then he'd settle in and follow the action in the OR.

I showed off Patrice to visitors with obvious pride. To be a surgeon faced with a life ebbing fast on the table, to be uncertain what was killing the patient, and to be without expert help or adequate tools are the makings of a nightmare. I had gambled on a distant memory and won.

I wrote to Dr. Frank Stinchfield, my orthopedic mentor,

about Patrice and listed the sorts of trauma patients that came in for surgery. To my delight, Frank sent me a military footlocker filled with orthopedic hardware and an operative atlas that outlined surgical procedures by the numbers. Frank was the chairman of Columbia's College of Physicians and Surgeons Department of Orthopedics. During my last two years at P&S, I worked for him in the dog lab, where he was experimenting with metal cup arthroplastic replacements in hip joints. I assisted him frequently in the operating rooms of the New York Orthopedic Hospital, where he taught me that if something went wrong during a procedure, turn around, rinse my gloves in the basin provided for this, and stay cool. The nurses loved him, and he was a role model and friend of mine for many years.

Medicine may be a demanding spouse, but surgery is a seductive mistress expert in caressing egos. One day I was driving across the main boulevard in Léopoldville preoccupied by things other than the traffic or the cop in the middle of a busy intersection. I ignored his signal to stop. He jumped off his white-and-black box and ran toward my car, shaking his police stick at me, incensed by my lack of respect for his authority. He bent over to look in the car, and suddenly recognizing me, a grin spread across his face. Straightening up, he tore open his shirt and pushed down his belt to expose a long midline scar on his belly.

"Remember, *docteur*? You operated on me!"

"Oh, yes," I lied. We shook hands.

He stepped into the middle of the crossroads, halting all traffic so I could proceed, and saluted as I drove past.

Chapter 16
Tshombe in Kitona

DURING SEPTEMBER AND OCTOBER, intermittent rains prepared people and the city's drains for the deluges and crashing thunderstorms of November. Most evenings great swirling clouds mushroomed into towering thunderheads with dark menacing bases from which lightning streaked and flashed on the horizon like bolts hurled down by angry gods. Thunder rumbled and echoed throughout the city, and people ran for shelter. The downpours cleaned the air and washed the dust off the flame trees and mango trees along the boulevards, but in the eastern Congo, the rainy season brought no refreshment, only more blood and dead bodies bobbing in muddy rivers. Rebels from Stanleyville loyal to Gizenga slaughtered and cannibalized twelve Italian airmen in Kindu. Their commander, Colonel Pakassa, watched the orgy from the sidelines. He was the same man who came close to murdering Mobutu in 1960. He had been thrown in jail then, but escaped and became one of Gizenga's rebel officers. While the rebellion in the east continued, in New York, the Security Council turned against Tshombe, and December saw a renewal of fighting in the Katanga between U.N. troops and Tshombe's gendarmes.

We went about our rounds with an unrelenting sense of foreboding. Among some expatriates, this foreboding turned into full-blown cynicism: anything bad could happen and probably would. Lightning could strike anywhere, even twice in the same place—especially given the many outside elements sidling in for their own self-interests.

By December 1961, hope had vanished that the United Nations or anyone else could bring about a reconciliation between Tshombe and the central government. On December 18, in the afternoon, I received a call from the U.S. embassy saying that Ambassador Gullion, who was with Tshombe in Ndola on the Zambian side of the frontier, requested that I meet him and Tshombe in Kitona, a military base on the coast, on the following day. Apparently Gullion was having a tough battle getting Tshombe to fly up to Kitona for a meeting with Cyrille Adoula, who had recently become prime minister, mainly because of Tshombe's fear for his personal safety. Since I had taken care of Tshombe when he had been under house arrest in the paratrooper camp, I suppose I was a source of security for him. The next morning I drove out to the American hangar at Ndjili and met Colonel Matlik, the U.S. air attaché who flew the embassy plane. We had to leave in a hurry. Another message from the ambassador asked us to be in Kitona before he and Tshombe landed in former President Eisenhower's Lockheed Constellation, the *Columbine*. The VIP aircraft had been sent over by the White House to further persuade Tshombe of the importance of the meeting with Adoula. Gullion also asked us to bring two Marines from the embassy detachment to give Tshombe an added sense of security.

Matlik's copilot was on leave, so he asked me if I would fly in his place. The plane was an embassy C-47. I told him that the last time I had flown a Goony bird was in 1946, but I agreed enthusiastically. We took off with some newspaper reporters aboard and had a pleasant flight downriver to Kitona. When we landed, the field was guarded by a company of U.N. troops from Nigeria in full combat dress, ready on the trigger, dug in, and dispersed up and down the runway. The colonel in charge said he had orders not to let any reporters on the base, so we took off again and hopped them over to Moanda, coming right back to Kitona just before the *Columbine* was about to land. We slipped in before them.

Tshombe looked tired and ap-prehensive when he stepped out of the plane, but he lit up when we shook hands and said how glad he was to see me. Then the whole party quickly proceeded to the abandoned base hospital where the meeting was to take place.

Tshombe under stress.

I had a short talk with Tshombe before Adoula and his party arrived. He was full of the horrors of the war down in the Katanga and apprehensive about security and his health. He was reassured when the ambassador told him that I would be present. I stressed that we hoped the solution to the divisions in the Congo would come from this meeting.

When Adoula arrived, it was obvious that the meeting would be rough going. He had with him Gbenye, the minister of interior; the minister of justice; the foreign minister, Bomboko; and U.N. officials Khiary, Gardiner, Bunche, and Dumontet. The Congolese delegation and Khiary had been anti-Tshombe for a long time.

A late lunch was held in the officers' mess, with everyone going over together. That afternoon Adoula and some of his men drove to Moanda for a swim in the Atlantic, and no negotiating took place. Everyone was housed in the hospital, some of us sleeping on the floor on mattresses. As we were getting ready for the night, Ralph Bunche, U.N. undersecretary for Special Political Affairs, came running downstairs in his bathrobe. He had just

(L-R) Ralph Bunche, Foreign Minister Bomboko, and Prime Minister Adoula.

heard a report that ANC soldiers had set off from Matadi and Banana heading toward us in Kitona. Their goal was apparently to eliminate Tshombe.

After an edgy night, Matlik and I got up at 4:30 and took off at daybreak to look for ANC formations along the roads to Matadi, Banana, and Kitona. We saw nothing. The whole thing was a false alarm.

Tshombe and Adoula and their men sat down around 9:00 A.M. and talked until 2:30 A.M. the next morning. They met alone. But in the evening, when Tshombe hesitated to sign a statement covering the points he had agreed to during the morning, the U.N. men and Ambassador Gullion pushed Tshombe for a settlement. The ambassador also pressured Adoula, telling him that if he did not loosen up, the United States might be forced to withhold its support for him and his government. At 10:00 P.M. the meeting broke up, with Adoula and his team clearly frustrated by Tshombe's vacillations. We prepared to leave immediately. Cars were called, and as everyone packed up, they started to talk again. But at 1:30 A.M., the talks collapsed once more. Hope for a joint statement had been shattered. More pressure was brought to bear, and in another hour, they came out with a joint statement. However, Tshombe held to his stipulation that Katanga's parliament and his cabinet would have to approve the document.

At 3:00 A.M., as soon as the statement was signed, we drove out to the airport. Matlik and I ran to the embassy plane and positioned it so that its landing lights lit up the Nigerian guard of honor, and the press, now admitted, gathered around Tshombe and Adoula separately. Adoula boarded the U.N. plane with his party, Tshombe boarded the *Columbine*, and the ambassador climbed aboard our C-47 and we flew back to Léopoldville.

If Tshombe and his people in Katanga would stick with the agreement made with Adoula, together they might be able to swing the tide against Gizenga and his people in Stanleyville. But the Gizengists were determined to have no part of Tshombe. It was hard to tell what would happen. For the time being, the fighting had stopped in Katanga, and in the northeast, Gizenga had been arrested and sent to the island of Bula-Mbemba in the Congo River delta where political prisoners were held in a coastal artillery barracks.

Chapter 17

The Boy with the Broken Leg

HE WAS DRESSED in a white T-shirt and khaki shorts, both smeared with dirt. We gathered, from the policeman who brought him in, that he'd been run over by a military jeep. He lay sweating and rigid with fear, gripping his left thigh. Sister Germaine, in her usual brusque way, snatched the boy's hands off his leg and placed them firmly on either side of his body, commanding him not to move. The boy clenched his teeth and grabbed the rubber sheet but lay still.

I patted his shoulder. *"Nkombo na yo*—What is your name?"

"Kumu Albert," he murmured.

"K'obanga te—Don't be frightened," I said. He nodded and closed his eyes tightly.

He had a nasty-looking gash in his leg, about halfway between the knee and ankle. Dark blood, carrying globules of fat, oozed from the wound. The leg was swollen and slightly angled outward. I touched the area around the laceration and felt the fragments grind under my fingers. The pulses in his ankle and foot were strong. It would have been nice to have an X-ray.

The sister wheeled him into the operating room, and with Pierre steadying the injured leg, we lifted him off the gurney and onto the table. The boy put his hand over his mouth to stifle a cry, and tears squeezed out of his eyes, streaking the dirt on his temples.

I pulled the anesthesia machine over, started an IV infusion, and gave him some pentothal. He relaxed, blinked, and with a deep sigh went to sleep. Makila placed a mask over the boy's face. I adjusted the oxygen and nitrous oxide knobs on the machine, and Makila pushed on the balloon.

Sister Germaine brought warm, soapy water and a nailbrush whose bristles were worn flat. She put on gloves and started to scrub the wound and leg. I went to the basin in the corner of the room to wash my hands. I was tired and the muscles in my shoulders ached; I did some shoulder shrugs and stretched my neck. I knew I still had to drive to the paratrooper camp and see what they had in the dispensary before heading home to bed.

The sister finished prepping the leg, sloshed iodine and alcohol over the wound, and covered it with a sterile towel. She laid out what we would need on the instrument table. I picked up the gown, opened it, and pushed my hands through the sleeves; it was still damp. Something was wrong with the sterilizer.

We debrided the wound, and with Pierre pulling on the leg, the fragments slipped into place. When he released the traction, the ends of the bones locked into each other, and the reduction was maintained. I brought the skin edges together with stainless steel sutures, then fluffed up gauze compresses to cover the wound and put on a light dressing and a thin, loose shell of plaster wrapped from the base of his toes to the upper thigh. As the plaster hardened, the boy awoke. With the fracture set and immobilized, he had little pain.

By the time I was through, the boy's father had arrived and was standing at the veranda door. I let him in, we shook hands, and he thanked me warmly for taking care of his son. He was a clerk in a bank. I told him about his son's injury and said that if the wound did not get infected, he would do well, adding that we would have to keep him in the hospital for a couple of weeks.

I showered, put on street clothes, and drove to the

paratrooper camp. After jabbing penicillin into a few soldiers, I went home. Trooper, my lovable, independent black Labrador, was there to greet me, and although I missed them, I was relieved that Tine and the kids were in Switzerland. It would have been nerve racking to have them here in the middle of such insecurity.

The next morning when I arrived at the hospital, Sister Euphrasie met me at the door. She had found the boy in bad shape when she came on duty and asked me to follow her to P6.

Sitting by the bed, looking worried and tired, was the boy's father. I shook his hand, then took the boy's. It was hot and sweaty. He looked sick and had the red, dry eyes and dilating nostrils of someone feverish with a toxic infection. His toes, poking out of the plaster shell, were swollen and blue. The cast had become a tourniquet overnight. I opened it along the top and spread the edges. I watched the toes, expecting them to return to a healthy pink—they didn't. Cutting into the cast padding, I pulled away the dressings. They were fouled with a gray, putrid exudate. I pressed the dusky skin next to the wound; it felt like a sponge. Although I had never seen gas gangrene before, the smell and the feel were unmistakable. I cut off the top of the whole cast, dressed the wound, and asked the sister to give him three million units of penicillin every four hours. Then I sat on a corner of the bed and explained to the boy and his father that the cast I had put on to immobilize the fragments had not allowed for the swelling that developed during the night; now there was a serious infection. I had every hope that the antibiotics would help. I would check him again in the evening.

All through the day I found myself regretting that I had not left the wound open with the leg resting in a partial cast. The organism that causes gangrene does not grow well in fresh air.

That evening the leg seemed about the same, but the

boy's pulse and temperature were going up: a bad sign. I walked outside with the father, and we sat on a bench near the OR.

"I must tell you," I began, "that if the infection does not come under control by tomorrow morning, I will have to amputate your boy's leg to save his life."

The father looked stunned, then buried his face in his hands. That night I hardly slept, and left before dawn to see the boy.

Sister Euphrasie and I removed the dressings, and even before the wound was exposed, the fetid smell banished any expectation that penicillin would be enough. Gray ooze seeped through the gauze. The gas had pushed farther up the leg, and the redness and swelling had progressed to a handbreadth below the knee. The boy had little pain—the nerves were destroyed. His fever was alarming. I covered the wound and sat next to the bed. He glanced at me, then looked up at Sister Euphrasie, who stood on the other side with her hand on his shoulder. I stepped to the door and asked his father to come in. He stood opposite the sister and held his son's hand. I told the boy that I had to take him back to the operating room and put him to sleep again and take off his leg. He cried out, "*Non,*" and his father hugged him tightly. I added that if I operated now, I thought we could save his knee. His father looked at me steadily for a moment, then lowered his head to hide the tears that welled up and ran down his cheeks.

"Do whatever you think is necessary. I have confidence in you."

Sister Germaine cradled his head in her hands as I put him to sleep. I did a guillotine amputation, leaving the wound open. After the operation I found the father sitting on the bench under the palm tree. I sat next to him. We didn't talk for a while. Then I turned to him.

"I will have the best artificial leg available in the

United States sent to your boy every year until he finishes growing."

"You can do that?"

"Yes."

We stood, and he embraced me. We both wept. I walked him back to his son's bedside and left them together.

In the shower, I scrubbed away the sweat and stains of surgery, then dressed and slipped out the back door. I walked to the Catholic chapel around the corner. The priest, a hospital chaplain, had shown me the loose brick behind which he hid the key to the vestry. The morning service had just ended. The fragrance of candles and incense lingered—a welcome contrast to the smells of the OR. I slipped into the front pew and sat staring at the altar, but all I saw was the amputated leg and all I heard was the father's "I have confidence in you." Would the boy have developed gangrene with a different dressing? Was I at fault with my choice of a closed cast? Had I been too cocky after saving Patrice? Probably. Was the tragedy retribution for turning my back on God's will according to the directors of Moral Re-Armament? Surely a loving God would not be party to such a thing. At that moment I was strongly tempted to quit surgery. I could go away . . . do something else where the stakes were not so high.

I rested my head against the back of the pew and gazed up at the cobwebs hanging from the hardwood beams. I was driven by what? My upbringing? My education in English schools? *Better to have tried and failed than never to have tried at all, my boy.* Flight training during the war followed by medical school honed my ambition and discouraged self-analysis. The amputation of a boy's leg had shattered my self-confidence. What was I doing here in the Congo? Right now, feeling sorry for myself for having made a mistake, for a cast that tightened like a tourniquet on a boy's leg.

I sat up. I'd have to get over it. Thank God I'd been able to save his knee. First thing in the morning, I would put in a call to my orthopedic mentor in New York. He would lead me to a service that could provide a below-the-knee prosthesis for the boy. I'd received the best training in surgery in New York, and now I would continue a tougher training on my own and fill a need for my patients.

I stepped outside, locked the vestry door, and pushed the key into its recess. I walked slowly to my car parked behind the surgical buildings. As I approached, a boy stepped out from the shadows with his hand outstretched.

"*Mbote, monganga,*" said Patrice, holding up a golden mango.

"*Mbote, mwana kitoko*—Hello, handsome child," I replied, kneeling down to take him and his mango in my arms.

I drove home. Mark and Martha were waiting for me. We sat down to eat. I told them I was exhausted and sick at heart over the kid whose leg I had amputated. They nodded their sympathy. I could have used a stiff Scotch on the rocks but had to settle for Earl Grey tea. Mark broke the silence.

"We've been seeking guidance about your work at the hospital. We are not sure that you are being guided by God."

"Who's not sure?"

"Martha and I."

"What do you think I'm being guided by then?"

"Ambition."

I thought, *Oh shit. Here we go.* "What's wrong with ambition to cure people, to relieve suffering, to make a difference in the lives of the sick or wounded?"

"You have a powerful ego," Mark intoned.

"That's probably true. So what? I wouldn't want a

wilting flower to operate on me." I stood up. "I've had a huge, exhausting, hell of a day. I don't have the patience or the energy to sit through your sermons."

Mark followed me to the door of my room.

I turned on him and shouted, "What gives you the right to judge what God wants me to do?"

Mark's voice quivered with conviction. "It's not *who* is right but *what* is right."

"And who judges what is right?"

He shook his head slowly. "We will pray for you."

I stared at his pitiful face. "Don't pray for me, damn it, pray for the poor bloody kid and his father."

He fixed me with soulful eyes. "You are the one who needs our prayers."

I slammed the door in his face.

Chapter 18
Article 15

IN JANUARY 1962, Mobutu asked me to become the chief doctor for the Congolese army. I accepted and was assigned an empty office in the headquarters building and access to a packaged field hospital sitting in the central depot, a gift from the Americans. As it turned out, there was no real medical corps, only Dr. Victor Ilanga, who had been trained in Belgium. He became my assistant and did much of the work of helping to resurrect hospitals destroyed and stripped bare by rebels and soldiers alike.

When Mobutu asked me to set up a field hospital in the eastern part of the country where fighting between central government troops and rebel units still raged, I

Dr. Ilanga and Bill (in uniform of honorary lieutenant colonel) at the destroyed Uvira Hospital.

had no problem admitting my total lack of experience in this sort of thing. His response, with a wave of his hand, was, "Just apply Article 15."

I walked downstairs to the office of a senior Belgian officer and asked him rather diffidently, ashamed to display my ignorance, "The general told me to apply Article 15 in setting up a field hospital in the east. Would you mind telling me what that means?"

The officer roared with laughter. "Article 15 means *débrouillez-vous*—work it out for yourself." The first draft of the constitution that "Emperor" Kalondji Ditunga adopted for his diamond-rich Kasai Province right after independence had fourteen articles with an unwritten Article 15 designed to cover anything the fourteen didn't. I saw Army Chief of Staff Colonel Puati, who was much more sympathetic and told me to do what I could. He suggested that Kongolo might be a good place to start. Puati was a courageous and dedicated officer with a wry sense of humor. I asked him, one day, why his ethnic group, the Bakongo, was a matriarchy. "It is always known who is the mother. But the father? . . . " I learned the reality later. The Bakongo belong to a matrilineal society. Power is held by men but transmitted by women.

As it turned out, a field hospital was not needed, but reports of a meningitis epidemic across the Lualaba River at Kongolo called for attention. Paul-Emile Dentan, my MRA colleague, and I flew to Kongolo in a twin engine Aztec with a Belgian pilot checking me out in the aircraft. Our pilot was a real bush pilot who thoroughly enjoyed his Primus and his Belga Jaunes cigarettes. He knew the country and the rivers and even the odd great tree standing in a vast undulating savanna, or a fishing village tucked into the forest beside a muddy stream. He was not a great instrument flier, and neither was I, so we often flew close to the ground and aimed for clear gaps in black clouds. I felt secure with him on board except when his intake of Primus was greater than his bladder capacity. During one fuel stop he drank two bottles of Primus, and an hour later, in the air, flying over dense forest, he reached back for a bath towel in his flight bag and peed in it.

In Kongolo we were met at the strip by the camp commander, a captain, and by Père Jules Darmont, the only priest to escape a massacre four months earlier. A plain pipe cross marked the site where twenty Belgian missionaries, Dr. Moreau from France, a seventy-year-old planter, M. Melkenbeek, and dozens of Congolese had been mutilated and hacked to death by Simba rebels from Stanleyville led by Pakassa.

Kongolo was one of the places where the army was doing a good job. The commanding officer had assembled the three local administrators and told them that they had to work together or he would arrest them. He had organized sports events between civilians and soldiers to encourage people to come out of the bush, return to town, and work.

That afternoon, we walked over to the military prison with Père Darmont, a humble man who spoke of the atrocities, leaving out details of the horrors. He showed us the cramped cell with its crawl-through door where a sympathetic soldier had made him hide during the killings. After sunset, Paul-Emile projected the army films *You Can Count on Us* and *Freedom* to a crowd of soldiers and civilians. The reception, as usual, was wildly enthusiastic.

The next morning I visited the regional civilian hospital. A badly burned patient, set on fire by Simba rebels, lay on a gray sheet stained with pus and urine. Next to him a man, gaunt and shriveled by dehydration, lay on a rubber mattress dripping liquid stool onto the floor. Clouds of hungry bluebottle flies foraged on the patients. The overpowering smell in the naked room, stripped of everything by the rebels and then the army and then the rebels again, forced us into the hot, damp air of the overgrown grass in the hospital yard. A wizened nursing aide was the only medical person for the population. He had nothing to work with, not even soap.

Bill (with his back toward camera) about to cross the Lualaba River to investigate a report of a meningitis epidemic in Sola.

Around noon, a Congolese adjutant and I crossed the Lualaba River in a pirogue paddled by two soldiers to check out the reports of the meningitis outbreak. At Kongolo, the river is about two kilometers across and moves swiftly. You have to paddle hard upstream to keep from getting pulled down beyond your landing site. On the other side, we wove through a marsh with high reeds and landed on a boggy island. We waded through muddy water for about a kilometer, climbed the bank, and walked three kilometers to Lumanisha, a village where a section of the fifth batallion was camped. One of the soldiers carried my black bag on his head, another a cardboard box filled with various medicines. I thought of Dr. Livingston and chuckled to myself. We climbed aboard a truck and drove thirty kilometers over a sand track to Sola.

Since the sun was approaching the horizon, I made a quick survey of the huts in which people were sick. Many villagers had apparently died of cerebral malaria. Whether meningitis was involved was impossible to determine. I left all the medicine I had brought with me.

Darkness overtook us by the time we reached the end of the road. The paddlers found the way through the swamp to the island where we had left the pirogue. Now the night was pitch black. We started paddling upstream, and this time the dugout developed leaks, and the adjutant and I bailed like mad. Starlight glimmered faintly in the water. I was sure we were downstream from the beach at Kongolo. All of a sudden a grass fire on the opposite bank lit up the night and we saw our landing place. It seemed to me as miraculous as Moses' burning bush. That night we slept on grass covered with sacking and awoke to a dramatic sunrise over the river.

On my return to Léopoldville, I reported to Mobutu that the trip had gone well and that we would distribute some of the equipment packaged in the field hospital to dispensaries that had been stripped clean by the rebels.

"There's one problem," I said. "It takes me forever to get past the military police at army headquarters to get up to my office. A laissez-passer would make it easier."

"I'll have one issued, but it won't do much good. When the soldiers know you and you have taken care of some of them, they will carry you upstairs."

Chapter 19

From Public to Private Practice

A COMBINATION of the minister of health and the United Nations through the World Health Organization succeeded in finding a young Belgian surgeon to take my place at the general hospital. I was burned out by the high volume and stress of operating, often around the clock.

Bill and Tine in home medical office.

And yet, I would leave the operating room crew and those extraordinary Belgian nursing sisters with a heavy heart. I left surgery at the general hospital in February 1962. My replacement and I worked together for a month, and I had no qualms about his taking over the service. Now I could function as a physician, occasionally operating at the Clinique Reine Elisabeth (later the Clinique Ngaliema), the hospital reserved for Europeans before independence but now open to any who could pay or promise to pay.

The Belgian nurses in Clinique Ngaliema were supremely competent and a joy to work with. My favorite was Sister Donatienne of Pavilion 5, who took care of the sickest medical patients. She had a clubfoot and made her way from the convent along the covered walkways to her pavilion on a bicycle with her African gray parrot, Jako, perched on the handlebars. Once when a particularly stuffy cabinet minister was lying in regal splendor in his private room, Jako crawled down from his perch on the sister's desk, waddled across the immaculate black-and-white tile floor, climbed up the foot of the bed and squawked, "*Zoba, zoba*—Idiot, idiot." The minister could not help but laugh and became easier to care for.

Nursing sisters from Clinique Ngaliema in Kinshasa in their retirement home in Brussels. (L-R) Sister Marie of Surgery; Dr. Jean-Francois Ruppol, born and raised in the Congo, a valued colleague and one of the first Belgian doctors to confront the Ebola epidemic; unidentified sister; Bill; Sister Donatienne of Pavilion 5.

During one of my frequent visits with Mobutu on his back terrace, he asked me if I would create a VIP hospital for senior members of the army and the government. I told him right away that I was not interested in taking care of VIPs exclusively, but that if he wanted a good medical clinic open to anyone, I would be happy to do that. This concept eventually became the Presidential Medical Services, in which care was available to anyone by appointment, something new for Léopoldville. Everyone was treated equally and well. An army general noticed a common soldier's wife in the waiting room. He remarked upon it and I reminded him that we were in the *Democratic Republic of the Congo*. He got the point.

One evening, Mobutu said, "I've been thinking of building a tourist center on Lake Kivu. We could attract tourists."

"I'm more concerned about the people living in conditions worse than before independence," I replied.

"We're dealing with that," he said. But he wanted to have his pavilion at the Organization of African Unity (OAU) connected to my office for a physiotherapy unit with sauna, massage, and rehabilitation. I didn't answer. I could see the office becoming a spa for the elite. My time in surgery at the general hospital had wed me to the needs of the people.

I missed working at the general hospital with the sisters, so one day, I stopped in to see Sister Euphrasie at the convent next to the hospital. Sister Germaine of the OR had left the order and become an air hostess with Sabena Airlines. Sister Euphrasie had retired from active nursing and was now the *mère de la porte*—mother of the door. I rang the bell and walked in as she shuffled out of the room devoted to receiving guests.

"Ha," she exclaimed, with a broad smile. "It is you."

I wanted to give her a hug, but we shook hands. She invited me to sit and busied herself making tea. She told me that she had returned to Belgium to retire, but after two months could stand it no longer and she'd returned to the Congo and her beloved patients. We drank our tea and she wanted news of the family.

"And you, *docteur*? How is it with you?"

"Too busy and so many things to attend to. I often wish that I was back here just doing surgery, just taking care of my patients."

Euphrasie, *la mère de la porte*, drew herself up and replied sternly, "I hear you are doing good work. That must continue. If the Savior wants you at the hospital, He will make it clear to you."

"*Oui, ma mère.*" I hugged her.

The Close twins, Billy and Teddy, at the age of seven, standing in front of the African pavilion of the International Colonial Exposition in Paris, 1931.

Lt. Gen. J.-D. Mobutu, President of the Democratic Republic of Congo, and Madame with children, November 1967. Children: Joseph 6, Jean-Paul 12, Felix 8, Françoise 1, Jacqueline 5, Marie-Antoinette 2, Marie-Louise 10.

Bill with Emperor Haile Selassie's pet cheetah in Addis Ababa.

Presidential Medical Service with the presidential gardens and Congo River in the background.

Boxing match in the paratrooper camp in preparation for training in Israel.

Bill and Mahele monitoring field events.

Bill and Mobutu enjoy a laugh on the president's boat.

The president's Alouette helicopter on the poop deck.

The president and his family on the upper deck, Tine and Nurse Tweedie on the lower deck, watching the helicopter take off from the boat.

Mahele leading bodyguards, aides, and Bill in morning exercises on the boat.

Jean Powis de Tenbosch (Mobutu's Belgian aide), King Baudouin, and President Mobutu visiting the president's zoo.

National journalists on the press plane between stops on a trip with the president.

Bill being congratulated by Mobutu after defeating the king of Morocco's military aide in a tennis match at the Rabbat Hilton.

General Mobutu's military aides.

Mahele, Bill, and military aides at picnic in Mogadishu during a state visit by President Mobutu.

Bill flying Bravo Hotel Alpha C-45.

Shadow of Bell helicopter over a village near
Lake Tanganyika during the rebellion.

Off-loading medical supplies in Fizi, which was surrounded
by rebels near Lake Tanganyika.

Father Angelo, Bill, Dr. Ilanga, and a local commander at the Uvira Hospital that had been ravaged by the rebels. We flew Father Angelo to the Mountains of the Moon to search for his brother priests who had been captured by rebels. That was the last time we saw him.

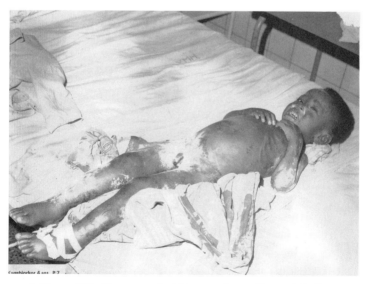

A refugee child with severe malnutrition, measles, and fungus infections.

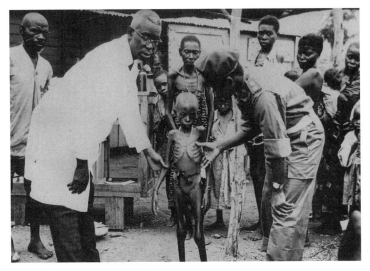

Starving refugees from the mountains above the Ruzizi Valley during the rebellion.

Rebuilding a village for the refugees in the Ruzizi Valley.

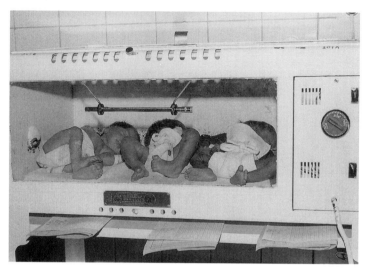

Premie service in Mama Yemo Hospital. Three infants packed into a single incubator.

Mothers of premies waiting to feed their infants. Two white spots = twins.

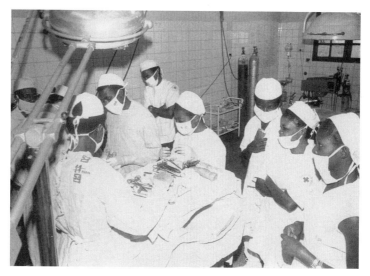

Gynecology operating room.

Sister Beata waving with other nursing sisters on the way to riverside dispensaries near Yambuku. Sister Beata was the first Belgian nun to die of Ebola fever in 1976.

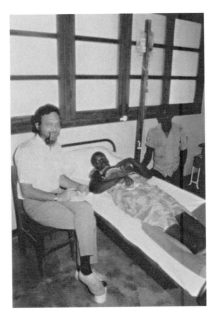

Epidemiologist Karl Johnson, of the Centers
for Disease Control, at Yambuku Hospital with
Sophie and Sukato, two of the rare survivors
of Ebola fever in 1976.

The main road from Bumba to Yambuku.

Glenn Close with villagers who pulled us out of deep mud holes.

Bill and Trooper during visit to Wyoming.

Dr. Miatudila and his wife, Pauline, with Tine and Bill in Big Piney, Wyoming, 2006.

Chapter 20
Psychologist, Sexologist, and Gorilla Hormone

IN MARCH OF 1962, I left for a much needed rest to visit friends in South Africa. The Rubridges were sheep farmers in the Karoo. I landed in Johannesburg and boarded the evening Karoo Express heading south. The Express was a picturesque little train in those days with comfortable red plush seats that were made up into soft bunks by white-haired blacks who called you "Bass." As the daylight faded and the telephone poles along the track cast long shadows in the setting sun, the train meandered through the countryside, in and out of the valleys and farmland that separated Johannesburg from the scrublands and desert of the Great Karoo.

In the morning, the porter brought me a cup of strong black tea and told me that we would be arriving at Merriman Station in an hour. I drank the tea, shaved, and went into the dining car for a breakfast of muscular porridge called "kaffir corn."

Charles Rubridge welcomed me at the station, and we drove for nearly an hour to Zoetvlei (Sweetgrass), his thirty-thousand-acre sheep farm. Charles and Stella Rubridge's families had come from Germany and England and had made the long trek from Cape Town in ox wagons with the early settlers during the 1860s.

The farmhouse was solid and homey, and the Rubridges were generous hosts. All the food at the farm was homegrown. Mutton was a feature of every meal, of course, and heavy cream on homemade oat cereal with brown sugar started the day. I was introduced to *boerebuskuit*, a rock-hard bread that became chewy only after dunking it in tea or coffee. *Boerebuskuit*, which means "farmers' biscuit," and *biltong*, the South African jerky, had been carried in saddlebags by the Boers during their war against the British.

I took long rides into the desert hills on an old pony and saw drawings scratched on rocks in shallow caves by bushmen long before the coming of the whites from the south and the Bantu from the north. Basking in the warmth of this Afrikaner family, I had been able to get some real rest, ponder the past, and wonder about the future.

Tine was back in Greenwich with the kids. I wrote to her:

> I've just come in from an indescribably beautiful two-hour ride on the veldt. I was riding a little mare called Daisy and had Rashes and Vicki, two black sheepdogs, as companions. It's been a beautiful day. Not too hot, but with the sun shining in a clear blue sky. You can see for miles and miles, not just flat, but mountains and valleys and never-ending plains.
>
> I saw a springbok this morning, and this afternoon flocks of ducks and geese and majestic herons and flamingos, rabbits and ferrets, cormorants, and many others I don't know, except for an ibis with a long curved bill and a spoon-billed something or other. How I wish you could have been with me. I took lots of pictures to send you.
>
> This morning Fred and I drove Mr. Kelly, a pensioner, who lives on the upper end of the farm, into Graaf Reinet to catch a bus. He is quite a character with a long white moustache. He doesn't want anybody to help him. He's sev-

enty-six. He thinks spirits are out to get him and hears things on the roof. As yet he hasn't heard any voices or seen anyone. When he does, it will be time to take him where he can get proper care.

P.S. Just got a call from the American Embassy in Pretoria with a message from Gullion and Gardiner asking me to get right back to Léopoldville. Things must be buzzing. Will keep you posted. Love, Bill

In Pretoria I met my troop carrier squadron commander, Tommy Mills, now an air attaché. We had lunch together, and Tommy, after three drinks, returned to the constant theme he had preached in the officers' club after a few drinks. "You have to be careful. People will use you." He repeated that on many occasions, always after a few drinks and usually with tears. I landed in Léopoldville and found out that Paul-Emile and Eric were on a trip in the interior. The MRA house looked wonderful except for cockroaches. The scarlet flowers on the flame trees were bursting open, and everything looked greener and more jungly. The rainy season was coming to an end, and the stifling heat and shirt-soaking humidity would soon yield to the dusty browns of the dry season.

The day after my return, I met with Mr. Gardiner in his office in the Hotel Royal, the U.N. headquarters building. He told me that the Russians were worried about Gizenga's welfare on the island of Bula-Mbemba. He knew that I had flown down to check Gizenga at Mobutu's request a little over a month ago, but apparently the Russians were still suggesting that Gizenga's life was in danger. Gardiner wanted to be able to tell them that the prisoner was alive and well. He asked me if I'd mind taking along Gizenga's personal physician, a Yemeni, who was anxious to see his patient. I had no objection.

In the early morning of March 30, 1962, I drove to the Ndolo airfield near the center of the city used by Air Brousse, nicknamed Air Frousse—Air Scare. The usual collection of bored soldiers slumped on benches at the gate. They asked for cigarettes and waved me through. The waiting room was empty except for a dapper little man on a bench, dressed in a black suit and a gray silk tie. He bowed as we shook hands and handed me a card introducing himself as Dr. Hussein Husseini. Under his name was printed "Doctor of Psychology, Sexology, and Endocrinology." His address was somewhere in Yemen. He opened his black patent leather briefcase and pulled out a glossy eight-by-ten photograph of himself taking blood from the arm of a gorilla.

"My specialty is the use of gorilla hormone in humans," he announced with authority and obvious pride.

Dr. Husseini and I climbed aboard a 1936 de Havilland Dragon Rapide and headed for the coast. The aircraft was a biplane with two midget engines on each of the lower wings, which, along with the fuselage, were covered with patched fabric. The pilot sat up in the pointed nose; the passengers wedged themselves into narrow canvas seats. We flew over gorges of the Congo River and jagged ridges of the Crystal Mountains,

The 1936 de Havilland Dragon Rapide.

weaving around towering cumulus clouds, porpoising and fishtailing like a stunt flier in an air show. The plane leaked where the canvas on the nose was patched, and the pilot had an umbrella over his knees when we flew through rain.

We landed on the airstrip next to Moanda, a resort

village along the scrap of beach that marked the western limit of the country. After a delectable lunch of shrimp and French fries on the terrace of the Mangrove Hotel, we were driven to the wooden pier at Banana, where we boarded a pilot launch and chugged out in pouring rain to the island called Bula-Mbemba in the middle of the Congo River's delta.

Pilot boat for Congo delta and Bula-Mbemba.

Bula-Mbemba in Kikongo means "territory of the eagles." The island had been a coastal artillery fortress during the Second World War. Massive cannons in concrete emplacements, a narrow-gauge railway, and rundown troop quarters remained. The guns and the rails had rusted and, for the most part, were hidden by thick vines and brush. Ancient baobab trees draped with soggy hanging moss gave the island a creepy, mysterious undertone. Part of the shore was mangrove swamp. The croaking of frogs and the whine of a million mosquitoes rose above the steady hiss and slap of rain on leaves and mud.

We were met by the prison commander, le Capitaine Welo. I had treated him for a recurrent infection, and we were on the best of terms. He was built like a sumo wrestler. I introduced him to my medical colleague, and we walked in the hot downpour along the railway to the central building, which had been the officers' club and was now a prison.

Political prison beyond the baobab tree on Bula-Mbemba.

Gizenga was delighted to see his Yemeni doctor, and after they embraced, he led us to his room. The heir to Lumumba's legacy wore a red brocade bathrobe on the back of which was an ornate, fierce-looking dragon—a gift from the Chinese during his reign in Stanleyville. He had grown a beard and put on a few pounds since my last visit with him. He looked well and seemed quite relaxed. He apologized for the spartan furnishings of the room and invited us to sit.

After a rapid exchange with his patient in Swahili that I didn't understand, Husseini turned to me. "Mr. Gizenga needs some medicine to make him feel better. I will inject him with a dose of gorilla hormone." He opened his briefcase and took out a syringe and vial.

I leaned forward and tried to see what was written

on the vial. "Look, *confrère*," I said, "I am responsible to the authorities for Mr. Gizenga's good health. I have no experience with gorilla hormone. I cannot let you give him that shot."

The Yemeni looked stunned. "What? Are you trying to prevent me from treating my patient?" I nodded. He stood abruptly and shouted, "You do not respect my opinion. I am a professor and an expert in gorilla hormone. I know what I am doing. Mr. Gizenga needs this now."

For all I knew, gorilla hormone might be the elixir of long life—or it could be poison.

"I do not think Mr. Gizenga needs the injection," I stated firmly.

"This is an insult! You know nothing about these things!" shouted the Yemeni, waving the syringe and vial in front of my face.

"I admit to that."

"Then you have no right to interfere," he declared triumphantly.

In desperation I turned to Gizenga, who sat watching our exchange with a smile. I said, "Let's leave the decision to Mr. Gizenga," and proceeded to make my case.

"Mr. Gizenga, I have taken good care of you in the past and I think you have trusted me. It is my opinion that you do not need gorilla hormone, and I do not want you to take that injection."

To my relief he laughed. "I agree. I don't need any gorilla hormone today."

Husseini, now livid with rage, shouted, "All right, then, I will give him his insulin."

"Insulin!" I exclaimed. "Why do you want to give him insulin? He's not a diabetic."

"He needs it for his appetite!"

"There's nothing wrong with his appetite. He's gained weight since the last time I saw him." I was on more secure ground and my voice rose.

"He needs insulin," countered the Yemeni, diving into his briefcase again.

"You will not give him anything," I commanded. "Mr. Gizenga is not a diabetic. Anyway, his food will not be here for several hours, and I assume you know as well as I do that if you give him insulin without food, you could kill him." I shouted for Captain Welo, who came running with two MPs. "Captain, please remove this man from the building. He is endangering the life of your prisoner."

The captain gave the order, and the two MPs took Husseini by the elbows and led him out, still screaming about my lack of knowledge. Gizenga and I spent a few more minutes together. He thanked me for the visit, and I left.

Welo and I walked back to the pilot boat. He asked me if I would call on his wife and kids in the capital and see that they were all well. He hoped to get leave in a couple of months. We shook hands and I climbed on board.

As we chugged back to the coast, the Yemeni doctor was all smiles. "You thought I was trying to kill Mr. Gizenga, didn't you?" I did not reply.

We flew upriver to the capital. I stepped into the cockpit and requested the pilot to radio the airport and arrange for security police to meet the plane. As soon as we landed, I told the officer to stay with Husseini while I made a phone call. I reached Victor Nendaka, head of security, and told him about the Yemeni's antics with Gizenga. One of the policemen took the phone and was ordered to tell Dr. Husseini that reports had come in indicating that his enemies were after him and that he would therefore be put under "protective custody." The doctor objected strenuously as they escorted him to a Jeep.

After the wild flights to and from Bula-Mbemba, I fell into bed exhausted. At 10:00 P.M., the telephone rang. Somebody in the American embassy asked me to rush to the home of the assistant military attaché, a lieutenant colonel, who had been murdered in his bed by a shot fired from outside the window. I drove to his house and ran in. Another American told me that the victim's girlfriend had been on top of him when he'd been shot. Apparently she was unhurt but in shock, and had been whisked away. The man was bleeding from a head wound and unconscious. We loaded him into the back of a station wagon, and a few minutes later, I had him on the operating table. An emergency craniotomy failed to save him.

A few days later, I received a call from Security Chief Nendaka, who had become a patient. "We need to talk to the woman who was with the colonel when he was shot," he said.

"I don't know anything about her," I replied.

"Now, *docteur,* you can tell me. We just want to ask her a few questions."

"Honestly, Victor, I have no idea where she is. She was gone by the time I reached the house. I have never seen her."

"That is strange. Your ambassador, Mr. Godley, told me that you were keeping her under sedation in a secluded place."

"Godley told you that?"

"Yes."

"That's a lie. Stay by your phone. We'll get this straightened out."

I called Mac Godley. "Did you tell Nendaka that I was keeping the colonel's woman under sedation in a secluded place?"

"Well, Bill, I had to tell him something."

"That's a goddamn lie and you know it, Mac."

"Well, you know, Bill—"

I shouted, "I know this. If you don't call Nendaka within the next five minutes and apologize for telling him a lie, I'll make the whole bloody thing public knowledge."

I slammed down the phone.

A few minutes later, Nendaka called back. Mac had apologized to him and Nendaka regretted having doubted my word.

Three days after this incident, I was asked by Nendaka to transfer the girl from Makala Prison to the Ngaliema Clinic. She had refused to eat while at Makala and had wept continuously. I borrowed an ambulance, drove to the prison, and transferred the girl from the jail to the hospital. That was my only contact with her. I was glad to hear that arrangements were made to send her back to the States.

At the end of March 1962, Stéphane d'Arenberg returned to Léopoldville and we had dinner. He was investing his own money in sending out teams of trained medical technicians throughout the provinces affected by the slow death of sleeping sickness—trypanosomiasis—carried by the tsetse fly. Prior to independence, the disease had been under control. Since independence, the pandemics, including sleeping sickness, measles, tuberculosis, malaria, and river blindness, were recurring with a vengeance. D'Arenberg provided the teams with Land Rovers, fly traps, and basic medications. We agreed that things were rugged in the country. Graft was universal. People were preparing for a nationwide strike to protest corruption and high living in the government. Two leading newspaper editors were in prison for publishing their convictions on these points.

Bribery was as devastating to the national health as the pandemics were to individual citizens and whole communities. The vast majority of officials were approachable only through *matabish*—tips and kickbacks. Overseas companies budgeted for these "door openers," and receptionists in most offices expected to be tipped or given "*cigarettes pour papa*." Washington's giving of money through the United Nations with no adequate control or accounting served to encourage leaders in their corruption and render the poor more bitter and jealous of those who profited from the system. Washington seemed afraid to insist on monetary discipline, and hesitated to lay down the law. They worried that the Africans would turn to Moscow. That attitude was rot. The European Economic Community (EEC) was strict and disciplined in dispersing their funds, and the Congolese respected them and did the work necessary to obtain EEC aid. America was losing respect because we were so often played for suckers. I was getting to be known as the "ugly American" around the embassy, because I was vocal in my criticism of this laissez-faire approach.

A few weeks after the trip to Bula-Mbemba, I was making rounds on patients in Sister Donatienne's medical pavilion in the Ngaliema Clinic. She told me that a doctor from Yemen, critically ill, had asked whether I would take care of him.

An MP let me into the room. Husseini was lying in bed on his back. I put my hand on his shoulder. He opened his eyes and said in a weak, shaky voice, "Thank you for coming, doctor."

"I'm sorry to see you are sick," I said, pulling up a chair.

He was deeply jaundiced and had the odor of a dying man. I slipped my hand under the sheet and felt his abdomen. His liver was enlarged and rock hard and his arms were covered with scratch marks. The itching produced by bile in the skin can be more unbearable than pain.

"I need someone to talk to," he whispered. "I know I am dying. I do not want to suffer. The pain and the itching are terrible. Can you help me?"

"We can certainly ease your pain and itching," I replied. He closed his eyes. For a long time, neither of us spoke. Then I said softly, "Look, Husseini, I don't know what your beliefs are, or where you think you're going when you die, but if you have anything to say, I will listen. Do you need a Bible or a Koran?"

"Thank you, but all I need is to talk."

It was widely known that the gold mines in the northeastern Congo had been looted by rebels. He did not tell me where the treasure was hidden, but then, I was his doctor and did not ask him. I suppose only he and his gorilla hormone patient knew its location, and by eliminating Gizenga, all the lucre would have been his. Some days later his liver cancer killed him. I know he died without pain. I think he died at peace knowing that our deathbed conversation might see him to a better world. His part of the secret died with him.

Chapter 21
Commitment and Peter

I WAS HIT by a car in Nairobi in 1964. When I regained consciousness, a white-haired African was holding me in his arms, humming a tune, and rocking me like a baby in the middle of one of the busiest intersections in the city. I was taken to the hospital, and after attempts at a closed reduction of my severe, comminuted fracture at the junction of the head and shaft of my humerus, the surgeon hammered a Kunchner spike into the shaft, right through my shoulder joint. The whole thing became infected, and for two weeks I received enormous injections of penicillin in my butt given through a large number 18 needle. A month later, I left the hospital with a frozen shoulder. From Nairobi I flew to South Africa to respond to a series of invitations to speak to government authorities, the Pretoria Ladies' Club, and a couple of universities. These audiences were interested in what was happening in the Congo, especially the question, Would an independent South Africa explode like the Congo at the moment of independence? From Johannesburg I flew directly home to Greenwich to spend time with the family.

During the last week of my visit home, I spoke to Peter Howard, head of the MRA, over the phone. I caught him up on my news, and he invited me to join him and a few other MRA men for a breakfast at Dellwood in Mt. Kisco.

I walked into the dining room. Peter stood to greet me.

"It's good to see you, Bill."

"Yes, finally," said Mark.

I greeted the others. The men were MRA leaders

from England and the United States and Mark from South Africa. I was happy to see Bunny Austin again, a Wimbledon champion, long-standing friend, and patient. He was living at Dellwood with his family and doing very well. I helped myself to sausages, scrambled eggs, and toast from the sideboard and sat down across from Mark.

"I apologize for being late, but I leave for Europe and Africa tonight on the red-eye and the telephone has been ringing off the wall."

Bunny said, "I've been fascinated by your involvement, really your adventures, in the Congo. What's the situation now?"

"The new twist is Tshombe's return from voluntary exile in Spain. The United Nations, having pushed Tshombe's gendarmes and mercenaries into Angola, is pulling out of the Congo, admitting that it's impossible for them to deal with the country's acute problems. Tshombe is backed by Belgian, British, and American mining interests in the Katanga. They hope he'll pull the country together. Mobutu wants to use Tshombe's Katangese troops to quash Gizenga's Chinese-backed rebellion in the northeast. It's a bloody mess."

"What's been your involvement in all this, Bill?" asked Bunny.

"My role is chief of the Congolese army medical corps and doctor to Mobutu and many others. Paul-Emile, Eric, Dave, and I visit army units all over the country showing *Freedom* and a film that Dave made with the paratroopers called *You Can Count on Us*. The army commanders invite the population and the local officials. Thousands of people come. They sit on both sides of the screen, cheering and commenting. It's a hell of a sight."

"Who pays for all this?" asked Mark.

"The army. I do medical inspections and treat those I can. We distribute medical supplies to army commanders who are officially responsible for their redistribution to local dispensaries and hospitals. The needs of the population are overwhelming. Our aim is to relieve some of the people's suffering—a huge challenge, but at least we have a start."

Mark cut in. "With whom do you actually have a common mind about the way you operate?"

I focused on my plate, purposefully spearing a sausage and chewing it slowly and deliberately. Mark's question hung in the silence. I put down my fork and looked around the table. Mark dabbed his mouth with a napkin and tipped his head forward waiting for my response with the forbearance of a spider on its web.

Peter smiled over the edge of his coffee cup. His look told me, *The ball's in your court, old chap.*

"Be honest, Mark. What you really mean is why don't I check my plans with you. Straight answer? I check with those whose opinions I value."

Mark blushed. "But, have any Africans changed?" he snapped. "Do you sit down with them and seek God's guidance?"

"Listen Mark, you don't know a damn thing about the people you classify as Africans. Are you talking about white Boers, bushmen, Bantus, Arabized Africans? Have you ever touched a black man or been hugged by one when you were alone and in need?"

He persisted. "I know that they need God's help through MRA."

"We all need God's help," I shouted. "But you can't sit on a man's head with your fat white ass, crushing his face in the dirt, and tell him he's free to find God. I know some of the blacks who puppy-dog you for the moment. One of them sticks with you because you give him money, a pittance, but it feeds his family. You patronize the Africans. You treat them like trained dogs. The way you operate is to exploit the actions of others, including me, to give yourself some unearned authority in this movement."

"But Bill," Mark counterattacked, "have any of the senior officers or General Mobutu said publicly that MRA is the answer for the Congo?"

"No. Of course not. Nobody would understand that movement jargon. The Congolese will meet their own needs and the needs of their country by actions, not talk. Christ healed the sick, fed the hungry, and gave a prostitute new hope. He preached action, not platitudes. He didn't jump on a man's back, adding to the weight of a pack full of miseries. He freed him from his burden and boosted him along his way to take care of other powerless miserables."

I pushed my plate away and stretched my legs under the table.

"So, what will happen in the Congo?" asked Bunny, the conciliator.

"I don't know what will happen. Tshombe was welcomed like a hero. He rode all over the city in the back of a Jeep, waving a briefcase that contained documents guaranteeing the Belgians continued grasp of the Congo's wealth. To the people, he seemed to promise a return of peace, an end to murder and starvation. Mobutu suspects that Tshombe will use his gendarmes and mercenaries to control the country as revenge for the U.N.'s brutality in the Katanga. I don't think Tshombe will last that long. The army, or rather the first paracommando battalion, which is completely loyal to Mobutu, may call the shots."

"Where does that leave you?" asked Peter.

"It leaves me, as well as Paul-Emile, Dave, and Eric, in the position of continuing to do combined psychological and medical work throughout the country in military camps. I personally will continue my private practice, which keeps me in close contact with many of the military and civil leaders, including people from the American and British embassies. It also provides money for personal expenses."

A few moments of heavy silence followed. Then Mark said, "The fact is that your ambition is to become a one-man CIA-Pentagon-State Department."

I pushed back from the table and stood. "It's nice to see some of you again. Excuse me, I've had enough of this conversation." I walked out and down the back road that led to the farm.

Behind me, Peter called out, "Bill, hold on."

I stopped and waited for him. "I'm sorry, Peter, but I can't take that crap from Mark. I know most people can't believe that what I do comes from my own conviction, my own training. Sure the CIA tried to recruit me a couple of weeks ago in Washington. Two agency people took me to a safe house and asked me whether I would report to the agency any illness of Congolese VIPs that might be of interest to the government. I told them I was a lousy liar. I could never take care of someone and then report to others about him. It would be like asking a priest to reveal secrets of the confessional. Anyway, I work twenty-four hours a day. How the hell would I find the time to be a spook? My involvement in the Congo is real, not just a lot of hot air."

"Listen, my friend, I have a lot more problems with those who criticize you than I have with you. I'm trying to get people to move beyond introspection and start making a real difference. I do worry about your safety sometimes, but if more of our people were involved in risky undertakings, the movement would be more effective."

"Let me be clear," I added, "I left the hospital, not because you insisted I do so in your letters, although the letters shook me to the core. I left the hospital because I was burned out and the U.N. came up with another surgeon."

We continued down the path together. "What are your plans now?" Peter asked.

"I'm flying to Europe tonight to pick up a bunch of visas, then I head back to Africa and visit contacts I've made in Morocco, Algeria, Guinea, the Sudan, and a few other places. I think I need to get a feel for these countries and not just stay isolated in the Congo, but my practice and my work with Mobutu will mean that my base is in the Congo."

"Go to it. I'm with you. How you and Mark settle your differences is up to you."

"Thanks, Peter. I'll stay in touch."

On my return trip to Africa, I stopped off in France, with its feel, its smells, and sentiments of early home. I rented a car and drove to Chartres. When we were kids, Dad drove us to Chartres several times on fun outings we called "benos." We would eat in one of the little restaurants around the cathedral and then wander through that impressive Christian monument and gaze at the stained glass windows and the lifelike sculptures around the nave. Dad bought me an ivory crucifix mounted on red velvet in a gilded box with carved doors. It still has a place of honor next to my bed.

Chartres Cathedral.

Memories of those rare outings with my father and the magic of the place itself, a memorial to a woman, Mary, the mother of Christ, drew me back to the cathedral at Chartres. Even as a child, I understood that the height and majesty of the vaulted ceilings were monuments to the faith of those who had labored so long to build them. Maybe some undefined part of that faith had penetrated my being and pulled me back to the cathedral several times during the war when my troop carrier squadron was based in Normandy. During those visits, I found an island of peace in the Lady Chapel behind the high altar. I could ponder and reflect surrounded by a spiritual presence that tempered the immediate and calmed my soul.

Now I returned to Chartres on my way back to the Congo. I strolled around the cathedral and finally sat on a prie-dieu in the Lady Chapel. The door of a confessional opened and a woman in black bent over her cane and hobbled away to kneel in a pew. Under the perfect symmetry of the ogives and vaults that reached to the heavens, she seemed to represent another lonely human searching for peace and her place in the world around her.

I pulled out Henry Drummond's pocket-size book, *The Greatest Thing in the World*. Drummond was born a Scotsman in the 1800s, an unorthodox Christian who didn't belong to any particular church. He was attacked by many religious people because he offered an active Christian program that involved the best that people had to offer rather than focusing on sin and guilt. It opened where the page was turned down:

> *Remember as you read the words to what grim reality they refer. Recall what Christ's program really was, what his society was founded for. This program deals with a real world. Think of it as you read—not of the surface world, but of the world as it is, as it sins and weeps, and curses and suffers and sends up its long cry to God. Limit it if you like to the world around your door, but think of it—of the city and the hospital and the dungeon and the graveyard, of the sweating shop and the pawn-shop and the drink shop, think of the cold, the cruelty, the fever, the famine, the ugliness, the loneliness, the pain. And then try to keep down the lump in your throat as you take up*

His program and read—
To bind up the broken-hearted.
To proclaim liberty to the captives.
To comfort all that mourn.
To give unto them—
Beauty for ashes,
The oil of joy for mourning,
The garment of praise for the spirit of heaviness.

At that moment, a brass band I had not seen in the choir burst into the Hallelujah Chorus followed by *Ave Maria*, Wagner's Good Friday music, and *The Grande Marche Jubilaire*, with prayers and time to think between. This service and music coming after the passage from Drummond renewed and confirmed the commitment I made with Tine so many years ago—our commitment to care for people and relieve suffering through medicine. I was content and peaceful with that decision.

Before returning to Paris, I stopped at St. André-de-l'Eure, where I'd been with the 306 Troop Carrier Squadron after D-day in Normandy. I drove out to the abandoned airstrip and dropped in on the bakery I'd been billeted above. It was on a side street behind the church, off the main square. The baker's wife was still there, and when I walked in, she was dumbfounded and gave me a hug. The African gray parrot I had bought her on a drunken weekend in Paris was in the bakery window. He still bit anybody that came too close, including the baker's wife, who loved him dearly anyway. She was a nice lady and remembered our troop carrier group with nostalgia. I was glad of that because my roommate, another pilot nicknamed Cookie, regularly took her to bed in the early hours of the morning when her husband was producing some of the most wonderful baguettes I've ever tasted.

I drove out to where our squadron tents had been set up in clinging mud next to the metal landing strip.

Another world away in 1944.

Back in the Congo I received a message from Peter: "I am grateful for your steadfast passion and commitment. Some of us get more worried about a lowering of standards than a lowering of aims."

In February of 1965, Tine forwarded a letter from Peter: "I am writing to you because I am not quite sure where Bill is. Just send him word that I am thinking of him and am enormously grateful for his memoranda and speeches and the news that he sent. I do salute you and your family. You are one of the bright lights shining out of America and heaven knows the world in darkness awaits such light."

Peter died in Peru of a severe kidney infection a few days after this note. His death came as a shock. I would miss him.

Chapter 22

Takeover

ON THE EVENING of November 24, 1965, Mobutu met with senior officers who supported his view that Belgian military counselors were helping the army find cohesion.

General Joseph-Désiré Mobutu takes over as president of the DRC.

Military courts had dealt severely with those guilty of corruption and abuse of power. The general also pointed out that the mercenaries were still necessary in the army to reduce pockets of resistance in isolated regions.

The Americans were caught off balance by the rapidity with which Tshombe was kicked out, and the policy swerved to the left with an opening of the river port to Brazzaville and the Chinese. After a couple of days, crossing restrictions were back in force for security reasons, the move ordered by Mobutu.

Once more anxiety gripped the population in the capital. Kasa Vubu was becoming unpopular. Aid from Europe had ground to a halt. Mobutu stayed in the political background but held the key to the country—the army, such as it was. Rebel activity had increased, especially in the Northeast. Mobutu announced that any rebel, especially from Brazzaville, who put his foot in Léopoldville would be incarcerated.

On November 22, 1965, after breakfast with Mobutu, I had talks with Mac Godley of the American embassy and Stéphane d'Arenberg, who had become head of the Belgian Medical Aid Mission. Mac thought the country was coming unglued, and d'Arenberg was sure that it would. Certainly the rebels, encouraged by the confusion and lack of authority in the central government, guaranteed a rough future.

That evening, at Mobutu's suggestion, I met with my former patient Tshombe in a darkened section of the Gombe suburb where he was more or less in hiding. The talk centered around the military crisis of the rebellion in the eastern provinces, the instability of the central government, and the need for a united front. Tshombe said he would seek out Mobutu. A stable, united government was critical, since disruptive elements backed by the Chinese in Brazzaville were fomenting trouble on this side of the river. To add to the tension, demonstrators burned a Belgian flag in downtown Léopoldville.

The rivalry between Kasa Vubu and Tshombe for top place in the country was at the boiling point. Kasa Vubu's men were reaching deeply into the country's till, and Tshombe had considerable resources from his Katangese followers and their industrial allies. The one with the most money would win. The solid element was Mobutu, who was working toward control of the army and had the certain loyalty of the first paracommando battalion in the capital.

A banner headline, "THE ARMY TAKES OVER," stretched across the front page of the newspaper *L'Etoile* of Thursday, November 25, 1965. At dawn, cities throughout the Congo awoke to a quiet day.

Below the headline a communiqué announced that

CONACO, Tshombe's party, supported without reserve the measures taken by responsible military authorities and rendered great homage to Lieutenant General Mobutu for this salutary decision. In a patriotic call to all its elected officials and partisans, CONACO launched an appeal that they support and help military elements to restore order and ensure the fundamental freedoms of people.

I was not surprised by Mobutu's takeover. I was excited at the possibility of doing more work with him and relieved that the coup had taken place without violence. Mobutu was in charge of the government, kept parliament in session, formed a new cabinet, and had it voted into office by a majority, all with no bloodshed. The country backed him more than they had ever supported anyone else. Like all people caught up in confusion and insecurity, they longed for a decisive man who would stick to his guns. That evening, I congratulated him by phone. I would see him again in the morning.

In December 1965, eighteen days after he had taken over the country, President Mobutu spoke to thirty thousand Congolese citizens gathered in the Baudouin Stadium to hear his diagnosis of the present severe illness of a "patient" called the Congo and the treatments he would impose.

"The problem in the Congo is that no one works," he stated clearly and forcefully. "I repeat, no one works. We have ceased being productive in the Congo." Mobutu spoke of the $42 million stolen by the politicians and the need for all citizens of the Congo to roll up their sleeves and work. He rolled up his own sleeves, and those behind him followed his example.

He illustrated the national distress with the following examples: "Before independence the production of corn amounted to 120,000 tons a year. Today, only 50,000 tons are produced. With rice, 100,000 tons have become 20,000, and with cotton, 143,000 tons have fallen to 15,000." He emphasized, "The country is forced to beg for help from abroad. Foreigners produce for the Congolese. The Congo can no longer feed or clothe its own sons. Hate, quarrels, waste, and corruption have replaced our common goals of fraternity, development, and well-being."

Mobutu went on to give examples of spending excesses especially among government functionaries. "In the Congo we produce only 80 percent of what we produced in 1960, and yet we spend six times more than in 1960." He made the point repeatedly that prices had gone up because production had gone down.

"To remedy this serious situation, I have decided to stay in power for five years. It took the politicians five years to lead the country into ruin. I give myself the same time to lead the country toward prosperity with your help."

The president detailed measures he would take against corruption, political self-interest, and the runaway prices of basic commodities. He touched on his plans for industrial development, which included a steel plant at Maluku, near the capital, and a hydroelectric dam at Inga on the Congo River, not far from the coast. He set goals for the production of basic agricultural commodities and underlined the need to increase local industrial production. Copper output, the major source of foreign currency, would have to be increased.

A few weeks later, in his New Year's message to the country, Mobutu again stressed the importance of working the soil and producing their own food. He ended his message with "Congolese men, Congolese women, I have confidence in you and I ask that you grant me your confidence. I repeat that the year 1966 will be hard, but if we work together, a glimmer of hope will soon shine on our country that has already suffered too much." Would that promise of hope grow to a reality, or would it die in a cesspool of corruption dug and filled from the top down? Trust betrayed shatters hope.

Many, including optimists like me, were hopeful that the new regime might be able to secure order in the country. Mobutu must do whatever necessary to restore Congo's credit with the exterior. Ghana, Nigeria, Burundi, Gabon, and the Republic of Congo recognized the new regime. Moscow was reserved, and to the Chinese, Mobutu was the beagle of the imperialists. Tshombe returned to Spain in voluntary exile. Kasa Vubu stayed at home in the Bas-Congo. The population was war weary, and knew that it was victimized by the corruption that consumed the politicians. The standard of living had plunged dramatically since independence. People asked with a sigh, "When will this independence end?"

Mobutu was thirty-five years old when he seized power with support of the army. Until then, he had exercised his influence in the background. But now the power was his at a challenging time that screamed for reform.

Chapter 23
Fausto and Big Bill

THE SILHOUETTE of a muscular bull with enormous testicles and the motto *Makasi*—strong with courage—was emblazoned like a coat of arms on the tail of each aircraft in WIGMO, the acronym for Western International Ground Maintenance Organization, a CIA front chartered in Liechtenstein. The Congolese Air Force had no pilots to provide air support for the army, so the United States provided WIGMO.

In December 1965, I rode in the cockpit of a C-46 transport flown by a "free" Cuban. Fausto Valdez, a former senior pilot in pre-Castro Cuban Airlines, was the pilot. We had become friends after I removed a kidney stone that had lodged in the wall of his bladder. Our mission was to fly across the country to Lake Tanganyika, pick up South African mercenaries in Albertville who were responsible for looting, brutality, and murder, and ferry them to Stanleyville. They would be replaced by gentler Spaniards who would protect WIGMO's operation.

On left, Juan, a free Cuban pilot, with Big Bill, a contract officer.

The airstrip in Albertville was on the shore of Lake Tanganyika. On the horizon of the deep blue water, banks of cumulous clouds climbed out of a distant haze. T-28 counterinsurgency fighters, with dive brakes for ground strafing, and A-26 fighter-bombers flew strikes on pockets of rebels up north near Fizi and Baraka. A Bell bubble helicopter, with metal basket stretchers strapped to its pontoons, clattered off on a medical evacuation mission eighty kilometers away. Before taking off for Stanleyville, we picked up a grizzled South African mechanic who had been injured in a road accident and needed to be hospitalized in Léopoldville. The veins in his hands and forearms resembled hydraulic lines. He was doped up and thirsty. We had no IV fluids, but Fausto passed the man a drink of warm water from a Beefeater gin bottle.

Stanleyville was a ghost town—astonishingly few vehicles and people on the streets. The rebel perimeter was twenty-eight kilometers around the city, with deadly infiltrations at night. We unloaded the South Africans, refueled, and took off for Léopoldville with a handful of army passengers and the injured mechanic.

The struggle for control of the Congo continued, each side with its proxies. The Chinese and East Europeans and Castro Cubans fought to turn the country over to Lumumba's heirs in Stanleyville. Those fighting for the "free world" included the U.S. Army Mission to the Congo (COMISH) and anonymous Americans, little touted in the dirty war of power grabs. Some of the counterinsurgency specialists were characters who fought for money and some for principles they seldom expressed. One of these was a naturalized American, Big Bill, an enormous "free" Pole who had flown with a Royal Air Force Polish squadron during the Second World War. It was hard to imagine him squeezing his bulk into a Spitfire or Hurricane. To our twenty-one-year-old daughter, Tina, he looked like a craggy-faced Polish John Wayne. To all of us, Big Bill was an example of a freedom fighter, today often referred to as "a civilian contract worker." Much of his work involved support of local antirebel militias in the east.

As acting coroner for the general hospital morgue, I

was contacted by the embassy to embalm an American citizen prior to sending his body back to the States in a sealed casket. I had never embalmed anyone, but found, in the morgue office, a stained booklet held together with adhesive tape that outlined the procedure. Walking into a stifling autopsy room, I switched on the light, a bare bulb hanging from the ceiling. An ancient Congolese morgue assistant followed me into the room pushing a cart with tubes, vats, and instruments. I asked his name.

"Dieudonné," he replied, as he handed me a pair of patched, yellow kitchen gloves and a cracked rubber apron. The air conditioner, hanging from a grimy window, was as dead as the body on the concrete slab in the middle of the room. The overwhelming stench of formaldehyde barely disguised the smell of body gas and sweet rot that leaked from the white body bag holding a large human being whose legs, from the calves down, hung over the end of the table. I stepped up and unzipped the bag. The assistant stripped it off the body. A bandage had slipped off the left side of the face. One glazed eye stared at me. His chest was crushed. My stomach retched into my throat. I had heard that Big Bill was killed near Albertville in a senseless jeep accident, but I never thought I'd see him again.

I stepped away from the table. I had to do this. I watched Dieudonné connect a plastic tube to the formaldehyde vat and another to an empty demijohn to receive Bill's blood. He handed me a knife and nodded encouragement. I made a small incision over his right femoral artery, then nicked the vessel and threaded in the plastic tube. I did the same on the left, with the exit tube leading to the jug. On the right, the assistant had attached a large glass syringe with a T-valve, which allowed me to aspirate fluid from the vat, turn the valve, and push the contents of the syringe into Bill's body. My first attempt met with resistance, probably clots in his large vessels. I pushed the plunger harder.

The tube flipped out of the artery and sprayed us with formaldehyde. Dieudonné handed me a length of used umbilical tape. I threaded the tube back in and tied it into the artery. The fluid went in with an initial shove, then with greater ease. Old blood, dark purple, dribbled down the left tube into the vat. The procedure took two hours. Eyes stinging and soaked in sweat, we washed Bill's body, drained the bloody formaldehyde from the bag, and zipped him back in. I stripped off the gloves and apron and gave them back to Dieudonné. I rinsed my hands in cold water and called the embassy. They would provide the casket and pick up Big Bill right away.

Chapter 24
Tine, Trooper, and Family

FOLLOWING A SHORT HOME LEAVE after Mobutu's takeover in 1965, Tine, the kids, and I returned to Léopoldville. We moved into an apartment provided by the army while a house in the paratrooper camp, two blocks from the president's house, was being refitted and painted. The apartment overlooked the Stanley Pool, now called Pool Malebo, a lakelike expansion of the Congo River, 830 square kilometers, that separates Brazzaville from Léopoldville. At night we could see the search lights of the Chinese communists sweeping the Congo River from a tower in Brazzaville. They were terrified that people from our side of the river would try to overthrow their puppet government. Some nights sirens wailed and then searchlights probed the banks and water searching for infiltrators. The Chinese had a stranglehold on the Brazza government.

Sandy, Tina, Glenn in the backyard in para camp, 1965.

I had breakfast with the president two days after his return from a successful tour of the interior. We reviewed my status as medical adviser attached to the presidency with the passes that went with the job. My job description, had one been required, would read: *Flexibilité. Disponibilité*—supple, bendable, unattached, and disposable. The honorary rank of lieutenant colonel, he thought, would be especially useful in operational or unstable areas. I would have the advantages of housing, transport, and communications from the army without being under their command or tied to them, since I was attached to the presidency. It seemed a near ideal situation.

Tina was spending a year with us and working at WIGMO as an assistant to the chief accountant and paymaster. Sandy and Jessie were enrolled at the American School of Kinshasa (TASOK). Sandy worked in the aircraft parts and maintenance department and later as a radio operator at WIGMO. Glennie was traveling all over the world with the singing group Up with People.

After we moved into the house in the para camp, we had to have a dog—a fundamental principle of the Close family. One afternoon, Tine and Jessie drove to the

Sunday on the river.

home of an American officer and picked up a new puppy. He was mostly black Labrador with soft silky ears, the right one angled out at forty-five degrees from his head. His coat was short and black with a white streak on his chest. His mother was a Belgian police dog, but her genes had been overwhelmed by those of his father, a Labrador. Jessie was ecstatic. We called him Trooper in honor of the people we lived among.

Trooper rapidly became an imperative reason for Tine and me and whatever kids were with us to spend Sundays on one of the many sand islands in the middle of Pool Malebo. Sunday morning, early, I would pack chairs, a tarpaulin, water skis, and the food that Tine prepared.

Troopie would jump into the trunk as soon as I opened it, and I had to pull him out each time. The river was one of his heavens. We had a Boston whaler with a big outboard motor that allowed us to skim across that huge body of water and set up our Sunday camp on one of the island beaches.

While we skied, read books, ate wonderful sandwiches, and dozed in the shade of the tarp, Troopie spent his time running up and down where the water lapped onto the sand, chasing squeaky little birds. We often took other families out with us, or they joined us in their own boats. I carried two radios in a duffle bag, one connected to the presidency and the other to the office. I don't remember once that our Sunday outings were interrupted.

Family on the beach with Trooper.

At home, Trooper spent many nights "out on the camp," so to speak, meeting and romancing his girlfriends. He would often return around two in the morning with his tongue hanging out to his toes and jump onto the bed, happy but exhausted. Once during a formal dinner he walked up the steps to the dining room with all four legs of a toad sticking out of his mouth. He was drooling foam as he slipped under the table. The guests all jumped up and helped us shoo him out.

Troopie not only loved the river, he also liked to fly copilot with me when we shot landings in my C-45 Bravo Hotel Alpha. He was a good copilot although he drooled on the throttle quadrant when the air was rough.

Tine kept an eye on many of the old mamas and young mothers, especially those who lived in the tent city across the street from our house. Often, a paratrooper or his wife would bring a sick child to Tine, and she would care for them or drive them to my office. One of the fathers, a paratrooper sergeant, brought a very sick little girl into our kitchen. Tine felt her forehead, and it was obvious that the child had a very high fever. She drove them to my office, where we treated the child for malaria.

When rabies killed some of the dogs in the camp, the order was given that all dogs had to be shot. The sergeant, the same man who brought the sick child to Tine, grabbed Troopie by the collar and shouted, "Don't kill him. He's the colonel's dog." The paratrooper carried Troopie home and advised us to keep him inside for a few days.

Chapter 25

Quel Bordel!

A FEW MONTHS after Mobutu's bloodless coup, I was called to the president's house to see madame, who had pressure pains in her abdomen from the child she was carrying. I had just finished examining her when the president walked in. He leaned his sculptured cane against the wall, tossed his leopardskin hat onto a chair, and sat heavily on the bed with a nod to his wife. He muttered "*Quel bordel*—What a whorehouse," referring to Brazzaville, from where he had just returned. He said the atmosphere was complete chaos caused by teenagers in the revolutionary youth movement. Castro Cubans had twelve antennas sprouting from their headquarters, and North Koreans, North Vietnamese, and Chinese swarmed all over the place.

Mobutu took off his glasses and rubbed his eyes. "What is over there? Nothing. So why are they there? Obviously they're aiming for us. If the countries that support freedom don't help us, it'll be a catastrophe." He had crossed the river with a good team. Tumba, the officer in charge of the household, had insisted that the drinks offered to Mobutu be taken out of fresh bottles and the ice cubes from the icebox in his room and not from outside. The atmosphere was tense and volatile. A man had been killed and his family arrested for demonstrating. One of the Africans assigned to help Tumba said that if President Mobutu hadn't arrived today, more blood would have flowed. The president had seen for himself how dangerous things were in Brazzaville. The telephone rang. The controller in the airport tower reported in great alarm that a fuel truck had backed into an airplane, causing a fire. "What shall we do?" the man asked frantically. "Put it out," shouted Mobutu, slamming the phone down. He asked me, as he often did, "How would you like to run a *foutu* country like this one?" My answer was always, "I wouldn't. It's tough enough being your doctor. "

A few nights later, all the lights went out in the paratrooper camp and most of the city. I was scared, really scared. Were the anti-Mobutu rebels crossing the river under the cover of darkness? Were they infiltrating along the river road? I jumped in my car and raced to the president's house. A guard at the front gate flashed a light on my face and, recognizing me, snapped to attention—"*Mon colonel.*" Other troopers pushed open the iron gates. Searchlights from across the river swept the presidential compound and the riverbank next to the road beyond the gardens. The lights left fleeting images of murky water and bobbing clumps of hyacinth. I drove past the house and swung around to park next to the front door. My headlights flashed across three security men in full combat gear.

Walking into the front hall, I shook hands with Lieutenant Mahele, who was, as usual, at his post near the president. "*Ça va?*"

"*Ça va,*" replied Mahele, handing me a flashlight.

I went upstairs to the president's room. The door was open. It was dark inside, and I didn't see him until a sweeping beam from across the river backlit his tall form at the window.

"*Bonsoir, mon général,*" I said, stepping into the room.

"*Bonsoir, docteur,*" he replied, without turning.

I sat on the bed; he remained at the window. We waited . . . waited for the lights to come back on, or for an attack. Rumors of assassination plots were rife. The feel of the snubnose .36 in my pocket gave me little comfort.

After what seemed like a long time, the lights flickered on and off and finally stayed on. I let out a deep breath.

The president turned toward me. *"Merci, docteur."*

"Bonne nuit, mon général," I replied, and drove home.

Chapter 26
The Horror of the Hangings

ON THE MORNING of May 30, 1966, Mobutu announced over the radio in his most emphatic and angry tones that irresponsible politicians had been caught in a plot against him and his regime and that they would be tried for treason.

The "plot" had been hatching in Colonel Bangala's house in the para camp near our home. We had no idea that anything unusual was in the offing until one of the WIGMO pilots, who lived in a house down the hill, brought us an automatic rifle and suggested we keep it handy in case of trouble, which he could not or would not define. One of our friends, a paratrooper officer, who was also a patient, came by the next day and suggested that we be careful and stay in the house as much as possible over the next twenty-four to forty-eight hours. Tine and I were nervous having an automatic rifle in the clothes closet. The para camp, most of the time, was the safest place to be.

Colonel Bangala, loyal to Mobutu, pretended to be sympathetic to the concerns of the four plotters: Evariste Kimba, who I'd taken care of when he was under house arrest with Tshombe; Jérôme Anany, who had been minister of defense; Mahamba; and Emmanuel Bamba, a prominent member of the Congolese Kibangist church. These men had been members of the parliament that Mobutu had closed a few days after his takeover of the government on November 25, 1965. With great courage, Bamba had objected strongly to Mobutu's power grab. The others had been more discreet. The four plotters hoped for a return to the aims of the army's highest commanders when Mobutu had taken over with their support. These aims had been to install a temporary regime that would elaborate a new constitution tuned to the realities of the day and return the country to democratic rule. Mobutu's announcement that he would take over personally for five years came the day after his coup. The four men were arrested by paratroopers hiding in Colonel Bangala's garden. Their trial had been short and their death sentence preordained.

The evening before they were to be hanged publicly, I was with Mobutu in his bedroom, the only room in the house he could call private. He was staring out of the window, wrestling with the awful choice between life or death. He mentioned that the pope and other leaders had urged clemency, but another voice in his ear may have come from Machiavelli's *The Prince* on his bedside table: "By making an example of one or two he will prove more compassionate than those who, being too compassionate, allow disorders which lead to murder and rapine. These nearly always harm the whole community, whereas executions ordered by a prince only affect individuals."

Looking back on those dark days, I think that executions ordered by a prince or president affect their lives for however long they can escape from their own violent death. For the first time in my life, I was with a man struggling with the naked bestiality of the death penalty. There were no murders to make "a death for a death" an argument for these public hangings that would feed the mob's worst instincts. But any death penalty was revolting to me. There may or may not have been a plot to overthrow Mobutu's growing autocracy. Until now, people who had been condemned to death had, at the last minute, been banished to their village in internal exile, or imprisoned.

Public murders, condoned by Mobutu, would escalate political opposition to way beyond "a tooth for a tooth." Such a move represented the preemptive killing of individuals, which was as futile a measure as a preemptive war against a whole population. So much for my personal views. Was there anything I could say? All I could think of was "If what you decide is not based on fear or favor, it will probably be all right." He said nothing, and I wished I'd kept quiet.

In the Congo, if you hit or kill a person in a driving accident, wherever the fault lies, a crowd will gather out of nowhere and you may be killed or maimed on the spot. A death for a death holds true. A person who kills another may be condemned to death by the village. However, the murderer's family can sometimes buy back the culprit's life by giving pigs or other animals to the family of the victim, but the murderer is banished from the village.

Mobutu could have commuted the death sentence of the four plotters to life in prison. He didn't. Could the reason have been another of Machiavelli's principles that it is better for a prince to be feared than loved? Certainly the hangings injected a dose of fear into the population that lasted fourteen years when, in November 1980, the opposition group, Union pour la Démocratie et le Progrès Social (UDPS) was born from within the legislature. Thirteen members of parliament signed an open letter to the president of the republic, a ten-point document cataloging corruption and abuse of power in the regime and calling for legalization of a second political party. The thirteen signatories were arrested and stripped of their parliamentary seats. They were not killed.

The morning of the execution, I stayed at home in the para camp. I was worried that as chief doctor for the Congolese army, I might be asked to pronounce the victims dead. If so, I would refuse. I heard rumors about the horror of the day. The hangings were botched.

Death was not instantaneous. The victims' bodies jerked spasmodically for up to twenty minutes after the trap door was sprung. Instead of cheering, a dreadful silence pervaded the thousands crowded around the gallows. Before the last execution, a sudden panic swept through the spectators. They ran away, bowling over women and children, leaving in their wake thousands of sandals and shoes.

The next day, when I visited the president, he expressed firmly the view that an example had to be provided to discourage more rebellion.

Later, Mobutu was quoted by Jean Kestergat, the noted Belgian journalist, as saying,

> The respect due a chief is something sacred and it was necessary to hit with an example. We were so used to secessions and rebellions in this country. It was necessary to cut all that short so that people could not start again. When a chief decides, he decides. That is that. I decided in the name of the high command that we are in power for five years. *C'est comme ça*—That's the way it is. It is not up to a group of politicians to go place themselves next to financiers to provoke more disorders or troubles in this country. They did it . . . an example was necessary.

Over the next weeks, I read with dismay, and some shame, press reports from Europe and the United States condemning Mobutu's cruelty. Acquaintances, both in and out of MRA, wondered what the hell I was doing with a man like Mobutu. Intimations that the whole so-called plot had been staged by Mobutu and his loyal colonel put Mobutu in the shoes of a Machiavellian prince "who truly understood 'virtue' in the sense of the qualities needed to perpetuate his state and his own power, would prefer the 'vice' of meanness to the 'virtue' of liberality." I was uncomfortable and insecure after the horror of the hangings. There was so much I didn't know and, if I was honest, didn't really want to know. Doctors were supposed to take care of those in need, but with Mobutu, I sometimes felt I was in way over my head. Those in MRA stuck to their mantra: human nature can change. I was learning that human nature doesn't change. It gets sublimated, suppressed, exploited, and, all too often, acted out.

Chapter 27

Mobutu and Some of the Belgians

IN DECEMBER 1967, d'Arenberg and I drove out to Nsele to report to the president about the murderous atmosphere created by an incursion of a handful of white mercenaries bicycling in from Angola. They were led by Bob Denard, the French renegade. Units of the Congolese army and the civilian authorities were sure that Katangese gendarmes and a larger body of mercenaries would follow on the heels of Denard to reclaim Katanga for Tshombe allies. In the panic that ensued, all whites were suspect, some were imprisoned, and a few were murdered. Panic spread across southern Katanga. With the authority of the president, and as members of the Presidential Rescue Commission, we had been able to free a Swiss mining engineer held by the army in Dilolo on the southwest border with Angola. The commission had been d'Arenberg's idea for improving Mobutu's image, especially in Belgium, where worries about the security of their citizens were ever present.

Mobutu was aboard his boat, which was docked at the presidential domain near Nsele. Bomboko, Mobutu's long-lasting foreign minister, was with him, and two trade union men from Belgium were his guests. The president invited us to join them for dinner. The Belgians were pompous and pathetic, and they thought the president and Bomboko were taking them seriously. One of them even attacked d'Arenberg for being a prince.

Later in the evening, when the men left and d'Arenberg, who was flying out early in the morning, was driven home, the president asked me about the trouble in Katanga.

"*Comment ça va là-bas?*—How are things going over there?"

"Not well. People are nervous."

"Why?"

"They're afraid of the army's reaction toward the civilian population, Congolese and European, following Denard's incursion from Angola."

He said, "The difference between now and 1960 is that then there was no control and no authority. Now there is some control all over."

"Yes," I said, "but many who know the country well, especially the Belgians, are worried by a lack of discipline in the interior."

"There won't be any trouble. My philosophy is to lead the masses, not have them lead me. A demonstration was planned for yesterday. I stopped it. There'll be one for the women tomorrow, but that's just the women for Women's Day."

I persisted. "The other thing that makes people nervous are all these newspaper attacks against the Belgians."

The general laughed.

"Wait," I said. "It seems to me that you go up the wall every time a European newspaper attacks you. There are probably press people in Brussels who say, 'Watch this. We'll push the button and the president will go right up through the roof.' You react just the way they want you to."

He answered, with force and emotion, "A student with a scholarship in Brussels told me yesterday that the cultural attaché at the Belgian embassy told some Congolese students who were to benefit from Belgian scholarships, 'You better stay put until we see how Mobutu behaves. If his speeches and attitude are acceptable, you can go to Belgium; otherwise, we may not be able to send you.'" He continued with tears in his eyes. "If you're going to help, you're going to help. Technical aid, teachers and such, cannot be used for political pressure; otherwise, the Congo will do without them and suffer but remain free."

I pointed out that he and the Congo were big enough not to descend into the nasty repartees between *Le Progres* and the *Libre Belgique*. Mobutu told me he had talked to Larry Devlin and Mac Godley in the American embassy and had asked them to intervene in Brussels to stop the Belgian papers from slinging their stuff. Only if they ceased their attacks would he stop his counterattacks. He added, "I give blow for blow."

It seemed obvious to me that Americans trying to influence the Belgian government vis-à-vis the Belgian press would be an exercise in futility. I suppose it was a sign of Mobutu's frustration and anger with the Belgians that had led him to call the Americans.

I said, "Well, that's fine, but it looks to me like you're heading for a rupture with Belgium."

He raised his voice. "I will never rupture. If they want to, we'll accept, but I will never rupture."

"I'm glad to get your thoughts, because I'm often asked questions and I'd like to know what to say. What if a senior man from Belgium came down here to meet with you? Maybe the two of you in a tête-à-tête could get the whole thing squared away."

Mobutu replied, "I wouldn't refuse to see anybody."

It made me wonder whether someone like Prime Minister Spaak could or would travel to the Congo.

Chapter 28
Mama Yemo and Mama Close

"LORD, IT'S HOT!" were my mother's first words when we met her at the foot of the stairs on the tarmac. She fished around in her purse and pulled out a lacy white handkerchief and dabbed at her neck and chin.

Tine and I each gave her a quick hug, and the protocol officer, with a formal bow and sweep of his hand, said, *"Madame, soyez la bienvenue. Suivez moi, s'il vous plait, il fait moins chaud au salon*—Madame, welcome. Follow me, if you please. It is less hot in the lounge."

Gran was charmed and, in her rusty French, said, *"Merci, monsieur."*

Preceded by the protocol officer, we broke away from the rest of the passengers and walked to the VIP lounge. The three of us sat down in comfortable, stuffed chairs. The protocol officer took her passport and baggage claim tags, saying that he would return promptly.

"We're so glad you came, Gran," said Tine. "Your room is ready for you and it's nice and cool. Sandy and Jessie are at school, and Tina is working at the airport. They can't wait to see you."

Before Gran could reply, a young woman wearing a body-hugging wraparound and matching bodice stood in front of her with a tray of soft drinks. Gran's eyes were fixed on the president's face printed on the material covering the woman's ample breasts. Loyal female members of the president's party wore green wax prints featuring Mobutu in his leopardskin hat, one over each breast and one across their bottoms.

"Gran," I asked, "would you like a Coke or an orange drink?"

Coyly, she pointed to a Coke. The woman smiled, batted her long eyelashes, and, to my relief, popped the top off with an opener. In less formal circumstances, the woman might have used her teeth.

On the second night of her visit, the camp commander, Colonel Bumba, arrived at the house to escort Gran to a party he was giving in her honor. We walked the two blocks from our house to his. Gran walked happily, with a jounce in her step, her arm tucked into the colonel's elbow.

As we approached his house, we could hear drums beating and people singing in that African harmony that is so natural when the people celebrate.

Gran with Colonel Bumba and Madame Bumba.

Gran turned to the colonel, pointing at her nose, and said, *"Sent bon*—Smells good."

I cut in, *"Ma mère veut dire, ça sent bon*—My mother means to say something smells good."

Bumba turned to me with a laugh. *"Je l'ai bien comprise, votre maman*—I understood your mother very well."

Mum poked me in the ribs. "See, Bill, my French is still pretty good."

We sat at a table at the top of the lawn, which had been turned into a stage and dance floor with colored lights strung through cactuses and bushes. In the cool evening air, the palm trees were silhouetted against a scarlet sky. The colonel introduced Gran to his "much loved" wife and the company commanders of his battalion.

Bumba's favorite Congolese dance group, dressed in straw and banana leaves, their bodies painted with black and white stripes, with bells tied to their ankles, danced, shouted, and sang to wild drumming and strumming of zithers. They charged forward stamping their feet and shaking their hands above their heads, then danced backward, ready for another charge.

During the entertainment, we were served roast suckling pig, plantains, chicken *mwambe,* and fish steamed in banana leaves, followed by Congolese staples: cassava, smoked fish, and, of course, roast monkey. After everyone had eaten, music was provided by a modern band. The colonel asked Gran for the first dance, and the rest of us joined them.

Early one morning, a few days later, I invited Gran to fly to Gemena with me to meet Mama Yemo. We drove out to the airport, and I parked in the WIGMO hangar next to my C-45, Bravo Hotel Alpha. I helped her through the door and told her to walk up to the cockpit and sit in the copilot's seat on the right.

"Where's the pilot?" she asked.

"I'm the pilot."

She looked surprised and nervous, but took her place. I strapped her in and explained that the aircraft had been given to General Mobutu by President Kennedy and that I had been thoroughly checked out and qualified to fly it.

We took off to the northeast and banked over the river with the city off our left wing. I dropped down to five hundred feet and circled tightly over Monkey Island isolated between cataracts formed by massive boulders in the riverbeds. I banked steeply away from the rapids, and Gran leaned to the right in her seat. Talk was difficult over the roar of the engines.

I said, "Just fly with the airplane. Let your body move with it, not against it." She nodded, and for a second, I could see a little girl on a fast-moving merry-go-round.

With the city off our right wing, we flew parallel to the paratrooper camp. I pointed to our house and the president's with its fountains and gardens and his office building and his private zoo. Army headquarters and the empty pedestal of the monument to Henry Morton Stanley marked the bay where river barges were built. Flying parallel to the bank, I pointed out embassy row with its immaculate lawns and mansions with terraces draped with bougainvillea. We flew over lines of rusting river barges beached on brown-stained sandbanks, then over the yacht club with its one dock and small clubhouse where *frites* and shrimp were served on weekends. Along the southern shore of the river's vast Malebo Pool, clusters of purple hyacinth floated in smooth, brandy-colored water between stretches of sun-baked silt. Kimpoko-Nsele and the president's Chinese pagoda and pineapple plantation, gifts from the Chinese government, flashed by, and then, still at low level, Maluku and its deserted steel mill, one of many monuments to faulty planning, passed under the wing. We flew on to where the inky waters of the Black River merged into the Congo, then below the sacred cliff

River scene on flight to Gemena. Man waving to aircraft.

of Mangengenge inhabited by particularly powerful *ndoki* spirits that guard the entrance to the pool.

A long, sleek pirogue, its gunnels inches from the water, streaked out from the bank. Tall, slim men in long pants and open shirts stood in the bow and stern of the narrow craft; a woman dressed for market in a red wrap-around sat between stacks of manioc and smoked fish. She waved at us, Gran waved back, and I waggled the wings. The men bent at their waist, and their powerful arms and shoulders pulled long paddles in synchrony through the water.

As the river widened, I waved my hand slowly, palm down, as we banked from side to side following the main channel, which weaved between forested islands. Still at five hundred feet, we flew upriver and dipped down to skim over the flat water and salute the people in tiny villages pushed by the forest behind them onto strips of sand that held their pirogues and fishing nets. They waved bright cloths and paddles. Gran, now thoroughly with it, waved back, and again and again I waggled our wings. We flew over wild buffalo, grazing in a swampy clearing. They tossed their heads and ran for cover. A bull pawed the ground ready to charge, then was hidden by the wing. Gran smiled in wonder but looked a little peaked. We climbed to ten thousand feet and set a course over the forest for Mbandaka. After an hour, Lake Tumba glittered in the distance beyond the swamps and forest to the east, and Irebu, where imprisoned Katangese gendarmes perished of malaria and dysentery, passed slowly below. The Ubangi, flowing into the Congo from the north, was ahead.

I shouted to Gran over the noise of the engines, "Five minutes to the equator."

Over Gemena, I circled Mama Yemo's house and rocked my wings, then headed to the airport and landed. I cut the engines. We sat for a moment.

"You're sure a good sport, Gran."

"Darling, that was an extraordinary experience."

Mama Yemo met us at the door. I introduced Gran as my mother: *"Mama na ngai."* Mama Yemo led us through her house to the back porch. Everyone was introduced to Gran one by one. In a sign of respect, they shook hands with her and nodded their welcome. Mama Yemo introduced Gran as *"mama wa monganga*—mother of the doctor."

Chairs were brought out. The grandmothers were immediately surrounded by children who stared at Gran, whispered, and giggled until Mama Yemo shooed them away. Neither lady spoke more than a few words of French, but it was obvious that they enjoyed each other's company; language was no problem.

The president's mother was comfortable in Gemena. She avoided the capital and all of her son's cluttered entourage. Her experience with white people had been as a cook or a maid or a nanny in Galveston, Texas. But she had a dignity and something of a chief in her makeup. Her quietness and her understanding were her forte. People came to visit because they knew she would listen. Gran had been brought up by a black nanny in Galveston, Texas.

In view of the long flight home, the visit was quite short. After I reviewed Mama Yemo's chart with her nurse (a young Congolese woman trained by the nuns), I gave her a brief examination and checked her medications. At the front door, she and Gran gave each other big hugs. She seemed happy, even proud, that I'd brought my mother up to Gemena to meet her.

In 1960, when I left for the Congo with MRA, Gran had stopped addressing her letters to me with "Doctor" or "M.D." I had reverted to "Mister" in her eyes. She dreamed of having a son with a prestigious surgical practice in New

York City, socially prominent, and terribly successful. Now she was flying in cloud valleys at eight thousand feet next to burgeoning thunderheads that gathered during the afternoons in the rainy season. Way below we caught glimpses of the river. I gave her a thumbs up and she blew me a kiss.

Chapter 29
Sandy

WE WERE LOST somewhere near Kikwit. Sandy, flying copilot, looked from the chart on his lap to the ground, which was all but hidden by a patchy ground-hugging vapor from a sweating forest.

"Pop!" Sandy pointed down. We caught a glimpse of a narrow river the color of milk chocolate flowing to the south.

"Good job, Sandy. Should be the Kwilu."

In five minutes we were over Kikwit, a town of four hundred thousand, easily recognizable. The sun burned off the ground mist, and another ten minutes south along the river brought Gungu into view. The landing strip was short and soft, but fifteen yards at both ends were

Our C-45 at Gungu.

hardened with crushed ant hills mixed with palm nut shells. I circled the field, lowered the gear and flaps, and the wheels touched down on the shells, then dug into the sand, and we stopped just before the end of the runway.

Sandy let out his breath. "Wow, Pop! Like landing on a carrier with the sand acting like an arresting cable."

By the time we'd taxied back up the strip and cut the engines, a crowd had come running from the village and surrounded the plane. With a train of kids behind us, we walked to the chief's mud-and-wattle hut. He gave me his report on the planting of peanuts we had provided to counter the severe protein deficiency in the area. Before walking through the village and out to the fields, he picked two masks hanging on his wall and gave them to us. He told us they were "named" masks, carved for special occasions and marked by the sculptors. They hang in our living room today.

The people were cultivating their fields, and only those too weak to work lay on mats in front of their huts, hollow-eyed and skeletal, without the energy to brush the flies from their mouths and eyes. These people had been overrun by Mulele rebels and the land stripped of anything edible. Pierre Mulele had been minister of education in Lumumba's government. He had traveled widely in Eastern Europe and received training in guerilla warfare in China. He and his rebels were most active in the Kwilu in a triangle between Kikwit, Idiofa, and Gungu. Mulele's rebellion began in 1963 and ended in September of 1968, when he accepted amnesty from Mobutu across the river from Brazzaville and was arrested and horribly tortured, with his ears and eyes torn from his head. The army had appeared, and the rebels melted into the forests until the soldiers had finished their looting and raping. The only difference between the army and the rebels was that the rebels did not rape. It was against the law of Mulele's spirits.

We walked to the fields where a dozen people, all women, hoed between rows of young peanut shoots. With the game killed and fish entrapped by rebels and soldiers, peanuts were the best hope of providing protein for a population where all the children, including some of the adolescents, carried the pot bellies, puffy cheeks, and red hair of kwashiorkor—the protein deficiency disease.

On the way to the local dispensary, we noticed tall stakes topped with human skulls on each side of the path. A male nurse with a patched white lab coat showed us his rooms. The place was swept clean but was bare, empty, no medicines, no equipment, nothing. Sandy approached a woman who was weeping as she tried to breastfeed her emaciated infant. Her breasts were like flat leather pouches, but that was not the problem—her baby was dead. The nurse and I tried to comfort the mother, but she hugged the little body tightly to her withered breasts. The nurse told us that her husband had been sent for. When she heard this, her crying turned to shrieks of fear. She knew that she would be blamed for the infant's death and probably beaten and abandoned. These double tragedies, filled with suffering and pain beyond the loss of a child, were repeated time and time again in areas where the population starved and no one gave a damn.

At the end of June 1967, I flew up for a quick visit to Mama Yemo in Gemena. She needed to be checked and her

Bill and Sandy.

medications brought up to date. Sandy came along for the ride, and an English WIGMO contract pilot, Terry Peet, flew copilot. We would stop in Mbandaka for refueling before flying on to Gemena. About halfway to Mbandaka, Sandy, who was sitting behind me, leaned forward and tapped me on the shoulder. I turned to look at him. He looked pale and pasty, sweating profusely. I took off my headset.

"God, Sandy. What's up?"

"I feel like puking and I have a hell of a headache."

I turned in the seat. "Can you reach behind and pull out my bag?"

He did, and started to retch. There were no paper vomit bags in any of the seat pouches. "Hang on, Sandy." I broke a vial of ammonia and held it to his nose.

He pulled back, "Jesus, Pop."

"Breathe it in as much as you can."

He nodded and wiped the sweat out of his eyes with the back of his hand. I replaced my headset and scanned the instruments. Mbandaka was a good half hour away.

He pushed against the back of my seat. The retching had returned.

"I've got her," said Terry, taking control of the plane.

I reached into my bag, pulled up a shot of Valium and, twisting around, gave him the shot in his shoulder.

"We're almost there, old buddy. Hang on."

He closed his eyes and leaned back in his seat.

"Try not to vomit, Sandy. Remember that in the air corps the guy who pukes has to clean it up."

He smiled wanly. I had to admit it wasn't very funny.

On the downwind leg into Mbandaka, Sandy cried out and vomited down the back of my shirt. I turned onto the approach and I felt him wiping my back. I glanced around and he had taken off his T-shirt and was trying to clean me up with it. I landed and taxied rapidly to the hangars.

As soon as I cut the engines, he ran to a clay mound next to the hangar and emptied his bowels. The mound was a Congolese latrine, made by clay packed around the top of a pit shaped like a cone with a hole at its apex. Whoever used it did so in full view of nature and humanity.

The Congolese airport personnel rolled out two barrels of fuel. It would take forever to hand pump the gasoline, so I waved them off and helped Sandy back into the plane and sat next to him. Terry took off, and an hour later we landed in Gemena. He would refuel and stay with Sandy while I was driven to Mama Yemo's house.

Sandy was groggy from the sedative I'd given him and slept on the flight back home. He remembers being pushed into the back seat of a blue VW bug, having some lab work done, and then being driven home to bed. He turned out to have black water fever, a severe form of falciparum malaria. The black water referred to urine that contained large amounts of hemoglobin released from red cells, exploded from within by the parasites. This form of malaria carried a high mortality rate. Sandy was critically ill for two weeks. Tine and I took care of him at home. He remembers crawling to the bathroom because he was too weak to walk.

By the time Sandy recovered, he had lost forty pounds. He returned to the United States, and my mother insisted that he attend a debutante party at the Sherry-Netherlands Hotel in New York, in spite of the fact that he looked like he'd come out of a concentration camp. The one girl he knew at the dance was horrified by the change in his appearance.

In 1969, the president had a four-day business visit to Athens, followed by four days in Germany, arriving in Paris on March 26. As I walked into my hotel room, the phone was ringing. Tine was calling from Greenwich.

"Bill, I don't know what's gotten into Sandy. He's acting strange. He won't tell me what's going on. Sandy, are you on the line?"

"Yes, Mom."

"Talk to your father."

"Sure. Hi, Dad." A pause. "Are you still on, Mom?"

"Yes."

"Would you mind hanging up?" Click. I could imagine Tine growling.

"What's up, Sandy?" My imagination was going wild—fatal accident, pregnant girl, flunking out of school?

"I eloped with a girl from Andover. We got married in North Carolina. Remember you and Ma looked into which states you could marry in without your parents' OK if you were underage?"

"Yes, I remember." Oh relief! Nobody dead or pregnant.

"Do her parents know?"

"We haven't told her parents yet. We're worried about their reaction. I was hoping you and Ma could go up to New Hampshire with me."

The panic returned with thoughts about minors crossing state lines to avoid parental interventions and kidnapping and who knows what. "Sure, Sandy. I'll catch the next plane to New York."

"Thanks."

"Get your ma back on the phone and I'll talk to her."

I remembered my call to my dad when I had just turned eighteen. After asking him to sit down, I told him I was leaving Harvard and the Navy V12 premed program, marrying Tine, and enlisting in the Army Air Corps Cadets. His immediate question was "Does your mother know?" I said no. He could tell her.

I walked down the hall to the presidential suite. "My son just eloped, he's underage, she's underage, her family doesn't know anything about it. It's a mess. I think I'd better go home right away and take care of it."

Mobutu reached into his pocket and pulled out a roll of money. "How much is a first-class round trip on Pan Am?" He covered the expense and I was more than grateful.

"Will I have to go through the same thing with my sons?"

"You'd better believe you will." Over the years, a Jesuit called Père Paul Dubois and I did a lot of thinking and planning for some of the president's kids.

I called Dr. Lipsitch, chief of staff at the American hospital, and he volunteered to cover for me if the president had any medical needs.

I caught an evening flight. Sandy had written twice that he was hoping to marry Kathy. Each time I had been unenthusiastic. He was struggling to graduate from Andover, and getting married seemed like first-degree foolishness. Now he was married. I couldn't help but admire his resolve, and, after all, Tine and I had been secretly engaged at sixteen and married at eighteen against my mother's will—she thought we were, or I was, too young.

Tine and Sandy were at the airport. We drove up to Andover and met Kathy's parents. Her dad turned out to be a nice guy, but her mother seemed eager to be rid of Kathy, an adopted child. The question came up about Sandy's new status and Andover's regulations about students who married. He agreed that it would be dishonorable not to tell the authorities that he was married. We waited with Kathy's parents while he went over to the school. He returned with the report that they were grateful for his honesty, that he couldn't live in a dormitory with his wife, they'd have to make other arrangements, but they'd keep him in school.

Chapter 30
Operation Survival

IN VIEW OF THE DEVASTATION caused by the rebellion in two-thirds of the country, I suggested to Mobutu that we organize a special operation working through the army to undertake the ideological and, where possible, the physical rehabilitation of the afflicted population. We called the effort Operation Survival.

This idea was born in my head following experiences I'd had after the Second World War in the Philippines where Tine and I spent some time in the mid-fifties with an MRA team. At that time, Jerry Palaypay and his wife, Linda, became good friends. Jerry had been President Magsaysay's military aide. During the operation to defeat the Huks, Jerry had dug his grave twice—once for each side—having been accused of being a double agent. President Magsaysay was confronted by communist-backed rebel Hukbalahaps, whose strongholds were in the mountains of Baguio. He offered the rebels the choice of coming out of the forests and reintegrating into a constructive society or suffering the military consequences. If their answer was positive, he sent in food, seed, basic agricultural implements, and medicines in ex-

Bell bubble chopper flying low over rebel pockets.

change for their weapons.

My first trip for Operation Survival was out of Albertville on Lake Tanganyika in a Bell bubble helicopter flown by a mercenary called Coucaracha, Spanish for "cockroach." Between his legs he kept a box of hand grenades to be lobbed onto unfriendlies if necessary. The space behind our seats was filled with cartons of Belga jaune, the cheapest cigarettes available. We flew at treetop level over rebel villages and dumped out cigarettes.

Flying over rebel village. People running.

The next day we dropped leaflets telling the people that if they wanted food and medicine, they should evacuate to open areas at the base of the peninsula and hoist a white cloth on a bamboo pole. On the third day, we landed in a number of villages and were quickly surrounded by expectant crowds. I snapped Polaroid pictures of them and passed them out, which delighted them and made them laugh. We distributed boxes of medicine to responsible people, saying that clothing would follow. Over the next days, C-46s flown by free Cubans dropped bales of clothes provided by Baroness von Leitz with the help of Lufthansa. This source of clothing was a windfall. Madame von Leitz had come to my office unexpectedly. She was an impressive lady, thin, energetic, and right to the point. With no preamble, she told me that she'd heard what we were trying to do and offered to help. I asked her whether there was any way of getting bulk quantities of secondhand clothes wrapped into bales that we could parachute to refugees from the rebellion in the east. In short order, new encampments, each flying a white flag, sprang up, and the rebellion in that area was over.

The Americans sent in elements of the 82nd Airborne. They were impressive, but perhaps not the ideal instrument for rebuilding pacified but shattered lives and communities.

It became clear that we would need to be able to fly all over the country for Operation Survival. The Congolese authorities gave me a pilot's license based on my American one. On February 22, 1966, I started twin-engine checkout rides in an eight-passenger C-45, a plane that had been used for training navigators and bombardiers during the Second World War. My checkout pilots were "Dinger" Bell from Australia, who flew the president's Aztec, and Terry Peet, both contract pilots with WIGMO. Fausto Valdez, a free Cuban working for WIGMO, flew with me in earlier instrument flights.

A few months after being checked out, I was practicing instrument landings at Ndjili Airport. After the third touch-and-go, I circled around for another approach and could not lower the gear. I pulled out of the pattern and flew to a safe altitude and tried lowering the gear again, without success. On the right side of the pilot's seat was an emergency hand-operated crank to lower the wheels. I tried to turn it, but it would only move a few inches. I began to sweat. I called the tower and asked them to notify the maintenance crew in the military hangar that I was having problems with the landing gear. Within minutes, Ray, who ran WIGMO, was on the tower radio talking me through the routine emergency procedures. Nothing worked. I heard the tower call several international airlines telling them that there was an emergency at Ndjili and that they would have to circle in a holding pattern.

Ray told me to climb to ten thousand feet, dive, and pull out abruptly to see if I could snap the wheels down. No result. He told me to keep flying in a gentle circle, and he would send up a T-28 (a counterinsurgency fighter) to fly under my plane and see if he could find the problem. Again, nothing. By this time my heart was pounding, I was drenched in sweat, and just able to control a rising panic. Dusk was over the horizon, the fuel tanks were full, and the C-45 had no means of dumping gasoline. If I landed with my gear up, the chances of a fire were high. I told Ray I would try the crank one more time. With fear providing additional strength, I pulled with all my might on the crank. The bicycle chain that activated the gear broke and the gear dropped down. I was relieved until I looked at the instrument panel and saw that the wheels were down but not locked. I reported to Ray and told him that I was going to land as gently as I could and hope for the best. I circled down to the proper altitude and came in on a long, gentle final approach. I eased the aircraft down over the runway inch by inch. The wheels touched down with a whisper. It was the smoothest landing I'd ever made. I turned off all the switches and the gas tanks and came to a stop surrounded by fire trucks and ambulances. I got out of the seat and took one step into the passenger cabin, and the landing gear collapsed slowly to the ground. I climbed out to be met by the American ambassador, who demanded to know why I was flying. I told him that it was part of my job with the president and not to worry. He shrugged and left.

Chapter 31

Hot Piss in the Bush

TO THE CONGOLESE, *la chaude pisse*—hot piss—as gonorrhea was called, was a serious disease, not because it caused burning and frequent urination, but because it affected their ability to have sex and children. An impotent man is not considered a man. Most soldiers were eager to do anything to cure the disease except curtail their exposure to it.

This bit of reality proved useful in my next military medical flight, which was again in eastern Congo at the end of January 1966. The task was to inspect another isolated battalion, this time camped on the outskirts of Baudouinville on Lake Tanganyika. A few ANC units had ended up in remote areas caught between the Stanleyville rebels to the north and Tshombe's Katangese gendarmes to the south. My job was to act as a link to headquarters in the capital.

I took off from Léopoldville and landed, three hours later, in Luluabourg. It was my first long solo cross-country trip in a twin-engine Aztec, and an adventure. I climbed rapidly through the overcast. With any luck I would be in sight of the lake within two and a half hours. Since no radio navigational aids were functioning reliably in the country, I would have to let down through the overcast to pick up the Lualaba River, then fly due east to the lake. I had learned to fly the rivers and had been lost enough times to develop a search-and-find-myself technique. The problem was that crossing a river didn't tell you whether you were north or south of your plotted course.

Turning on the autopilot, I stretched my legs around the rudder pedals and settled into the seat for the flight. I had synchronized the props, but the sound of the engines still undulated slowly, recurrent, and symphonic as higher-pitched tones crept into the harmony of the engines. I scanned the instruments. In the air corps, we had been taught to fly the plane and leave the navigation to the navigator and the engines to the crew chief. My ignorance kept me alert.

After two hours I started a gentle descent. Going down through an overcast when the ceiling was unknown wasn't something I liked to do, but the central part of the country was quite flat, and I figured if I let down very slowly, I'd see the ground in time to pull up if necessary. I broke out at four thousand feet. The visibility was to the horizons. The Lualaba River lay ahead, running north and south. To the north, I could see Kindu, where Italian airmen flying for the United Nations had been slaughtered. To the south, the Luvua River formed the eastern fork of a Y flowing into Lake Moero, while the Lualaba continued south to the copper country. Lake Tanganyika appeared on the horizon, and after flying over the lakeshore, I turned south, looking for the prominent Catholic mission on a hill near Baudouinville. I buzzed the church and circled the area. A collection of huts and tents appeared not far from a dirt landing strip. A breeze off the lake bent the tall grasses next to the runway. I landed to the east and taxied back to the west end of the field to be in position for takeoff. Aside from boxes of penicillin for gonorrhea, I had no fixed ideas of what to expect on this inspection trip. I hoped they would be happy to see me. I planned to make this mission as short as possible.

As I gunned the right engine to spin the Aztec around, armed soldiers rose out of the grasses and surrounded the plane. A rush of fear squeezed my belly. I pushed my black bag out onto the wing and followed it, leading with my shoulders so the men could see the red crosses that Tine had sewed on the night before. "*Monganga, monganga*," I repeated, smiling and waving. They seemed to relax a little. They needed a doctor. They looked ragged and miserable.

With no supplies for months, these troops had terrorized the people of the area and lived off their meager crops of corn, manioc, and papayas. Abandoned troops without logistical and command support become a menace to the population. The local women provided their only recreation, and as in many army units, gonorrhea was the major medical problem.

I walked to the camp with a lieutenant. The men who had been at the airstrip followed in a disorderly group, chattering among themselves. I told the officer that I had been sent by General Mobutu to bring them medicine and see how they were doing. The lieutenant, who was young and seemed well educated, apologized for my reception. He explained that the red markings on my aircraft made them think it was a Katangese plane, like the Fouga-Magister that had strafed them on their trek south. He ordered a soldier to run ahead and tell the commanding officer that a doctor had arrived.

After a few minutes, we came to a hut guarded by a corporal armed with an automatic rifle. I noticed with relief that no magazine was clipped into the weapon. The lieutenant brushed past the guard. As I entered, he was standing at attention saluting an officer who sat behind a rough wooden table. The officer, a captain, got up and, reaching across the table, shook my hand. He was a heavy man with a scar on his temple, extending to the outer corner of his right eye, and a long drooping mustache. His features were more finely chiseled and his skin lighter than most Congolese.

"Sit down, *docteur*," he said. I sat on a stool the lieutenant put behind me and noticed a young woman squatting in a corner behind the captain. Her hair was braided into sharp spikes projecting from her scalp. She stared at me with big brown eyes, the whites like young ivory. Her naked arms and shoulders were strong and shapely. Copper bracelets clinked softly as she raised her hand to cover her mouth and nose in the presence of a stranger.

"General Mobutu sent me to inspect your battalion and do what I can for your men," I said.

"You are the first person from headquarters we have seen in a long time. We have not been supplied for over a year."

"I'll tell the general. I have brought some antibiotics to treat any infections in your men, including *la bleno* [short for *blennorragie*—gonorrhea]. If they will line up, I can check them quickly and do what's necessary." The captain gave the order, the lieutenant saluted, then left.

"I doubt whether I have any disease, *docteur,* but with these women, you never know," said the captain. "Give me a shot of penicillin. And give one to her."

As Air Corps Cadets during the war, we were subjected to weekly "peter parades." We stepped up and unzipped in front of a medical officer seated on a stool. After obeying the order to "skin it back and milk it down," those who showed evidence of a venereal disease were sent to an office for treatment. Those who passed the test buttoned up and walked out, happy and relieved. I gave peter parade instructions to the lieutenant and sat on my medical bag at the head of the line.

The men stepped up for inspection, and I divided them into three groups. The largest was made up of those infected, as evidenced by a drop of pus clinging to the end of their penis. The second group consisted of a handful of men without the disease. Men in the third group were seriously ill with hot, red, swollen genitals filled with galloping gonorrhea. Was it a coincidence that some of the sickest looked the surliest? They were withdrawn and hostile. I told them that their disease was serious enough to warrant special care. The other, less critical "positives" would be given penicillin injections by the battalion medical aide as soon as I left.

After turning over supplies of syringes and penicillin, I boarded the plane surrounded by soldiers who wanted to shake my hand. I shooed them away from the door, started the engines, and bounced down the strip with soldiers running beside me leaping in the air, shouting and waving their weapons as I pulled up and became airborne. I retracted the gear, climbed to a thousand feet, banked steeply, and dove to the strip buzzing the troops, then climbed up and away for the short hop to Albertville. I made arrangements for a military plane to pick up the men who had been chosen for special treatment.

Chapter 32
Hôpital Mama Yemo

IN THE FALL OF 1968, Mobutu asked me to take over the fifteen-hundred-bed Hôpital des Congolais in Kinshasa, where I had worked as a surgeon in 1960 and 1961. I hadn't visited the hospital since then. I knew that the place had become a death trap and that only a handful of sisters remained. The staff was overloaded with unqualified personnel: "brothers" or "cousins" of those who ran the hospital for their own profit. I thought about the president's request for a long time and finally submitted a paper to him stating that I would reorganize and rebuild the general hospital on condition that I reported only to him. I would submit an honest budget for capital improvement and operating costs, and expected the budget to be respected 100 percent. I assured him that the usual budget game of asking for more than was needed to do the job would never be my policy. In addition, I would require full hire-and-fire authority with no interference from the ministry of health, the labor unions, or his political allies. I was doubtful that he would accept such conditions, but he did, with no hesitation.

After several visits with Stéphane d'Arenberg, we agreed that his nongovernmental organization Fonds Médicale Tropicale (FOMETRO) would have a little sister called Fonds Médicale de Coordination (FOMECO), whose main charge would be the renewal, restaffing, and direction of the old hospital and surrounding health

Bill, president of FOMECO.

institutions, including the prestigious laboratory of the Institut de Médicine Tropicale (IMT). I became the president of FO-MECO's board of governors. The other members of the permanent board were Dr. Roger Youmans, chief of staff, and Dr. Georges Bazunga, director general. When warranted by the agenda, other department chiefs were invited to attend the meetings. Because the board was made up of men and women who managed key departments in the hospital, our meetings were short and effective. All who attended were expected to have done their homework, and the meetings rarely lasted over an hour.

I did a lot of management over a beer or cup of coffee on the back porch of our home. My main jobs were to run the monthly board meetings and yearly budget exercises and keep the president aware of our problems and accomplishments. I knew nothing about the management of a large public hospital, but I recruited some extraordinary men and women who were experts in their fields and, above all, were enthusiastic members of a team characterized by hard work and humor. Because those

Dr. Georges Bazunga Nganga Munama.

who made policy were the same as those who executed the policy, the distance between the bosses and the workers was minimal. I had the final signature on budget and especially paychecks, all approved by the president, so I had a little extra clout that helped smooth the way.

A few years after we had renovated and staffed the hospital, I received a call from the British embassy that an English officer, Major Roger Chapman of the Green Howards, had been admitted to Mama Yemo Hospital (formerly the Hôpital des Congolais, renamed by Mobutu in honor of his mother) in critical condition. I was informed by the military attaché that the Green Howards was a Yorkshire regiment, loyally serving the Crown since 1688.

I hurried over to our surgical intensive care ward and found the major in bed next to the nurses' station. One of our staff surgeons, Bob Turk, was with him. I introduced myself to the patient.

Bob said, "Major Chapman has just been flown in from Kisangani. He's with the British Army Zaire River expedition. A Canadian nurse with the expedition flew down with him."

"Sorry to be a bother," said the major groggily.

"Has he had something for pain?" I asked Bob.

He nodded and continued, "According to the nurse,

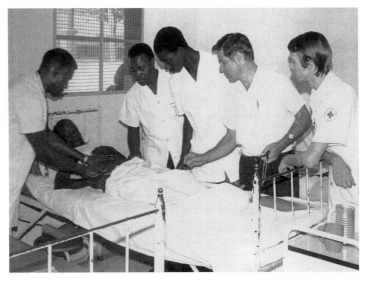

Surgical teaching rounds with Dr. Youmans.

the expedition doctors operated on him for appendicitis. When they found that his appendix had been removed at some other time, they explored his abdomen and, finding nothing but a little pus, had closed him up. They drained his belly with a Penrose."

"Gentlemen," said the major, exhaling the word, "all this happened on Friday the thirteenth."

"Interesting," I replied. "Would you mind if I examine you?"

His abdominal wall was tight and tender. He did his best to relax. I percussed his abdomen gently. The right upper quadrant was the most tender, and light percussion of his rib cage over his liver made him cry out.

"I'm sorry. You may have a liver abscess," I said.

"Is that serious?"

I asked for a spinal needle. "Yes, it is. I'm going to insert a needle into your liver to confirm our diagnosis. Do you want more pain medication?"

"No. Just do what you have to."

Bob and I prepped and draped the area. I pushed the needle into his flank just below his rib cage, aiming up into his liver. He was whispering to himself and let out an "Ow!" I pulled back on the plunger, and the barrel filled with chocolate-colored pus with cherry-colored streaks. I pulled out the needle.

"You do have a liver abscess, major. Probably formed by amoebas nesting in your cecum that were stirred up when they operated on you in Kisangani."

Bob left to check with the OR crew.

I put my hand on Roger's shoulder. "We'll give you more medicine to help with the pain and deal with the abscess in the operating room. We'll take good care of you, major."

Bob reported that the OR would be ready in an hour. I walked out of the ICU into an early night and strolled along the covered walkways between the pavilions. The smell of freshly mown grass had replaced the pungent odor of stagnant sewage that had pervaded the hospital grounds a few years ago. The laundry, recently reequipped, was in full swing. The smell of hot soap and wet linen reminded me of going on rounds with my dad in his Paris hospital. The personnel in his laundry had baptized him "Papa" Close. He'd stolen a chef from the Ritz and was rightly proud of the cuisine in the American Hospital.

I strolled through central supply, where gas sterilizers were used to resterilize plastic syringes so that "use only once" equipment could be used many times. Years earlier, when I had been the only surgeon in the hospital, the nuns gave post-op patients bags of gauze wads that had been used in the operating room, retrieved, and laundered in bleach. The wads had to be separated, flattened, and folded into pads for reuse. The aide at the entrance of the endlessly long maternity ward awoke from her snooze as I passed by. With a sleepy yawn, she said, *"Cigarettes pour Papa?"* a code for "What do you have for me?"

I smiled and replied, *"Pas ce soir*—not this evening."

Muted strains of Congolese music, with its repetitive drumbeat, floated across the lawns from the transistor radios in the GYN ward. I walked in and said, *"Bamama, mbote."* They raised their hands and answered with soft *"Aaaaahs."* Patients and their families sat on the narrow, freshly scrubbed terraces that surrounded each pavilion. The visitors brought food to their relatives, others chatted quietly. From Pavilion 6, men's surgery, where a dozen soldiers from the fighting in North Katanga had been admitted with war wounds, occasional groans of suffering and cries of pain breached the peace and quiet. The night *mère* and I greeted each other formally as I headed for the OR and she continued her rounds.

Early on, Pepo Eskenazi had supplied us with one thousand new red plastic mattresses, pillows, and sheets. Pepo was and remains a good friend and successful businessman. He invested his own money in his fabric and plastic factories during some of the worst times in the 1960s. His workforce at Solbena-Plastica remained loyal and devoted because he protected their jobs and cared for them and their families when other industrialists abandoned the country. Pepo and I met at the riding club in Léopoldville, the Cercle Hippique, and at dinners with mutual friends. He was a delightful bon vivant who rode Arabian stallions and enjoyed the most attractive mistress in town.

(L-R) Bokassa laughs, Mobutu glares, Bobozo sweats, and Pepo is diplomatic.

The television sets in half of the pavilions had been provided by a businessman close to Mobutu. He had called on the president one evening when we were playing checkers. I suggested he could supply television sets for every pavilion in the hospital. Mobutu added that this would be a great gesture, and the televisions were installed gratis during the following weeks. Pepo contacted directors of companies making good money in the country. A truck, an ambulance, a minibus, refrigerators, and many other items were donated. Pepo used the fact that *le Patron* would be informed and pleased by their gifts.

Through a large trochar, we drained over half a liter of pus from Roger's liver and brought out hard rubber drains from a stab wound between his ribs. We returned him to the ICU for the night. The next day, I loaded him into the back of my car and drove him home, where I could keep a good eye on him and he'd be comfortable under Tine's care.

Mobutu stuck to the agreement he and I made when he asked me to rehabilitate the hospital. He followed the developments in the staff and buildings with keen interest. The money required was deposited regularly in FOMECO's account over my signature. From time to time, I drove him to the hospital in my car, without bodyguards, and we made rounds together. He was impressed with the cleanliness and order in the wards and admired the equipment and efficiency of the nine new operating rooms, surgical supply, and the expanded emergency services completed during the early seventies. He shook hands with the nurses and technicians and doctors and thanked them repeatedly for their good work. His encouragement was thoroughly appreciated.

The rounds that were special, in my eyes and I think in his, were when we spent time, usually in the ICU, visiting with the patients and families. These rounds were never announced. I'd see him first thing in the morning, and on a whim or a hunch, I'd suggest we check on some of the patients.

"*Pourquoi pas,*" he'd answer, and we'd go.

On these private visits, I saw a side of Mobutu's character that was more engaging and simpler than his public, self-assured persona.

I read from a chart hanging on a clipboard at the foot of a bed. "This young man was in an auto accident yesterday. He suffered a concussion, a broken forearm, and a laceration of his forehead from the windshield."

The president patted the patient's hand. *"Bon courage."*

Tongue-tied, the patient replied, *"Aaaah . . . Merci."*

Whispers of "président" came from other patients following our slow progress from bed to bed.

A woman watched us through a peephole in a heavy bandage around her head and face. I looked at her chart: acid thrown by her husband. She grasped Mobutu's hand and pressed it to the slit in the gauze by her swollen lips.

"Mama, bon courage," he said quietly, then turned to me, "I'll give you something to help pay for her care."

Usually, Mobutu's personal contact with the patients, his questions about their conditions and their families, brought smiles and shy responses from the patients. They were surprised when he stood by their beds and leaned

Mobutu waves his cane at the crowd during the opening of the new X-ray department.

over to shake hands. Most of them had only seen him at mass meetings in the stadium, if they could afford a ticket or had a cousin at the gate.

As far as the effect of these visits on the president, they brought him closer to the people. When he was in the public eye, he put on a bold front, stepping from his helicopter like a man who owned the stadium and the winning team. He pumped his legendary cane, with a pregnant woman carved near the handle, toward the heavens, then brought it down and held it by his thumb, waving to the crowd, not unlike Leonard Bernstein when he tucked his baton into his palm to give his arm a rest.

At home, Tine read poetry to Roger and fed him her great cooking. I fed him amoebicides and sang "Vincerò" along with Pavarotti to speed his recovery and add a little Italian passion to his cure. He was eventually ready to fly home to England and his family. We've stayed in touch through the years.

FOMECO was increasingly involved in the search for better health care delivery systems to meet the needs of the country. At all administrative and professional levels, Zairians worked with expatriate counterparts whose contracts ran for two years. Whenever possible, the expatriates worked with and trained their own replacements.

In coordination with the national university and the ministry of health, FOMECO participated in the development of physicians trained to meet the needs of people in rural and isolated areas as well as in the mushrooming urban centers. The national government asked FOMECO to survey hospitals in the interior of the country for reorganization.

The Hôpital des Congolais of Léopoldville started as an outpatient facility in 1910. The services increased slowly, and the first inpatient pavilion was built in the 1920s. Other pavilions were added until 1958. By 1960, it was the main public hospital for the capital city, which had a population of 400,000. Between 1960 and 1970, due to other pressing problems in the country, little or no improvements were made in medical facilities. The population of Léopoldville had increased by 312 percent, to 1,250,000. Seventy-four percent were women and children. At the time of independence, the hospitals run by missionaries or colonial civil servants were designed for the care of large numbers of Congolese. The colonial health system was one of the very best in Africa, probably because the Congolese provided the muscle power to transfer the wealth of their country to their colonial masters. During the ten years that followed independence, the momentum for the care of the population slowly ran out of money and competent professionals. "One for all and all for one and I'm the one" became the modus operandi of some who maneuvered themselves into positions of responsibility. They became bleeders and looters of the system.

Within a few months of FOMECO's taking over the hospital, the transformations began to take place. The renovation of two city blocks of hospital wards, clinics, walkways, operating and emergency rooms, kitchens, and offices were well under way. The sewage system had to be completely dug up and rebuilt. All electrical wiring was replaced. The one non-functioning telephone was replaced by a switchboard open twenty-four hours a day with 15 outside lines and 192 extensions.

Hospital renovation.

Those who delivered the care were people from five continents, twenty-five countries, and from all over Zaire. The variety of backgrounds was stimulating, and made for a confluence of ideas and

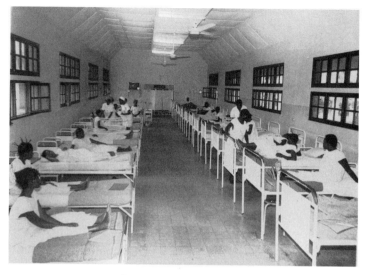

Renovated women's ward.

opinions. A staff of 1,821 cared for a daily inpatient census of 1,594.

Internal medicine admitted 304 patients during August 1970. A year later, the admissions were up to 442 per month, and the average length of stay had dropped from twenty-nine to fourteen days. In 1972, 4,819 patients were hospitalized, with an overall average stay of seven days.

In surgery, the number of major operations in 1970 was 5,496. By 1972, the number had increased to 10,284.

The hospital's twenty outpatient clinics saw over four thousand patients a day, sixteen hours a day. New methods of mass screening were developed to handle the large volume of patients.

In child care and nutrition, classes were held every day for mothers whose children were being treated in the pediatric clinics. The food was purchased at the local market, prepared, and eaten in class.

In emergency medical care, the volume of emergency patients increased steadily; the facilities were expanded

Major surgery in 1970, 5,496 cases. In 1972, 10,284 cases.

three times in one year. The variety kept pace with the volume, sometimes staggering the imagination: one hundred victims of a two-bus crash, a snakebite, and an esophageal burn could come in at the same time.

For mother-child health care, an outpatient clinic for mothers-to-be averaged 330 patients per day, all year long. An average of 130 babies were born every day at the hospital. It stretched to 170 on occasion. One of the pediatric outpatient clinics treated 113 critically ill children daily.

In specialty medical care, the average patient had two and a half diseases that required input from specialists. Intensive care units for surgery, maternity, and cardiology were developed under modern guidelines. In-service training programs for nurses were essential in the development of a better cadre of professional personnel.

An army of midwives averaged 130 deliveries a day.

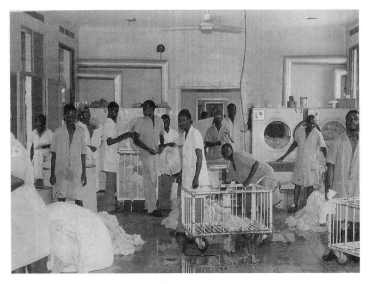

The laundry.

Each day, the laundry processed and distributed over 1.6 tons of laundry. More than three kilometers of corridors and walkways were scrubbed with soap and water daily. Maintenance crews were busy throughout the hospital. Twenty Catholic nuns provided years of experience in administration and logistics. Above and beyond the medical staff were the secretaries, administrators, accountants, plumbers, and pharmacists. The entire operation required imagination, patience, guts, and a healthy sense of humor.

How does one marry technical excellence with humanitarian goals? FOMECO was an organization that attempted to do just that, to coordinate the best efforts and resources available in the most effective

Three kilometers of corridors scrubbed with soap and water daily.

and humane ways possible. It sought to train, to teach, to research, and to implement.

"The gross national happiness . . . Perhaps one day the universal standard will be man instead of money," declared the optimistic president Mobutu on December 5, 1972, in a speech before the National Legislative Council of Zaire.

Chapter 33
Ordre du Léopard

THE CONGO'S NINTH INDEPENDENCE DAY, June 30, 1969, was celebrated with the usual parade, visiting heads of state, and the official opening of the International Industrial Fair in Léopoldville.

Downtown, on Boulevard Albert, in front of the Regina Hotel, military bandsmen, dripping in braid and sweating under tall black bearskins that hid their eyes, tooted or emptied spit from their instruments waiting for the arrival of President Mobutu and his guest, President Obote of Uganda. The diplomatic corps, members of the government, and significant businessmen worked their

Mobutu pinning on the Order of the Leopard.

way into the grandstands on either side of the presidential tribune. A crowd gathered behind the band and along the boulevard vying for a spot with a view. The smell of hot tar and horse manure was blended with sweat or cologne, depending on where you stood or sat. The people, some straddling lampposts, or balanced on the ledges of the Regina, waited with anticipation. Any spectacle added color and zest to a struggling, humdrum life.

The band was ordered to attention and struck up a march with repetitive phrases and rhythms imposed by the thunder of a bass drum. In the distance, the presidential cavalcade made its way slowly down the avenue. The two presidents stood in an open car acknowledging the cheering, waving crowd, whose roar rose and fell like a tidal wave as the presidents, surrounded by the presidential motorcycle escort, passed by. Finally the car and escort stopped in front of the band, and the presidents were ushered by Louis Tshibambi, the chief of protocol, to their stuffed chairs in the front row. Mahele, Tshibambi, and I sat on hard folding chairs guaranteed to cut off all circulation to the buttocks after the first hour or so.

With a trumpet call and ruffle of drums, General Victor Lundula, Lumumba's uncle, president of the Congolese veterans of the Second World War and chancellor of the National Order of the Leopard, stood before the dignitaries and the people and called forward President Obote of Uganda. After a short statement of praise, the chancellor handed the decoration to President Mobutu, who placed the sash and decoration on his guest. Then I heard over the speakers, "le Docteur William Cloooose." Tshibambi pushed me out of my chair, and I walked out to stand next to the chancellor, who launched into a statement in Lingala and French about this American doctor's service to the people of the Congo, an example of selfless devotion without seeking material gain, now the president's doctor, and so on. The president pinned the decoration on me, Officier de l'Ordre National du Léopard, kissed me on both cheeks, and we turned to face the band while they played the national anthem. Tine was sitting among the diplomats. The gentleman next to her said, "That's my doctor." Tine replied, "That's my husband."

Mobutu salutes the national anthem, June 1969.

At the time, I was proud of the decoration, which I considered as recognition of medical services rendered to the Congolese people and other patients, including the president. My nature was to meet a challenge head on with, as my English schoolteachers had reported years ago, "boundless enthusiasm" and "singleness of purpose." My training allowed me to do just that, and most of the time, Tine and some of my colleagues tempered my enthusiasm with reality. In my mind, people like the old midwife who walked for miles to get to work deserved recognition. She had neither money nor an American passport nor the choice to stay or leave.

Chapter 34
A Flame-shaped Hemorrhage

MOBUTU OFTEN TEASED ME. If I gave him medical orders he didn't like, such as diet, exercise, or rest, he'd pull the stethoscope out of my pocket, listen to my heart, and say, "Tonight nothing at all to eat or drink and tomorrow morning you go to the lab where they will bleed you." I would reply that I hated needles, I was *pas d'accord* —not in accord—and would find another doctor. This somewhat casual approach to his health care changed on July 2, 1969.

The phone woke me up at 3:30 A.M. "*Le Président a besoin de vous*—The president needs you."

"*J'arrive*—I'm on my way," I replied, jumping out of bed.

Only his wife called at night. I pulled on clothes, grabbed my bag, and drove out of our yard. What the hell was going on? The occasional street lamp shone feebly through clouds of moths and mosquitoes. I drove past the camp commander's house; the guard saluted from the comfort of his chair. So far, so good. The headlights startled goats munching refuse in the gutter. I turned in at the president's gate. The troopers saluted and waved me through. The place seemed asleep except for the security detail at the front door and in the entrance hall. In the cool hours before dawn, the peepers sang in the grass.

Upstairs, I found Mobutu standing in the middle of his bedroom in his bathrobe holding a handkerchief over his left eye. He removed it and blinked.

"I can't see on the left. It just happened."

I picked up a book from his bed table. "Can you read?"

He looked at the text, squinting and trying out each eye. "I can see with the right eye, but not the left. *C'est flou*—It's fuzzy." He sat on the corner of the bed.

I pulled an ophthalmoscope from my bag, took a deep breath, and focused the light beam on the back of his left eyeball. A fresh flame-shaped retinal hemorrhage was clearly visible at three o'clock adjacent to the ivory-colored circle of the optical nerve. I let him rest for a moment and controlled the tremor in my hand. The arterioles in the red bowl of his retina were narrow and stiff, like silver wires. His right eye was normal, but his blood pressure was up to 150/100: arteriolar sclerosis and hypertensive retinopathy. One brittle arteriole under excess pressure had leaked blood into the retina near the optic nerve, blurring his vision on the left: a clear-cut dangerous precursor to a stroke. And he was only thirty-nine.

I explained to him what had happened, the seriousness of these warning symptoms, and the immediate need for us to get his pressure and weight down, and control his blood fats. I told him I was very concerned and would call Professor Vannotti and ask him to fly down from Switzerland for a consultation as soon as possible. In 1966, I accompanied Mobutu for what would become his yearly medical checkup with Professor Alfredo Vannotti, the chief of medicine in Lausanne and director of the prestigious Clinique Nestlé. The professor was born in the Tessin, the Italian part of Switzerland. After his education in Milan, he made his home in Lausanne. He brought with him an Italian sense of humor, delivered with gestures to make a point, and a melodious voice. He was a small, *soigné* gentleman with thick horn-rimmed glasses and a floppy Borsalino perched at a rakish angle on his bald head. He was a much-respected scientist and a wise clinician armed with a healthy realism about human nature. He pioneered the use of radioactive iodine in the diagnosis of thyroid diseases and, in his later years, was an artist and author. He appreciated good cuisine and fine wine.

Professor Alfredo Vannotti.

I gave Mobutu a sedative. I could have used a double dose myself. He must have read the worry in my face, because he accepted what I told him without trying to make light of it.

From his bloodless coup in 1965 to his retinal hemorrhage four years later, I had checked his pressure and responded to minor problems like diarrhea or a cold, usually when I was called over to see one of the children or one of the innumerable family attachments. If I checked his pressure then, everyone, including the children, had to have their pressures checked.

Forty years later, the same blood pressure cuff lives in my bag. It's as accurate as the newer ones and carries memories that hiss softly from its black bulb when the air is released slowly to reveal the pressure in a brachial artery. Over the last few years, I had occasionally checked his pressure and found it slightly elevated, especially when he was stressed out, frustrated, or thoroughly annoyed by the stupidity and demands of his family and their hangers-on. Vannotti would have more authority than I to impose a strict diet and medications to bring down his weight and pressure. I told him he should rest in bed until I checked him again around noon.

During the short drive home, I was hammered. What if he died from a massive stroke, or worse, what if the next bleed in his head left him alive with a crippling paralysis, unable to take care of his most basic functions?

Flame-shaped hemorrhages in the retina of a man with hypertension, even intermittent and stress related, at least doubled his chance of a full-blown stroke. Up until now, taking care of Mobutu had been an offshoot of taking care of members of his family. Mobutu was never sick. Our yearly pilgrimages for checkups with Professor Vannotti were pleasant breaks from his constant dealings with trivial or crucial affairs of state. I was always more comfortable when Vannotti signed off on my medical records and added his wisdom to Mobutu's prescriptions. Now, a flame-shaped hemorrhage in his left eye and threatening hypertension changed all that.

Once at home, the air conditioner cooled the sweat on my body. My head throbbed. My whole body shook. In bed I threw off the soggy sheet and curled up under a Turkish towel like a fetus. Malaria? That would be so much simpler. I dreaded the chaos and killing if Mobutu died. I would be found guilty of deadly incompetence by those who basked in the president's shadow. I forced myself to think more rationally. If the flame-shaped hemorrhage had appeared in anyone else except the president, I would take it as a stimulus to exercise all measures of stroke prevention without compromise. Because he was president, and I was his doctor, I was trapped by his precarious health. Nobody close to Mobutu who had a personal stake in his survival would let me off. If he died, so would I. I thought of Tine and the children, and my fear congealed into something cold and sharp in the pit of my stomach.

Mobutu had taken over the country in a coup in 1965 and given himself five years to put right the mess dumped on the country by the politicians—his way of putting it. There was no reason to believe that he would step down in a year when his promised tenure would be over. Since the hangings of the four conspirators in 1966, a year after his coup, the country and the politicians had been scared into submission. No one was powerful enough to take over. If Mobutu died, a deluge would destroy the Congo.

The next day I rechecked the president at noon and at 6:00 P.M. By then he was completely asymptomatic and relaxed, but his pressure was still up. The next morning, after a good sleep, his blood pressure was normal and he had no visual symptoms. I ran complete lab studies on him to show the professor.

That evening, I met Vannotti at the airport and drove him to the residence. He confirmed my findings, and we discussed a treatment protocol of medications, together with less stress and more rest. Such advice had faint hope of affecting our patient's schedule or modus vivendi. The thought of apoplexy filled me with apprehension as I imagined an overweight, stressed out, hypertensive chief raising his voice in thundering conviction during yet another meeting with the population and collapsing with a fatal stroke. We would have to control his pressure in spite of the stress in a man who found it hard to delegate. At this point I had to be with him. I had no choice. Shortly after this episode, I received a terse note from Mobutu's personal assistant for special deals stating that if anything happened to *"Le Guide,"* I would be dealt with summarily. I showed the president the handwritten note. He shrugged it off and said, *"C'est rien."* The note and Mobutu's reaction to it did little to settle my nerves, but from then on, at the president's insistence, I took his blood pressure at least once a day. His pressure remained subject to the amount of effort he required to maintain an external appearance of equanimity.

After this frightening episode, which was really a ministroke, I was indeed the dictator's doctor. I was on call day and night, and saw him regularly at least once a day. I soon learned that I was also expected to travel with him on all his trips inside the country and abroad.

Chapter 35
Washington Visit

ON OUR FIRST DAY, we stood on the steps of our national cemetery where President Mobutu placed a wreath at the Tomb of the Unknown Soldier. The historical setting of Arlington Cemetery, our national anthem played by the Marine band, the close order drill of the honor guard with flags snapping in the breeze under a bright blue sky brought tears to my eyes. I was so proud to be an American showing *le Patron* one of our most sacred monuments to those who had given their lives for freedom.

On August 4, 1970, at 8:00 P.M., Mobutu's official party dined at the White House. Tine sat next to Donald Rumsfeld, who was silent throughout the meal. Unhappily, I

Nixon hosting Mobutu at the White House, August 1970.

forget who the people were on either side of me. In his toasts, President Nixon said that the former Belgian territory was a good investment because it was a strong, vigorous, and stable country. These remarks were reported by the *New York Times,* which added that President Mobutu, who was visiting the United States in search of investments by American business, smiled delightedly and thanked America for its aid. He issued a warm invitation for Americans to invest in his stable country, whose philosophy did not include any concept of nationalization. After dinner, we were entertained by André Watts, who played Chopin's *Ballade No. 1,* Scarlatti's *Three Sonatas,* and Liszt's *La Campanella.* Then the Marine band took over, and Tine and I had such fun dancing that we had to run to catch up to the official party as they walked down the White House drive to Blair House.

Mobutu was received royally. His meetings with senior industrialists were facilitated in every way. Occasionally I translated for him during private luncheons. Most of the time, I observed with fascination the interactions between Mobutu and these captains of industry seeking American investments in the Congo for their own gain.

After the state visit, President Mobutu was joined by his children, who had been flown over from the Congo. The whole party flew back to Los Angeles for a special tour of Disneyland. Tina was living in Pacific Palisades. She and Shona, our granddaughter, joined us. We all boarded the *African Queen* riverboat and chugged into jungle scenes with sound effects from Disneyesque hippos and crocodiles. Everyone enjoyed the exhibit with the two people up a palm tree and the white hunter's rear end inches above the horn of a rhino. We climbed the gangplank of the pirate ship. As we progressed past a Wild West fort, rifles poked through loopholes in the logs, and the president's security men reached for their weapons. I shouted, *"Non, non, c'est du* Mickey Mouse," in time to avoid a counterattack. It was a happy time with the president and some of the family. I was embarrassed that we were ushered into the rides and exhibits ahead of people who had stood in line for some time.

A tour of Hollywood and Beverly Hills in a VIP minibus with an attractive French-speaking guide was arranged for the president and his family. Tine and I and a couple of security men went along. After viewing the houses and flowered lawns of some of the movie stars, the guide announced that we would now see properties owned by some of the wealthiest people—the doctors and lawyers of the rich and famous. When we drove slowly by the mansion of Howard Hughes' physician, the guide announced, "This man makes millions of dollars and he only has one patient." From the back of the bus, I asked her to repeat the salary, which she did. Then I asked her to repeat how many patients he took care of. She turned up the volume and answered, "Just one." Mobutu swiveled in his seat and said, with a frown, "*Tu exagères*—You exaggerate, you go too far," an expression he used often when I approached the edge of the envelope.

At first, state visits were exciting, but as time passed, and the number of trips accumulated, they became increasingly tiresome. I loathed coming back to a mountain of patient charts, hospital documents, and so on piled on my desk. I was happiest when I was involved with medicine, not puppy-dogging the president. The family accepted our separations gracefully, but the trips took their toll and even left scars over the years.

Back in November 1969, Tine and I reviewed our personal accounts and found that we would have a hard time paying for a Greenwich, Connecticut, wedding for our daughter Glenn. I talked to the president about this, and he suggested that he pay me $20,000 a year as a retainer. For the ten years of earlier service, he volunteered to pay $40,000, or two years' worth. That seemed like a lot of money, and I accepted gratefully, especially since our expenses were covered, and at that time, an American working overseas could earn up to $20,000 tax free. This gave us enough money for a nice wedding and a down payment on a small ranch in the western mountains of Wyoming.

It seemed funny to some of my friends that I never signed a contract. In fact, I never even talked about a contract with Mobutu. No contract was needed. When Tine and I moved permanently back to Wyoming and bought a small ranch, we signed the usual papers, but the old lawyer, who became a friend, told us that a word and a handshake was enough of a guarantee of honesty in this part of the Rocky Mountains.

Chapter 36
Games

MOST EVENINGS I called on Mobutu at his home in the paratrooper camp. He liked to play checkers, making his moves with lightning speed. I rarely won even when I caught him cheating, which he did frequently. Sometimes, to tease me, he played a recording of de Gaulle's speech attacking American policy in Vietnam. Mobutu thoroughly enjoyed his victories and my defeats, especially when my patience wore thin.

After winning two of the thirteen games I had set as a maximum number I would play in one evening, he offered me a cognac. As we moved out onto the terrace, he laughed and proclaimed, "As Napoleon said, *J'ai failli*

"I come here to catch fish!"

perdre—I almost lost.'"

"I almost lost" meant that he had to win. "I almost lost" added excitement.

Mobutu also liked to fish. On a trip to the interior, we stopped at a fish farm where artificial ponds produced tilapia, sometimes called the "new orange roughy." Mobutu sat in an armchair next to a pond. A bodyguard threaded a worm on the hook at the end of a long string attached to an even longer bamboo pole. The president dipped the worm into the pond and pulled out a fish, which was plucked from the hook and dropped in a bucket. Another bodyguard applied a new worm and the president caught another fish.

I said to him, "That's not fishing. There's no sport in that."

"I am here to catch fish," he announced. How obvious and how stupid of me to mention sport.

Looking back, it seems to me that "I am here to catch fish" and "I almost lost" were expressions of his intolerance to any proposition that he might be wrong. When he set his course, he could not admit to error, and doubt played no part in his thinking. Messianic convictions tend to be guided by the gut rather than the head and, in a chief of state or an imperial president, can be downright dangerous.

Sometimes others would join us at the checkerboard. Holden Roberto, a Western-backed Angolan leader, dropped by occasionally. He played checkers just as fast as the general but let him cheat without objecting. It made me wonder how strong a leader Roberto would be.

When General Gowon, president of Nigeria, was visiting the Congo, Mahele called my office to say that *le Patron* wanted to see me right away. Still in my white coat, I hurried over to the presidency and found both heads of state sitting in the living room. Mobutu introduced me to his guest, pointing out in broken English that "My *docteur* speeks leetel Inglish." General Gowon struggled to greet me in French. I interrupted in good American English and told him not to believe his counterpart. We laughed, and I stayed to translate between the two heads of state.

Another call came in the middle of the night on July 20, 1969, seconds after Neil Armstrong stepped onto the moon. Mobutu wanted to be the first African head of state to invite the astronauts to the continent. I awoke our ambassador, who relayed the message to Washington.

The three *Apollo 11* astronauts visited the Congo on October 24 and, in the midst of a celebration with music and dancers, received the Ordre du Léopard decoration from the president. They gave him copies of the plaque they had left on the moon. Tine and I had the pleasure of having their flight surgeon as our guest for the night. Over dinner I remarked that taking care of these astronauts must be quite a challenge.

"Not really," replied our guest. "They're former test pilots. All they need is a routine commercial pilot flight physical." The doctor told us that when one of them felt he needed to exercise, he lay down until the feeling subsided.

The Congo was the first and only African country Neil Armstrong, Buzz Aldrin, and Mike Collins visited, and the Congolese danced to a song, *"Apollo onze, cha-cha-cha."*

Chapter 37
Mobutu, *Oyee*

ONE NIGHT, on a trip upriver, the president and I leaned on the wooden railing to watch the shoreline illuminated by a searchlight from the bridge. Crowded by the forest behind, giant trees bent over the water and groups of people on strips of sand flashed by in the beam of light. Moments later, darkness had reclaimed the people. Their shouts, "Mobutu, *oyee*—Mobutu, hooray," reached us across the water.

"That's what you call the voice of the people," said Mobutu with a dry laugh. "It's Mobutu, *oyee* when beer and bread are cheap. If prices rise, they'll shout Mobutu, *à bas*—down with Mobutu—and shake their fists at me."

Riverbank village.

These trips up the river with Mobutu and his family were relaxing and fun, especially when Tine and sometimes Tina were invited to come along. When we stopped at villages along the way, a long gangplank was lowered to the riverbank so people could come aboard, one at a time, to shake hands with the president. On these occasions we sat on low rattan stools, and Mobutu welcomed each person warmly.

An old man hobbled up the gangplank and shook hands with the president, who referred him to me as a doctor who might help with a leg swollen with elephantiasis. Even with such severe conditions, the quiet attention given by the president and his doctor were greatly appreciated. Two men carrying a huge *capitaine* fish on a pole slipped and stepped on

Bill examining newborns with Presidents Tombalbaye of Chad and Mobutu watching.

the fish's tail as they struggled to bring their gift aboard. Everyone cheered and clapped as they made it on board with their trophy. An old mama approached with three small pullet eggs cupped in her hands. She offered them to Mobutu, and he received them as he would gold nuggets. Next, a woman with white paint covering her face showed him her newborn twins. The president congratulated her warmly and asked his ordinance officer to give her a reward.

Mobutu had a way of putting everyone at ease, whether a stuffy diplomat or an ancient, arthritic mama from an obscure village on the river's edge. His charm could disarm an angry man, who might even forget the cause of his anger and come out from the interview with a smile on his face. I never saw him angry at a stranger,

Welcoming a citizen on the boat.

although he was sometimes furious and frustrated by the incompetence of some of those around him. He could imitate, to perfection, foreign ambassadors, especially Americans. I remember the day President Carter was elected. I stepped out onto the terrace to see Mobutu, and he greeted me with a smile that exposed all his teeth and said, "*Il a gagné*—He won!"

Out of our talks during river trips came the concept of the floating hospital. The hospital riverboat was a 700-ton unit built by Chanic, the Belgian firm of naval architects that built the tugs and barges that plied the Congo River.

Sandy and I helped with suggestions for the floor plans of the various decks. The idea behind the boat was to work segments of the river to update public health services and training as well as to care for acute needs. The vessel was

Catfish for the president.

baptized *Marie-Antoinette* after the president's wife. The captain, crew, and medical staff were all Congolese except for Sister Lucie, a Flemish nun, who kept the key to the supply cabinets.

The floating hospital was such a showpiece, with two operating rooms, screening clinics, X-ray, lab, and wards, that the president insisted that as many river villages as possible should be reached so that the people could see the boat and be treated. He would have been happy to have it sail all the way to Kisangani, a trip of over fifteen hundred kilometers, on every outing. Two boats, hoisted on davits on the afterdeck below the helicopter pad, were used to speed nurses to destinations for preliminary screening prior to the boat's arrival. Frequently, patients were admitted on board for surgery or other acute care and dropped off in their villages on the return trip. This was not the ideal use of the boat, since there was too little time to retrain the village medical personnel and attend to more general public health needs. The log of one such trip reflects a frenetic pace:

> *May 3, 1971: The* Marie-Antoinette *returns. She left Léopoldville April 13, returned May 2. She visited 109 villages. The doctors did 77 operations and saw 5,134 patients. They had 17 work days. There were 15 serious hospitalizations, two deaths, and one birth.*

Hospital boat *Marie-Antoinette*.

Although the president was pleased with the boat's activities, this impressive unit taught me a lesson: a sound operation and maintenance budget for any medical facility was critical for success. The hospital boat proved to be far too expensive to operate. After several years of service, it was lashed to an abandoned dock and allowed to rust.

Chapter 38

Mama Yemo

ON MAY 13, 1971, the president called me to say that Mama Yemo had been ill during our long trip to France, China, and Taipei in April, and that she had taken a turn for the worse. We flew up to Gemena in an air force plane, taking with us Dr. Amin Jazab, who was on the staff of our presidential medical services. Amin, with his wife and children, lived their Bahá'í faith, adding trustworthiness to his work as a doctor.

Mama Yemo was breathing with difficulty and unable to talk. We examined her. She was clearly in severe congestive failure. I suggested to the president that we would do our best to stabilize her, but in view of the limited medical facilities in Gemena, we should transfer her to Léopoldville. Mobutu stood at his mother's bedside watching her struggle for air. "My mother told me she would die and be buried in her birthplace. I must follow her wishes. Do your best here, in her home."

With the help of a local physician, we brought a portable X-ray to her bedside. The films revealed an enlarged heart and congested lungs. We started oxygen and intravenous medication. Within thirty-six hours, she showed some improvement. Sharpness returned to her mind, and recognizing her son, she was able to speak clearly. Her younger son, then the ambassador of Zaire in Sweden, came and gave her great joy. President Bokassa arrived from Bangui for a visit. I sent for Dr. Beheyt, our cardiologist at the general hospital. He ran several electrocardiograms and confirmed that Mama Yemo's cardiac failure had been exacerbated by a heart attack.

At 2:00 A.M. on May 18, Amin called: Mama Yemo was in extremis. I notified the president and joined him at her bedside.

He leaned over to catch her whispers.

"Mobutu. Mobutu."

"Oui, Mama." He took her hand.

"Mobutu, *tu dois aimer ton peuple. Tu dois aimer ton peuple*—You must love your people. You must love your people."

"Oui, Mama . . . Oui, Mama, je te promets—Yes, Mama . . . Yes, Mama, I promise you."

Her whispers faded, but she repeated, "Mobutu . . . *aimer ton peuple . . . aimer ton peuple . . .*" She died with those words on her lips.

The family, who had been waiting in another room, rushed in and cried out their grief, and the keening took over.

The president walked down the back steps and into a patch of corn husks. I followed him. His shoulders shook with his sobs. He turned, "Why did she repeat that?"

We both wept.

Dr. Jazab lays wreath at Mama Yemo's grave.

Much later I wondered whether she was reminding him of their humble origins, mother and son. Was she admonishing him to care for the people among whom he'd been born? Had she seen him lose touch with the mothers who struggled each day to feed their children? To fail in the eyes of his mother was tantamount to destroying her faith in him.

Chapter 39
Medical Militia

IN 1971, Lovanium University students demonstrated against Mobutu and his regime. They issued a statement that when Mama Yemo died, the whole country was given four days to mourn, four days for a "whore," but nothing had ever been done to memorialize the Lovanium students shot by the army during a demonstration in 1969. Mobutu was livid. He kicked a cup of coffee across the room and

Dr. Miatudila on right with fellow medical militia.

shouted, "They can insult me, but not my mother." All university students were immediately drafted into the army for two years in spite of the objections of certain generals and prelates whose sons were students.

Thus, in November 1971, nine young men in starched, pressed khaki uniforms stood before me, their campaign hats balanced at various angles. These men were some of the "medical militia" created by order of the president. One stepped forward and introduced himself as Dr. Miatudila. He had been president of the medical student association. He handed me an official paper stating that they had been assigned to work at Mama Yemo Hospital. I welcomed them and called the hospital director, Dr. Georges Bazunga, to tell him that these new doctors were on their way over to see him for assignment.

At that time, the rebuilding of the hospital and recruitment of medical cadres from Europe and the United States were well under way. Our primary goal in FOMECO was to train medical students and young doctors from Lovanium University in the practical aspects of medicine and surgery.

Even before the graduation ceremony, the Léopoldville newspapers had published the assignments of graduates in medicine to hospitals in the interior. Congolese doctors had no right to engage in private medicine, but non-Congolese graduates were free to engage in private practice anywhere in the Congo.

Dr. Miatudila had been requisitioned for service at Bosobolo in north Ubangi, the most northwestern part of the country. From the age of five, he'd never been outside Léopoldville, and he admitted freely that the university had certainly not prepared any of them for the formidable responsibilities of being a doctor in the bush. Although they had the ponderous title of Doctor of Medicine, Surgery and Obstetrics, most of them were incapable of performing the simplest surgical operations.

Years later, my friend Dr. Miat told me how shocked he had been when some of his fellow students had dared to call Marie-Madeleine Yemo a whore. In the eyes of the party-state, this offense was all the more punishable because this mama, the venerable mother of President Mobutu, had done nothing to the students, but had died. Miat was outraged at this loss of respect that Bantus normally had for their dead. The other event that shocked him occurred two hours before his graduation. He heard over the radio that Mobutu and his close collaborators had decided that his country, Congo, would be called Zaire. He would be called Zairian. His heart ached, and it took time for the idea to sink in.

Miat's first interview with Dr. Roger Youmans, chief

of staff, swept away any prejudices he and his colleagues felt against the Mama Yemo Hospital. They realized right away that important changes were taking place since FOMECO had taken over. Over the past two years, since the president had asked me to run the general hospital (at the time the Hôpital des Congolais), and accepted my conditions, the expansion of the operating rooms and emergency service and the renovation of the various wards and pavilions had kept pace with the recruitment of doctors from the United States, Canada, and Europe under the leadership of Dr. Youmans.

Dr. Youmans and I had met in 1968, when he was finishing a term as surgeon in Wembo Nyama, one of the largest and most efficient protestant missionary hospitals in the interior. Together, we operated on a patient at Ngaliema Clinic. During the long procedure, we

Dr. Roger Youmans, Chief of Staff, Mama Yemo Hospital.

spoke of the challenge of training newly minted doctors from the university into competent, practical professionals. I was impressed with his sense of reality, and knew that he would make an outstanding chief of staff of the hospital I'd been asked to manage. Roger was interested but, at that time, had his fill of the Congo. Later, while on a short trip home, I flew out to Kansas City where he was teaching surgery and put the proposition squarely on his plate. With some reluctance, he accepted the offer and returned to the Congo. Sight unseen, he took over as medical director of a huge two-thousand-bed, dilapidated, filthy, ill-staffed Hôpital des Congolais that stank of sewage. With perseverance and high professional standards, he performed miracles.

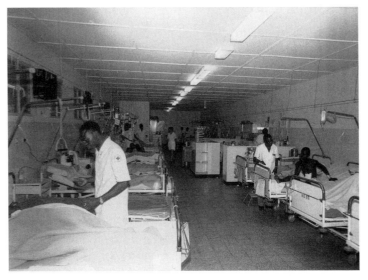

New ICU, Mama Yemo Hospital.

Roger and the heads of departments elaborated a fifteen-month internship program, which included rotations in the major services: emergency, internal medicine, pediatrics, surgery, and gynecology. The work was divided into two shifts: 8:00 A.M. to 8:00 P.M., and the night shift, 8:00 P.M. to 8:00 A.M., followed by a day of rest. Miat went to work on Monday, December 6, two days after his wedding. He was assigned to the emergency room, where two hundred to three hundred people were seen every twenty-four hours. It was not his idea of a honeymoon, but he knew better than to complain.

Fifteen months at Mama Yemo Hospital transformed the interns into competent doctors of medicine, surgery, and obstetrics. The program was much like the rotating internships offered in our best hospitals before we in the United States became so specialized. During Miat's internship, the hospital registered an average per day of 2,000 outpatients, 140 deliveries, and 30 surgical operations. At the end of the internship, most interns were transferred back to the ministry of health and assigned to government hospitals in the interior. FOMECO kept a few to build up our teaching staff. Dr. Gabriel Ngoma was attached to the hospital boat to work with Dr. John Ross. Dr. Sylvain Muteba was assigned to work with Dr. Youmans, and Dr. Miatudila was assigned to the British Missionary Society hospital in Bolobo that had recently been taken over by FOMECO. In the years that followed, more interns were prepared for duty in other critical areas.

In August of 1974, I arranged, through the U.S. Agency for International Development, for Miatudila and two of his colleagues, Etienne Mvuni and Faustin Ngwala, to receive scholarships from Tulane University in Louisiana for degrees in public health. Miat graduated summa cum laude, and this eventually led to the establishment of the Kinshasa School of Public Health.

Chapter 40
Parades and *Meeting Populaire*

PARADES MARKED every presidential visit. Toward the end of December 1971, we were in Bukavu, the principal town of South-Kivu tucked between the shores of Lake Kivu and its surrounding mountains. The presidential grandstand was on the main avenue. The national police band led the parade in their black furry shakos and red tunics trimmed in white. The musicians wheeled into position across the street facing the grandstand. A good band, but the Zairian Jesuit who wrote the new national anthem told me they were putting in too many of their

Mobutu addressing popular meeting.

own twists and trills. Although Mobutu had brought a sense of nationhood to the disparate regions of Zaire, massive doses of Jesuit-like faith and the triumph of hope over reality would be needed for the country to sing in unison.

So here we were again, sitting behind *le Patron*. The day started cool and cloudless, with high-flying white-striped crows. But soon the atmosphere turned hot, damp, and noisy with the usual exuberant crowds pushing to see Mobutu. They shouted in unison, *"L'homme seul*—the Man Alone—the Only Man." I asked him if the people shouted *"l'homme seul"* because they distrusted the politicians who operated in his shadow. He chuckled. "No, it's the title of a book about me."

The primary school kids marched by, followed by other children strutting past, stiff-legged, with their left arms held rigidly by their sides, their right fists clenched over their hearts—the Mouvement Populaire de la Révolution (MPR) youth salute. Then another section came along, swinging their arms across their bellies, followed by a group of kids each proudly waving a paper national flag, all serious, rubber-necking to steal a look at the president.

I dozed in the heat. The repetitive beat of the drums and musical phrases were soporific—*da-da-dum-te-te-boom-boom, da-da-dum-te-te-boom-boom, da-da-dum-te-te-boom-boom*—for hours on end. Every time I saw the band, I wondered why it didn't melt away in the sweat pouring from their fur shakos and heavily braided uniforms.

I thought of previous visits to Bukavu, this beautiful but rundown town hanging on steep hills and spreading into Lake Kivu on numerous *presqu'îles*. In 1967, the city was held hostage by white mercenaries, who were finally chased out by the army. I returned a few months later with Mobutu to view the damage after the fighting, mostly between the army and the citizens of Bukavu. In the Commune of Bagira, I was grabbed by a wild woman who thought I was a mercenary riding as a captive in the security jeep behind the president's car. I jerked free and yelled that I was a Congolese albino, and the security men almost fell out of the jeep laughing.

More kids marching, strutting, shuffling, jigging, jogging, swinging, or stiffly staring. Diversity of style in unity of action. *Le Patron* sat and waved in time with the music, his right elbow resting on the arm of his chair, his hand in a perpetual salute. The civil service marched by, jillions of them, many chewing gum. This was something new. There must be a new chewing gum man in town! There is talk of cutting parades down to a maximum of two hours. I would not have thought this possible in the past, but with the new disciplined way of doing these interior trips, maybe it would be possible. This trip saw a minimum of cocktail parties and no *soirées de gala* and *diners dansants*.

As I sat there in the heat and dust, I thought of Tine and the kids. Surely after a few more years, after earning enough money to pay off the ranch we had bought in Wyoming and getting something medical under way in the Congo, it would be nice to retire and live the simple life. A simple life for us might involve writing, which leaves something behind as a residue of lessons learned. Tine and I would have something to leave to our kids and grandchildren. I wondered whether, for me, events would lead to a completion of work here in Zaire, at least a launching of the hospital and national health plans along constructive lines, and le *Patron* into the good hands of a national M.D.

The parade continued with varied groups of three or four huddled together, obviously from the bush, the women with babies on their backs. The better organized urban groups filed past with some of the mamas dancing to the rhythm of the band, every articulation moving in a different direction. A farm group passed, each member waving aloft an egg, a cabbage, a carrot, a manioc root, a tomato. They wiggle-waggled and their hips gyrated more or less to the beat of the bass drum. Then came the market women, as high-powered a segment of humanity as can be found anywhere: powerful in voice and body, with hearts that must be massive muscles to push blood through the rolling mountains of flesh and fat. Quite a few of those parading had goiters that were endemic to the region due to a lack of iodine. No people parade like the Africans.

Chapter 41

Heartbreak at Christmas

DECEMBER 23, 1971: Aboard the president's boat near Kwamouth, a hundred miles upriver from Kinshasa. At 5:30 P.M., I took the chopper off the boat and flew to the capital, which had just been renamed Kinshasa, for more medical supplies—actually a good excuse to see Tine. I landed right next to our house in the camp. The visit was painfully short. I wrote these lines flying back, low over the river, as the sun set:

Standby

They also serve who stay at home and wait
For news, or calls, or whisperings of Fate;
Alone at home.

To snatch a moment out of time and try
To plumb the depths, when both hearts cry
To be as one alone.

Imperative duty cuts across their heart's desire
As on the rocket wing of time the schedule must be
    met.
Thus, off he goes again with heavy heart,
And she remains. The moisture in her eyes
Betrays the calm exterior of peace.

And so she waits again;
But he waits too
For Fate to make these separations cease.

As we skimmed over the glass-smooth water that reflected the sunset, I thought back to Tine's and my meeting when we were sixteen. Our first encounter, so I've been told, was when we played in the same wicker bassinet in 1926, eighty years ago, as infants in Greenwich, Connecticut. We bonded in a wicker basket!

The next time we met, my twin brother Ted and I had just come from England and France at the beginning of the Second World War. We were at Tine's Aunt Margaret's house across from the Round Hill church in Greenwich. Tine wore riding britches. She loved horses, was shy and terribly dignified. I had my hair parted in the middle and spoke with an English accent. She recalls meeting "two little English boys."

She visited St. Paul's School to see her brother, Johnny, who was two classes ahead of us. This gorgeous young lady in a light summer dress smiled at us from the first row of the visitors' gallery in the chapel. She wore a stylish wide-brimmed straw hat decorated with a blue velvet ribbon that rested on waves of copper-toned blonde hair reaching to her shoulders. I remember thinking how unapproachable she seemed.

In 1940, we both turned sixteen, and Tine's mother announced to her children, "The Closes are old friends. We want you to give a dinner party for their twins." In fact, Arthur Moore, Tine's dad, was my brother's godfather. Our fathers had been through divorces together, which I suppose sealed their friendship and understanding. My mother announced to Ted and me, "You two are going over to the Moores' for dinner. They are good friends and I want you to get to know Bettine and John." The young Moores and the Close twins reacted the same way: "We don't want to meet your friends' children just because they're your friends' children."

We were sitting on the back terrace sipping tomato juice when a gray bunny rabbit ran out from a flowerbed.

Tine's Irish Setter, Paddy, bounded over and picked it up gently. Tine held Paddy and I eased the rabbit out of his jaw. We carried the petrified rabbit to the end of the lawn and set him down in the long grass on the other side of a stone wall. After a wonderful dinner and some intermittent talk, we drove to Port Chester to see a movie. I don't remember the film, because Tine and I whispered throughout the picture, much to the annoyance of the people around us. She had on Blue Grass cologne! A passionate potion for a sixteen-year-old who'd been raised like a monk in an English school where the school matron was the closest thing to a real, live, mysterious female. Tine was my first love, and we spoke to each other about our deepest dreams as though we'd been together for a lifetime. That evening, in the dark movie house, surrounded by shushing people, we discovered that we both wanted to use our lives to help people and relieve their suffering. That commitment, even in far and lonely places, has remained steadfast.

Ted and I had an agreement: whichever one of us spoke up first for a girl, the other would not interfere. Walking out to the car after the movie, I said to him, "She's mine."

Throughout the summer, Tine and I met before dawn at the Moore stables. We rode into the woods and were together when the soft light of summer dawns came filtering through the maples and the oaks. Tine rode her chestnut hunter, Skookum, and I followed her on Clinker, a big palomino gelding. During the afternoons, we played tennis or swam in the lake. In the evenings, we rode across the pastures and through the woods in the twilight. My memory tells me that all those nights were moonlit, the woods enchanted, smelling of warm earth and leaves, and Blue Grass cologne. I followed her along the woodland trails that she knew like the palm of her hand. We sat or lay in the moonshade and listened to the peepers and the snorting of the horses nosing through the leaves. We talked about our dreams, our hopes, and our love for each other. She was the first girl I ever kissed. I gave her a gold engagement ring. Unhappily, the ring slipped off her finger while we were swimming in the cold water of the Moores' lake.

Tine's dad and Johnny had built a log cabin in the woods overlooking the lake. We decided to paint the inside white. The cabin was just big enough for one bunk and a loft, but the job took all summer.

That Christmas Eve, 1971, I sat behind Mobutu for midnight mass in Matadi's cathedral in the port city, with four bishops attending. As an official practicing Catholic, the president sought to retain the Latin liturgies. The presiding bishop was barely audible and tottery. The whole service was in Kikongo (the Bakongo language), in spite of the president's request.

During lunch at the villa, Mobutu talked with the minister of the interior about a program of authenticity, integrity, and honesty in the villages. Had they given up on honesty in the cities?

In public meetings, Mobutu worked the crowd and pumped them up with slogans like *"Bomba, bomba*—To hide the truth, to hide the truth"—and the thousands shouted back, *"Mabe*—Bad." Then the president: *"Naloba?*—Should I speak the truth?" The answer followed with a roar, *"Loba*—Speak it." "I am the chief of state for every man, not for a particular group, not for a special clique." I longed for him to tackle his own robbing of the national till and set an example for those closest to him and his ever-expanding family. His friend, the king of Morocco, had almost been eliminated because of corruption in high places. Following an attempted coup, his majesty was forced by public pressure to haul many of his ministers before the bar of justice. Could kings or imperial presidents remain blissfully unaware of the crooks that share their table?

Boma, downstream from Matadi, had replaced Vivi as the second capital of the Congo Free State. The Congo Free State was a kingdom privately owned by King Léopold II of Belgium. That included all of the Democratic Republic of the Congo. Eventually, Léopold II had to accept annexation by Belgium in 1908 because of the horrendous atrocities and mass killings of the indigenous people carried out during his autocratic reign.

The governor-general's house, a steel skeleton covered by corrugated tin and wood, could have been a museum. It was built around 1890 by German contractors. A Congolese woman told us that it was in the governor's house that Congolese were first whipped.

I called Tine on Christmas morning. I could hear recorded carols in the background. As usual, she was a good sport about yet another separation over a holiday, which was normally a family affair. I was miserable with gut-clawing guilt. My "sacrificial" medical duties were nothing compared to the sacrifices imposed on the family. Tine was the vital, selfless presence that commuted from our home in Connecticut to Switzerland and Africa, providing the glue and the care that kept the family connected through both happy and stressful times. Her forte was common sense. Sometimes, when the rest of us were sitting around the dining room table, she would walk in and announce, "I've been thinking." "Oh NO!" we'd wail. Tine had been an archery champion in school. We all knew that her thinking would hit the bull's-eye.

At 10:00 A.M. the next morning, we attended a two-hour parade in town. Nothing unusual except that all Congolese parades are unusual. A soldier marched by with a baby boa constrictor wrapped around his neck. I gathered later that apparently he was punished for not having permission to march past the president with a baby boa wrapped around his neck. I noted many new and uncomfortable-looking plastic shoes, especially on the kids marching by. This must be the result of the president's statement that when King Baudouin was last in the Congo, he mentioned the fact that many more people wore shoes than before. This was considered an indication of progressive social development. By the look of the shoes with pointed toes and sagging arches, I wondered whether, in this climate of hot feet, modern footwear was really anything more than another curse of civilization.

Toward the end of the parade, a woman with triplets approached the president and received a handsome gift of cash. His largess was at first admired, then expected, and finally required for loyalty.

On December 30, 1971, we were off Kwamouth, again, in the president's boat. We flew to Kinshasa in his chopper, landing in the middle of the stadium packed with over a hundred thousand people who welcomed Mobutu with wild cheers. He gave a rousing speech on authenticity, which included pulling down all the monuments to Belgians and renaming all citizens with European names to African ones that reflected who they were and where they came from. Léopoldville had become Kinshasa in October 1971, Boulevard Albert had become Boulevard 30 Juin, and the statue of King Albert at the far end had been pulled down, leaving the monument naked. Elisabethville had become Lubumbashi, Stanleyville had become Kisangani, and so forth. Mobutu dropped the Joseph-Désiré and defined "Mobutu" by where he came from and what he was, starting with "Sese Seko." Another side effect of *authenticité* was a change in diet on the president's boat and in his home. Prior to the return to authentic Congolese customs, names, dress, and cuisine, the president's home and boat offered gourmet European dishes and vintage wines. One of Mobutu's treats was *osso buco*—braised marrowbone—which he sucked out with relish. With a return to originality, Congolese classics replaced colonial dishes. Some of these were *pondu*—cassava leaves; *porc-épic*—hedgehog; hippo, which tasted like something between beef and pork; *moamba*—chicken cooked in palm oil with peanuts and *pili-pili* (hot peppers); *maboke*—steamed fish, usually *capitaine*—cooked in banana leaves; *chenilles*—caterpillars of various colors with hard black heads to be cracked between your teeth; *fufu*—manioc flour, eaten, when possible, with smoked fish to add taste; and finally *cousin*—monkey meat. The first time Mobutu introduced me to *cousin*, he told me that he could call it that, but not me. Although Mobutu still enjoyed his prodigious wine cellar, he also drank fresh palm wine, pouring a driblet on the ground or on the deck for the ancestors.

In the stadium that day, addressing the crowd, the president talked about the control that certain Belgian firms still had on land resulting from preindependence concessions that should have been abrogated and all land returned to the Congolese people. He said that it was easy to criticize foreigners, but that everyone in the country must begin a serious self-criticism. "Ministers, after three months in office, build big homes. Where do they get all the money? An investigation will be undertaken to correct this." The speech met with loud approval by the audience, who had waited for a long time for such a statement.

Perhaps the president needed to listen to his own advice. He had been unable to rid himself of a handful of crooked family members, and seemed to live with the illusion that, as an African chief, whatever he did himself was beyond reproach. In truth, that attitude was more in keeping with Machiavelli or Napoleon than with the traditions of African chiefs. In some ethnic groups, in days gone by, the chief carried a vial of poison around his neck as naturally as he waved a fly whisk. If the Council of Elders concluded that his behavior was improper or his judgment faulty, he was required to take poison so the power could be passed on.

Chapter 42

Diplomacy?

IN 1974, Tine and I were invited to tea at the U.S. embassy residence with the newly arrived Ambassador Dean Hinton. He carefully stuffed his pipe and lit it with a wooden match. I pulled out my pipe, preparing for a relaxed conversation. I lit up with a Zippo.

The ambassador remarked, "You shouldn't light a Dunhill with a Zippo."

I shrugged and we puffed away while his charming but nervous wife poured tea.

"Dr. Close, you've been here a long time. What do you think is the most critical need for the country?" asked the ambassador.

I replied, "I think the real need in this country is that the mothers and the fathers have some small hope that their children will be better off than their parents, that they will be fed and educated decently."

Hinton examined his pipe. "Really?"

"Yes, sir. Really. That hope is the basis of stability in the country; it must not be betrayed."

"That's the sort of answer I'd expect from a doctor," he replied, waving aside such an uninformed opinion.

"Mr. Ambassador, you've been here two days. What do you think is the most important thing?"

"The army needs better equipment."

"That is sheer baloney," I snapped. "I've been working with the army for several years, and that's the least of the country's needs.

We drank our tea in the silence that followed and soon

took our leave. Mobutu had remained in power with the help of American arms and more than $1 billion in U.S. economic aid. Congress suspended military aid to Zaire in 1990 but continued the sale of arms.

A few days after the tea party, I walked out to the terrace and found Mobutu staring at the river as if he'd seen a ghost.

"What's the matter?" I asked him.

"Your ambassador! He was just here giving me economic advice. I called the governor of the bank and passed on the ambassador's suggestions. When I hung up, your ambassador said, 'Calling the governor of the bank is not the way to deal with the situation.'"

I learned years later, from the other American diplomat who was at this first meeting of Hinton and Mobutu, that Hinton, in his very bad French, declared, "*Vous est un malade international*—You are an international sick man." Mobutu, according to this version, walked off.

On the morning of June 16, 1975, I picked up the *Elima* newspaper from a chair in the front hall of the president's home to take it upstairs to him. The headline: "The CIA in a Plot against Mobutu." I ran upstairs to his bedroom and threw the paper on his bed. I was furious.

"You know that's not true. What will happen to my American doctors? Will people attack them?"

He waved off the question. "It's just politics. No one will hurt the doctors."

I was worried that the doctors would suddenly feel insecure—like me at the moment. I suggested forcefully that if the headline was not true, he should have it retracted. Mobutu picked up the telephone and called *Elima's* director, Esolomba, and told him that the paper had exaggerated and that he needed to back off. The whole thing seemed crass. I knew that Major Andre Mpika, an American-trained paratrooper, had been thrown in jail upon his return from an advanced course in the U.S. Army War College, accused of writing a paper on plotting a successful coup against Mobutu. Rumor blamed an ambitious intelligence officer of leaking the paper to the president. Whatever the facts or truth of the rumors, Mpika was in a basement prison cell in the paratrooper camp. My assistant, Dr. Ilanga, reported to me that part of the concrete floor he slept on was wet all the time. I told Ilanga to provide Mpika with a stack of blankets. I could do nothing else, even though I was profoundly upset that one of the elite paratrooper officers who had just returned from training in the United States should be treated in such an inhuman and unjustified fashion. Tine and I considered Mpika and his wife as friends. Before the couple left for training in the United States, Tine taught Mbudi some American cooking and a few English phrases. For me, the gut-churning nights of June 1966 returned, when serious people suggested that Mobutu had engineered the pseudo-plot against him that led to four hideous hangings.

Shortly thereafter, Hinton was declared persona non grata and left Zaire.

Chapter 43
Scrawls on the Wall

BY 1976, the economic situation had become critical, especially for state-run hospitals and schools. I walked over to the president's office and found him reading reports out on the grass terrace off the living room. He was sitting at a white garden table in the shade of a striped umbrella. He had an unobstructed view of the Kinsuka Rapids and part of Pool Malebo, where the massive power of the Congo River narrows after the pool and starts its wild race to the coast. Distance muted the roar of the cataracts. Nearby, the cries of peacocks and parrots in the presidential zoo blended with Congolese music coming from a radio set on the table.

"Good morning, *docteur*. You have a problem?" asked the president.

"*Oui, mon général*. We need more money to feed the patients at Mama Yemo, especially the children. We budgeted for enough, but prices have gone way up."

"I cannot authorize any out-of-budget expenses," he replied.

"I know that, *Patron*, but I have an idea. Independence Day comes next week. Air force jets will fly over the grandstands as they have in the past. Why not cancel that and give me the fuel money to buy food?"

"That's impossible. Of course, the jets will fly in a salute to the country."

"But what about money to feed the patients?"

"You don't know anything about politics. The government has to show its strength. *Comment va madame?"* He turned back to his reading.

The blood rose to my head. "Madame is fine. But we need to be able to feed at least the people in the hospital who are sick. Most of the kids have *kwashi*. They're in terrible shape. Surely feeding your people is good politics," I added, raising my voice.

He replied angrily, "You cannot speak to the chief of state that way."

"I'm sorry," I said more quietly, "but what can I do to feed the patients in the hospital we named Mama Yemo after your mother?"

He looked out over the rapids for a moment. "How much do you need?"

I told him.

He picked up the telephone and called the governor of the national bank. "Le Docteur Close will come to your office. Give him the money he needs to buy food for the hospital." He hung up and went back to his reading.

"Merci, Patron," I said, and left.

Tshibambi and Mahele had heard the heated exchange from the living room. "Everything all right?" they asked anxiously as I brushed past them.

"Just fine," I said. *"Pas de problème."*

I collected the money, and the jets buzzed his grandstand. It became more and more difficult to see the president. The handwriting was scrawled all over the wall.

A couple of months later, I fired the Zairian doctor in charge of the hospital morgue when I discovered that he was selling hundreds of placentas for the extraction of gonadotrophic hormone to an Italian pharmaceutical company for his own profit. Mobutu asked me to rehire the man, who was also the hospital coroner. I refused. Full hire-and-fire power had been one of the main conditions of my accepting Mobutu's request that I operate the defunct hospital in 1968. The ability to fire people who were not qualified for their jobs, but were simply "cousins" or "*petits frères*" of some authority figure linked in any way to the president, was of critical importance to the honest and effective staffing of a hospital. In government-operated institutions, especially in Third World hospitals, unqualified personnel are sometimes as many as 30 percent of the staff, creating an extra burden for qualified professionals and a useless drag on the budget. For a couple of weeks, Mobutu kept insisting that I rehire the coroner, mumbling something about the political importance of a small tribe. Eventually, the subject was dropped. The doctor kept his position and there was nothing I could do about it. He was fired in principle, but other factors kept him in his position.

I learned, years later, that Dr. Mbomba (the hospital coroner), Dr. Ilanga (my assistant with the army medical corps—such as it was), and Joseph Nsinga Udjuu were all from the same ethnic group, the Sakata from Lac Mai-Ndombe, a freshwater lake in western Congo. Nsinga had been a member of Mobutu's cabinet in various functions, but even more significant, Nsinga's father was one of Mobutu's practitioners of fetishism. No wonder I could do nothing about the entrepreneurial coroner. I would have been as lost in the dark forest of Congolese relationships and traditional bonds as I would have been in the disease-ridden shores of Mai-Ndombe—Black Water Lake.

The economic collapse of Congo/Zaire was caused by a series of events in the early 1970s. Some of these were international. The Arab oil embargo of 1973 hit the developing world harder than the West. Africa's wars of independence against Portugal closed down the railroads through Angola and Mozambique. Over 80 percent of Congo's revenue came from the sale of copper, and the railroad provided the most efficient means of exporting it from the mines. Furthermore, the value of copper and other strategic minerals hit bottom with the end of the Vietnam War. Added to critical decreases in revenue, Congo's imported consumer products rocketed out of reach of all but the wealthiest.

Other causes of the economic catastrophe were Mobutu's responsibility. In November of 1973, exploiting the Bakajika law that stipulated that everything on top and below the soil belonged to the state, he launched the national program of Zairianization. Goods and properties had to be transferred to Zaire's nationals. The symbolism was understandable, but the execution of the transfer from foreign owner to ill-prepared and corrupt cronies of Mobutu's regime further devastated the economy of a country already bankrupt. Even the shops in the interior owned by Portuguese, Greeks, and others who had lived in the country for generations were taken over by Zairian elite. The new owners promptly sold everything in sight and left behind the skeletons of ruined businesses. The effect on the population was immediate. Farmers of cotton, palm oil, rice, and other saleable produce had no reason to make money, because the bolts of cloth and earrings for their wives, the batteries for their transistor radios, cigarettes, matches, and thimblefuls of salt and spice had been sold off and were no longer available. People work for what they want, not for what they need. The failures were visible to the world and devastating to those who still hoped for sounder policies in Zaire. The fanciest grocery store in the capital, SARMA-Congo, was grabbed by Litho, Mobutu's "uncle." In a few weeks, the store's stock was reduced to little more than coarse soap, canned chickens in their yellow, liquid fat, and shelves of expensive wine like Chateau d'Yquem.

Mobutu had encouraged our opening of mother-child health centers (MCH) in some of the more densely populated slums of Kinshasa. The purpose of these centers was to provide midwife services for normal deliveries, to do well-baby checks, and to provide training in hygiene and nutrition for the mothers. One morning, I drove Mobutu to one of the MCHs to show him the delivery service and the nutrition training. When we arrived, a class was under way. We stood outside the room, within earshot of the teacher.

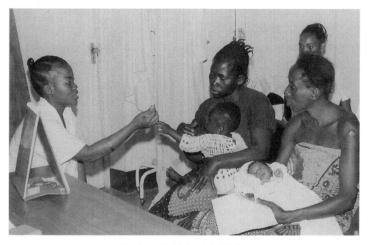

Mother-Child Health Clinic.

"You do not have to go to Litho's expensive grocery store to buy canned milk and fancy foods for your children. You need simply to follow the recipe I will give you, and your children will be healthy."

Mobutu whispered in my ear angrily, "Did you tell her to say that?"

"No, *Patron*. Everybody knows about Litho."

The Zairian woman was surrounded by new mothers and children. She demonstrated how to make a gruel, high in protein, using tiny fish sold by the kilo in the marketplace as well as grubs, insects, and soya seed. The kids loved it and would do well on it.

Litho was caught at the Swiss frontier driving a Rolls Royce, its trunk stuffed with foreign currency and gold ingots. Mobutu bailed him out. I told the president that Litho was his worst enemy and that nobody could understand why he didn't bring him to heel for all his lavish living and corruption. I even refused to be in the helicopter if Litho was also there. Mobutu agreed to that, but nothing else changed. Why? Because he was "family."

With a country in economic collapse, brutally expensive projects such as the Maluku Steel Mill (which never produced steel), the traffic cloverleaf in Limété (which was never completed), and the World Trade Center and the Voice of Zaire building (which were unfinished or became useless because of faulty design) were typical of prestige spending. Profiteers from the West made fortunes on these projects. The Inga-Shaba Power Line Project was controversial and expensive, but over time, Bisengimana and those who fought for the project were proven partly right: the Inga Dam now exports electricity to some of Zaire's neighbors.

After that meeting with Mobutu over money to feed the children, I was acutely aware of the change in his attitude. In his early days, he united a disparate country with four major languages, over 230 dialects, and unnatural borders within and at the periphery of this immense and complex country. His energy had been exhausting for those of us who traveled and worked with him. But his enthusiasm, his broad smile, his optimism, and his self-assurance had been stimulating and enjoyable. But by 1976, he had become a tired, morose, and lonely man. Slowly but surely he had surrounded himself with sycophants and profiteers. Was he beginning to feel trapped in the international web of intrigue and corruption, a web of his own spinning?

In the early seventies, three men close to the president told him the truth, good and bad. He listened to their reports, often without comment. The first was "BB," Bisengimana, the director of the president's bureau. The second was Colonel Omba, his intelligence chief. And the third was me. On many occasions, I gave him a piece of paper without heading or signature that said, "The problem is a, b, and c. The solution is x, y, z. See annex 1, 2, and 3 for details. Approved or unapproved?" I called the one-page memos "Eisenhower documents," because I read somewhere that Ike didn't like to read. "BB" resigned and died of hepatitis, Omba spent time in prison for knowing too much, and soon I would be moving to Wyoming.

Toward the end of 1974, when Mobutu turned 44, I persuaded him to take a break in Germany's Black Forest for serious rest and physical rehabilitation. Bookings were made at the famous Brenner's Park Hotel and Spa in Baden-Baden. With all the problems of the Arab oil embargo and the country's economic woes, and with fewer people that he could trust, he was exhausted, overweight, stressed out, and prickly. His usual good humor was in short supply. The specter of a stroke was never far away. I could travel with him, check him daily, and speak to him bluntly about diet and exercise. But talking to a man with one of the more impressive wine cellars in the world about drinking was a challenge I did not undertake. I knew his response: *"Et comment va madame?"* The plan had been for the president to relax in the spa, exercise, walk, and ride a bike in the forest.

During dinner with Mahele, who was still in charge of Mobutu's security detail, I expressed my frustration and anger that le Patron had spent all day cooped up in his suite with madame and her entourage of large women. Later, I was called up to the president's room. He was furious that I had criticized his program and his wife's entourage. He did not shout. His tone was flat and decisive, his emotion repressed. I was ordered to take the next train back to Brussels and return to Zaire. He told me that I could see him anytime if I had problems at the hospital, but that Dr. Amin Jazab, who had previously helped in the care of his mother, would be responsible for his care. I am sure that my criticism, given with much steam, was not constructive, to say the least. He was not only upset that I had criticized him but that I had done so to someone else. Mahele was devastated, but pointed out that he had his duty to perform. I congratulated him on his integrity and left.

I called Amin in Kinshasa and asked him if he could fly up and meet me in Brussels. He took the next plane to Europe.

The long train ride running along the Rhine was as peaceful as it was

Bill fixing Mahele's tie in happier times.

beautiful, and I had plenty of time to think. I hated being fired—leaving with my tail between my legs—but damn it, I was his doctor . . . or was I? I had become his flunky, trailing along doing what I didn't want to do. This episode was really the end. I had fought just as hard for him in the past to act sensibly about his blood pressure and overindulgences. One result had been the successful exercise program with a gymnast, followed by a swim and healthy food in Morocco. Both Vannotti and I had leaned on him heavily to take a break and get back in shape. That time it had worked well. And we had fun steaming ourselves in the hammam and then running to the pool and racing underwater. Those days were over.

The gorgeous Rhineland countryside fed my spirit: there was more to life than being on constant call to one man and having a radio hanging from my belt. After a while I was surprised that I felt more relieved than angry or put upon. I arrived in Brussels in time to meet Jazab at the airport, hand him my medical bag, and speed him on his way to the president. I thanked God for a colleague like Amin. I hadn't realized how heavy that bag had become until he took it.

Tine's and my commitment to help people remained firm, but in 1976, she saw clearly that our usefulness in Zaire had come to an end and that insecurity and even danger were in the air. She was also clear that her own time in Africa was over. After a severe and prolonged illness with hepatitis, her energy waned, and living in Kinshasa became a physical burden that, even with her extraordinary perseverance, was unacceptable. She would return home regardless of what I did. She wasn't fierce in her decision, just resolved and sincerely leaving my moves up to me.

Chapter 44

On the Way Home

I TOLD MOBUTU I would be leaving for a vacation in Wyoming in June, then return once more to hand over my responsibilities to others. When he learned I was taking my black lab Trooper with me, he knew my time in Africa was coming to a close. I would miss the earlier years working at the old Hôpital des Congolais taking care of Mobutu and his family. I had enjoyed the adventure of working with some of the better officers in the army, flying all over the country in an effort to improve the condition of a population at the mercy of venal politicians and ruthless soldiers. I would miss some of the earlier trips with the president until they became unbearably dull and repetitive. I would certainly miss what Mobutu could have become: a real father of the nation, listening to his people and the Ngbandi elders in his family. I would not miss the vulgar increase in his trappings of power, like his jungle palace in Gbadolite, when the capital was largely a stinking slum. A personal DC-10 and Concorde when he wanted it were criminal luxury when the roads, railways, and riverboats had become all but useless. He was like the man who pocketed money given to him for a road through his village. He used the money to buy a car, only to find no road to drive on.

On my way home to Wyoming in June 1976, I lay over in Geneva after an eight-hour flight from Kinshasa so that I could spend a day and a night with my old mentor, Professor Alfredo Vannotti. As the other passengers headed for the terminal, I went to the rear of the plane and waited for Trooper. Two baggage handlers came out of the hold carrying his cage and set it on the ramp. When Trooper saw me, he barked and his tail strummed on the bars. I let him out, and he looked up at me and smiled with his gray muzzle as he emptied his bladder against a lamp post. His gums were bleeding from efforts to chew his way through the bars. I was relieved to get him out of Zaire. Next to my wife and kids, he was my closest buddy.

We headed for baggage and customs. The other passengers had long since reached the terminal. Suddenly Trooper put on the brakes and deposited a sizable mound on the Swiss-clean floor. Nobody was around. The only paper I had was *Time* magazine. I covered the mess with it. Carter, Reagan, and Ford were on the cover. I meant no disrespect. At customs I said to the inspector, "I'm terribly sorry, but my dog pooped in the hall. We have just come in on an eight-hour flight from Africa."

"Never mind," he replied. "The Italians will clean it up."

He chalked my suitcase, we headed to a car rental desk, and finally were on our way to Valmont in a little Renault. There was no rush. It was a beautiful summer day, and Vannotti didn't expect us until after lunch. The Swiss countryside, neat and without litter, helped to restore order in my cluttered mind. Scarlet geraniums and variegated petunias in a riot of color grew in farmhouse window boxes and in brass pots hanging from roof beams. The lake shimmered in the distance, and the French side was ill defined in the morning haze.

I was hungry. The food on Air Zaire had been awful—leathery cold cuts and a chicken *mwambe* swimming in cold grease and palm oil. There had been plenty of warm beer pulled from a wooden crate dragged along the aisle by a sweating air hostess.

Just before Lausanne, I pulled off the main road, drove down to the lake, and stopped at a little restaurant with a terrace overlooking the water. It was early for lunch, and the place was empty. Trooper and I sat at a table under a grapevine trellis. Dogs are allowed everywhere in Switzerland. The waiter came, neat and efficient, a folded napkin hung over his left forearm.

"*Bonjour, monsieur. Ah, quel bon vieux chien*—What a good old dog," he exclaimed. Trooper gave the waiter a smile and lay down. I explained that we had just flown in from Africa and were very hungry. He handed me a menu and disappeared. A few minutes later he returned with a red enamel dog bowl with "*Le Chien*" written on the side. It was filled with a succulent hash of raw meat and cooked vegetables. Trooper wolfed down the food, crawled under the table and, with a contented sigh, went to sleep. I ordered Wiener schnitzel and a bottle of Swiss white wine.

After eating, I sat back and looked out across the lake to the distant peaks of the Dents du Midi. The edge of the red-and-white checkered tablecloth fluttered in the breeze. I ordered an espresso and a cognac. No need to rush now.

The last month had been frantic. I had to get away. I wanted to be with Tine and the kids at our ranch in Wyoming—our place to get off the world, our retreat, my escape. So many things whirled around in my head. So much needed to be done that couldn't be done in Zaire. How could the black bag I had carried to the Congo sixteen years ago have become such a burdensome load?

I reached under the table, found Troopie's head, and softly scratched behind his ear. The lake was glassy smooth, but occasional light breezes nudged patches of ruffled water gently ashore and rustled the vine leaves on the trellis. I tried to relax in the tranquility of the place. I couldn't remember *not* being on call. I couldn't remember being somewhere where people who had a right to demand my time and attention couldn't find me. Now, for once, no one knew where I was, and no radio was strapped to my hip to tell them. I had been on call for so many things. On call to the hospital and to my practice. On call to the president. On distant call to Tine and the kids. Too distant.

The waiter came and I paid the bill, with a good tip.

Trooper woke up and stretched.

"Come on, old dog, time to move on."

I drove through Vevey, along the lakeshore into Montreux, then up the steep, narrow road to Glion, and the clinic at Valmont. This institution was, and still is, old world and prestigious. People with means went there to recover their health and sometimes their perspective and humor.

The building hung on the side of the mountain with a view of the lake through the tops of pine trees. A bridge connected the third floor to the access road. I parked the car, opened the windows so Trooper had plenty of air, and walked in. The elevator took me slowly and sedately down to the first floor and the concierge. I introduced myself.

"Ah yes, doctor, the professor is waiting for you in his office."

I walked down the hall, opened the outer soundproof door, and knocked on the inner door. "*Oui*," resounded from inside, and I went in. Vannotti came from behind his desk with his arms outstretched. "*Cher ami*," he said as we embraced. "Sit down. How are you?"

He was in his early seventies but had looked the same for the last ten years. A black stethoscope stuck out of a pocket in his immaculate starched white coat.

"I'm fine," I answered. "Maybe a little weary."

He acknowledged this with a smile. "Sit down, please. We will have a little talk now, then I will finish these charts, and we can go for a walk." He settled behind his desk, his back to French doors that opened onto a balcony. I pulled up an antique chair. He folded his hands and waited for me to speak.

"I hated to leave, but I had to get away. It was impossible to keep the hospital going. Most of the children have *kwashi,* and I had to fight with the boss even to get local funds to buy the simplest foods in the market."

"How is the president?" asked the professor.

"Tired. Annoyed that I'm leaving." I paused. "He sends you his regards."

Vannotti acknowledged the thought with his hand. "Did you bring your old dog?" he asked.

"He's sleeping in the car."

"Give me half an hour to finish my work, and we'll go for a stroll on the mountain."

I walked back to the car, let Trooper out, and walked down the steps to the garden terrace. The day was clear and fresh. High up, a plume of cloud like a pennant on a mast marked the peak of the Rochers de Naye. The lake was deep blue, and the smell of pine sap filled the air. I sat on a bench, put my feet on the low granite wall, and looked through the trees to the sky. I thought of the last time I had seen Vannotti.

Bill with his mentor, Professor Vannotti of Lausanne, Switzerland.

The president was on an unofficial visit to Tunis. His fatigue, to which he would never admit, and some other medical signs were worrying me. I finally traced Vannotti to Milan, and he agreed to hop a plane to Tunis. I met him at the airport, and during the drive to the Hilton where the president was staying, I told him of my concerns.

As I parked the car, he said, "You must call me Alfred, not always *Monsieur le Professeur.*"

I replied, a bit embarrassed, "I couldn't do that. I wouldn't be comfortable calling you Alfred."

"It means much to me to have followed your work in Africa. And remember that I have known you for a long time, even back when you were trying to change people and the world at Caux. You call me Alfred, or I do not come again when you call."

"Well, if you insist, *Monsieur le . . .* I mean Alfred." We both laughed. He donned his Borsalino and followed me to the elevators and up to the presidential suite.

The visit went well, and my concerns proved to be of no major account. Vannotti encouraged the president to get some rest and exercise, and afterward I drove him back to the airport.

A hand on my shoulder awoke me. I got up and stretched the stiffness out of my limbs; Troopie was doing the same, with a big yawn.

"I fell asleep," I said to the professor. "What a peaceful place. So calm and well ordered. Why can't the Africans be so organized?"

"They are when they're allowed to be," he replied. "Let's drive up the mountain. We can walk and then have something to eat in the café."

We drove up the steep narrow road past Caux in Vannotti's Alfa Romeo. We climbed up to Les Avants. Leaving the car next to the café, we set out along a narrow dirt road that followed the mountain's convolutions. For a while neither of us spoke. Trooper walked ahead, his tail rotating with pleasure. Around the next corner we came to a bench overlooking the lake. We sat. I whistled for Trooper to come back.

"You have done a good job in Africa," said Vannotti. "Now it is time to return to your country, and your own people and family. You say you wish the Africans were organized as we are in Switzerland. Much of our organization is a product of our climate and our culture. Much of it is a thick crust overlying our humanity. We are terribly civilized and controlled, but we have as many suicides and alcoholics as most civilized countries. Did you see many suicides in Africa?"

"No," I replied. "Many people were killed during the rebellion. But that was war. Now children are dying for lack of decent food."

We were quiet. Then I continued, "Violence is different in Africa. In New York City, the violence we saw in the emergency room was more calculated. It was expected. No one got emotional about a floater, a jumper, or a murder. In Africa, when the police and army fought, or ethnic groups clashed and people were killed or wounded, crowds gathered outside the operating room crying and screaming in distress over the brutality. Civilized violence is calculated. Uncivilized violence is more emotional, more glandular."

Vannotti nodded his agreement. "I have two patients who want to kill each other, but not in the usual way with guns or knives." His English had a musical lilt, and kill became "keel."

"Each is the head of an international holding company. If one died, the other could easily appropriate the dead man's assets. Although they are what you Americans would call high livers—good cigars from Cuba, and the best wines and cognacs—they are both well educated, civilized gentlemen." He painted the picture with a flourish of his hand. "One has coronary artery disease and hypertension; the other, bleeding ulcers. Their maneuvers against each other's companies are sure to increase blood pressure in one and gastric acid in the other. I do the best I can to treat them, but someday one will die first and the other will win. *C'est comme ça,*" he said, raising his hands and eyebrows, and shrugging his shoulders in a salute to immutable fate.

He turned to me and, shaking his head with a smile, said, "*Beel,* you would go after them both. You would explain to each that he must not be so aggressive. You would fight to change their ways: no more cigars, no wine, no cognac. You would try to impose on them a regimen not even a monk could follow. You would try and remake them into what they are not—what they never could be. You want to cure *everybody.* You can't—*c'est la comédie humaine.* Sometimes it's funny, sometimes sad, and all you can do is listen carefully, sympathize, and go home. Maybe that is enough." He paused and we looked out over the trees to the lake.

Fight, impose, remake. He is so right, I thought to myself.

The breeze off the mountain set little dust devils dancing next to the bench. Trooper chased a squirrel up a tree, barking slowly and hoarsely like old dogs do. I felt lost and useless, like flotsam on a beach washed up after a storm at sea. I looked at Vannotti. He smiled and said, "As you used to say in Africa, '*Ça ira*—It will work out.'"

"I hope so," I said, and added, "we also used to say, '*Ça ira, peut-être*—It will work out, perhaps.'"

"Look," he went on, putting his hand on my shoulder, "you have done things *fantastiques* during your years in Africa. It has been *la grande aventure.*"

"None of it was planned. One thing just led to another," I retorted, feeling a little defensive.

"Of course, of course," he replied, laughing. "How

could it be planned? Adventure is never planned. It is marching through the door of opportunity into the unknown, with enthusiasm. You endured the storms and built up something *extraordinaire* in an impossible place."

"Probably too *extraordinaire*," I replied. "I think a lot of what we built will fall apart. The country's broke, and the profiteers in the hospital were starting to move in before I left."

"*Et alors*—So what? That is politics . . . another form of *la comédie humaine*. Now you must go to your mountains in Wyoming, look back, and look forward, and write. Write so people feel what you have felt, and so people will see what you have seen. And be with your family and, of course, your old dog."

I took a deep breath of that clear pine-scented air and my shoulders relaxed as I exhaled. I stood up and stretched my arms and body.

"Thanks," I said. "That's a good prescription. I'll do my best."

"And relax a little. Then you will do better," he said, with a smile.

I spent the night in one of the clinic's rooms, and the next morning, after saying good-bye to my much loved mentor, Trooper and I drove back to Geneva for the flight home to Wyoming.

Chapter 45

Once More into the Breach

LIKE MANY THINGS IN LIFE, my involvement in Zaire's first Ebola epidemic in 1976 was unplanned. I was in Wyoming when I received word that something unusual was killing people in the northern regions of Zaire. I decided to return to Africa immediately.

Arriving in Geneva, I found that the Air Zaire plane I was scheduled to board had been canceled. By a stroke of fate, I was given the last seat available in the economy section of a Swiss Air DC-10. I wedged myself between two passengers in the center section, resigned to the long, dull night flight to Kinshasa. My neighbors looked quite intellectual. One had wild gray hair and a beard to match, the other had neat black hair and beard.

As we took off, Black Beard leaned across me and said to Gray Beard, "Now that there's no way you can go back, let me tell you about Zaire." I found out quickly that they were both from the CDC—the Centers for Disease Control and Prevention in Atlanta.

We introduced ourselves. The gray-haired man was Karl Johnson, the head and founder of Special Pathogens and the Level Four, Maximum Containment Lab, at CDC. His colleague was Joel Breman, a senior epidemiologist.

I told them that I was on my final trip to Zaire to hand over many years of work to others, but that I was returning a little early because of reports of a mysterious disease in the north. Neither scientist had been to Zaire. Karl had never been to Africa. We crawled out of our seats and spent a good bit of the night in the galley talking over the situation.

We landed in Kinshasa at dawn. Karl and Joel were met by people from the U.S. embassy. I told Karl that if I could help in any way, he should let me know. My own people from the Presidential Medical Services whisked me through customs and into town. Two days later, Karl called.

"I've never been in such a fucked-up country!" he exclaimed.

He wanted help with French-English translation and with people in the government whose cooperation would be needed to deal with an epidemic in the rain forest more than six hundred miles from the capital. In short order, the team of international scientists headed by Karl appointed me head of logistics. Working in close collaboration with Minister of Health Dr. Martin Ngwete, we mobilized the personnel of the National Pharmaceutical Depot, which I ran along with the Mama Yemo Hospital.

The first outbreak of the African hemorrhagic fever that came to be known as Ebola occurred in a place called Yambuku, at a Catholic mission hospital deep in the equatorial forest. The hospital had little of the equipment we associate with modern medicine, but it did have syringes and needles, IV fluids and injectables. But with roads in disrepair and fuel lacking to run the generator, the syringes and needles were only sterilized properly once each morning. Throughout the rest of the day, they were swished out with a weak disinfectant that had no effect on viruses.

Thus, when a very sick man came to the clinic for a shot of antimalaria medicine, other patients who followed him were injected with the same syringe, and the sick man's virus spread. That man was Mabalo Lokela, who turned out to be the first Congolese victim of Ebola.

Karl Johnson, Joe McCormick, C. J. Peters, and many other scientists and virologists have written extensively on the research undertaken to identify various viral diseases, including Ebola. They are the experts in so-called emerging viruses. My interest over the years remained more focused on the human, political, and social dramas associated with these violent diseases. That interest was renewed in 1988 by my daughter Glenn, who saw in the story of the scientists a potential for a book or a movie. We traveled to Yambuku and met many of the people involved in the epidemic. Our efforts eventually became a book, *Ebola: Through the Eyes of the People,* published in 2002.

The Ebola epidemics are not controlled by modern medicine but rather by isolation of the sick, a traditional practice that tribal elders imposed in the face of any threat. Today, neither modern nor traditional medicine has provided a cure for Ebola. We still don't know where the virus hides between epidemics, even though some evidence is emerging regarding the role of bats as probable hosts of the agent.

Certainly Ebola is dramatic. Any disease with a mortality rate of 88 to 90 percent is dramatic. In Yambuku, a priest wiped sweat and blood-tinged tears from the face of a dying nun and then wiped the tears from his own eyes.

A nightly meeting of the scientific team dealing with the Ebola virus. (L-R) Guido Van der Groen, unidentified team member, Peter Piot, Pierre Sureau from the Pasteur Institute, Karl Johnson, Bill Close, Margaretha Isaacson from South Africa, and Joe McCormick with his back to the camera.

In September 1976 a field team was assembled in Yambuku to confirm serologically that the survival rate during the first Ebola epidemic was 15 percent. (L-R) Sister Mariette, Guido van der Groen, Stephan Pattyn, Peter Piot, Karl Johnson, Sister Genoveva, Sister Marcella, Malonga Miatudila (kneeling), unidentified Frenchman, unidentified Zairian, unidentified man, Mbuyi, Kintoki, Joe McCormick, and Joel Breman.

Drs. van der Groen, Pattyn, and Piot were from the Institute of Tropical Medicine in Antwerp. Drs. Johnson, Breman, and McCormick were from the Centers for Disease Control in Atlanta, Georgia. Dr. Miatudila was head of the Community Health Department at Mama Yemo Hospital. Mbuyi and Kintoki were from the Department of Internal Medicine at the University of Louvanium.

A week later he developed the shattering symptoms of the hemorrhagic fever. Seven days after that he was dead.

During the first outbreak of Ebola, some four hundred people perished. In 1994, in Kikwit, the epidemic killed some three hundred more. Yet, in reality, Ebola is nowhere near as serious a problem as other diseases, once controlled, but today explosive and pandemic: measles, drug-resistant malaria and tuberculosis, AIDS, sleeping sickness, and river blindness, not to mention malnutrition and diarrhea. Each of these will kill, in a single day, more people than have died from all the Ebola epidemics.

Chapter 46

"We Got Us a Doc!"

I STRUGGLED with the fly on my stiff blue jeans. Finally, after releasing my new belt buckle and starting from the top, I could peel the tin buttons out of their small button holes, and relief became possible. The door behind me opened and slammed shut. A cowboy in fringed chaps and an impeccable black Stetson stepped up to the other hole, unzipped, and peed, blowing his breath out in relief.

"Hi. You new here?" he asked. "Ain't seen you around before."

"I'm new. We bought a little ranch next to Round Mountain."

"Great. You aimin' to push cows?"

"No," I said sucking in my gut to button up. "I'm a doctor."

"Jeez, ya don't say." Zipping up, he barreled out the door, yelling, "Hey, you guys. We got us a doc!"

I rejoined Tine on the bleachers.

After the water truck dampened the soil in the arena, young riders carrying the American flag and the flag of Wyoming galloped in, followed by the rodeo queen and her attendants. More riders, carrying western state flags, galloped around the ring. We cheered with the crowd as they reined in their horses to form a line of state flags behind the Stars and Stripes and the Wyoming flag.

The cheering stopped. A horse stamped and shook his bridle. A child cried. A bull raked the bars of his pen with his horns. In the stillness, the air was heavy with the smell of dust and manure and the scent of sage. From the announcer's booth, a trumpeter started to play our national anthem and everyone stood. Men held their hats over their hearts. It was hard to keep away the tears. How long we'd been away!

Rodeos are rodeos. Men get tossed, cowgirls race around barrels at impossible angles, calves are roped and tied, steers are wrestled and slammed to the ground. The bulldogger loses his hat. Kids are peeled off the railings only to climb back up again. The young ride sedately between the pickups, the beer shack, and the sloppy joe trailer. The last event, the one that holds the crowd, the ambulance, and the doctor, features the bull riders.

After sixteen years in the Congo, Tine and I wanted to "get off the world." We picked the least populated county in the least populated state. Our plan was to relax, read, ride, maybe write, and spend time with the kids. But a few months after moving to Big Piney, I became immersed in a rural practice, twenty-four hours a day, seven days a week. I loved it, and frankly, after all those years of high-intensity work in Africa, I would have gone nuts sitting around pondering the past and wondering about the future. I kept in touch with my friends and colleagues in Zaire and some of them came to visit.

In 1978, two years after I left Congo/Zaire, a management team that had no real interest in patient care took over and profited personally at the expense of the patients. FOMECO lost its capacity to recruit and keep cadres with valid experience. Decent salaries were less and less available, and the conditions of work that had protected people from material worries were replaced by a national kleptocracy that had become endemic. A few Congolese doctors tried to counter this trend, but in vain. Such attempts cost some of them their jobs, and three Mama Yemo Hospital doctors were forced into exile to avoid attacks by those who were systematically pillaging the hospital. The quality of care hit bottom, but patients kept coming.

Between 1977 and 1979, Dr. Miatudila was the head of the community care department. During this time, Mobutu asked him to fly up to Gbadolite, where he had built a wide range of social infrastructures for the people of his mother's village, including a brand new modern hospital staffed by German medical specialists. Miat learned that in spite of the president's determination to help his people, his lack of sensitivity to local customs provoked grumbling instead of gratitude. The first problem was the airport, hacked out of the forest, to handle Concordes, C-130s, and other traffic from Kinshasa and Europe. The people complained that the noise of the airplanes scared away wild game, which was basic to their diet. Mobutu shipped in frozen beef and chickens. The people complained that the beef was tasteless and the chickens inedible cadavers.

The second problem Mobutu wanted solved was why people were reluctant to patronize the Gbadolite Hospital. Apparently, a steady stream of men and women continued to walk some eighty-five kilometers to the Loko Mission Hospital for their medical needs and, even more disturbing, to the old and decrepit government health center at Mobayi-Mbongo on the Ubangi River adjacent to the Central African Republic.

The nurses in Mobutu's new, modern hospital were too young, and none spoke Ngbandi. The patients resented having to speak Lingala and other foreign languages to health providers and to communicate with foreign physicians through interpreters, thus revealing their problems in public. Miat drove up to Banzyville and interviewed a male nurse in a tattered lab coat who was in charge of a decrepit dispensary filled with patients waiting for their fever medicine. The ancient nurse told Miat that in the Gbado Hospital, people with fever had blood drawn for a test and told to return the next day.

In his dispensary, he not only spoke their language, but treated fever with antimalarials and aspirin right away.

Miatudila then tackled the problem of the houses that Mobutu had built for the people of Gbadolite. These were modern, well-appointed homes with glass windows, allowing the occupants to see outside and, of course, to be seen inside. Cherishing their privacy, the occupants covered the windows with banana leaves. When the weather turned cold, fires were lit in the houses. Mobutu was furious. He chased the people out and told them to go and live in their traditional huts on the outskirts of town. But as was their custom, the Ngbandi had buried their dead next to their houses. To leave their departed relatives was not an easy option. Mobutu had Lingala-speaking people from Kinshasa and other outsiders move into the ancestral area, compounding the confusion and discontent.

Chapter 47
Concern from Afar

THE CHALLENGING WORK of a rural doc continued, while in Zaire the economic and political situation degenerated beyond disaster and despair—the medical crisis an incredible tragedy. Mobutu chose to be surrounded by rogues like General Kpama Baramoto, former defense minister, and Presidential Guard Commander General Etienne Nzimbi. These generals were said to be involved up to their necks in the exploitation of "blood diamonds" from Zaire to international markets. They protected the president in return for his blind eye. My heart ached for the people. I was frustrated that the U.S. government could do or would do nothing to change the situation.

In April of 1990, Mobutu announced that Zaire was entering a new era—the Third Republic. He had traveled around the country in an exercise of direct democracy or "popular consultation" and claimed that he had received 6,128 memoranda from the people, most of whom wanted to retain the single-party status of his government. With a real flair, he announced to the country that he had opted for political pluralism, establishing a system of three political parties and indicating to his critics that he was even more for democracy than his citizens. He assumed no responsibility for the country's problems, nor did he acknowledge that his "great initiative" was a reaction to pressures from Western creditors and many African states. Most importantly, he would serve as chief of state and, as such, would be above political parties, functioning as the final arbiter of last resort. *Plus ça change, plus c'est la même chose*—The more things change, the more they remain the same. He could have given Machiavelli lessons in a prince's retention of power.

In September of 1991, Zaire blew up again. The army, unpaid for months, looted and destroyed what little was left in Kinshasa. The population joined in the looting. Belgian and French troops flew to Brazzaville and crossed the river to evacuate foreigners. Mobutu huddled behind a few hundred troops at the core of the Division Speciale Présidentielle (DSP), his palace guard. Washington waffled, refusing to send a strong public message to Mobutu. Hank Cohen, assistant secretary of state for Africa, carried private letters from President Bush Sr. to Mobutu, apparently exhorting him to share power with a divided opposition. Mobutu never revealed the contents of these letters; he simply waved them in front of the press to show that his American counterpart had written to him. Two years later, Kinshasa was ravaged by another eruption of looting. Many believed that Mobutu staged these destructions to prove his point: *"Aprés moi, le déluge."* Apparently, Zaire's dictator wanted to put an ugly face on the democracy, which many, including the U.S. government, were promoting for the less developed countries in general and Zaire in particular.

In February 1992, I wrote a letter to the two senators who chaired the foreign affair's subcommittee on Africa, Senator Paul Simon and Senator Nancy Kassebaum:

> Five days ago somewhere between 40 and 69 people were shot dead by President Mobutu's troops in Kinshasa as they left church services and marched in a peaceful demonstration. They were demanding the resumption of the Sovereign National Conference. Those brutalized by Mr. Mobutu's army will not be encouraged by the pap offered by the Republican Administra-

tion in response to the killings. Washington's messages "deploring" his actions, or the actions of his troops, are as ineffective as ever. Mobutu continues to thumb his nose at the American administration and the world. White House proclamations in defense of human rights and support of democracy must ring hollow to the families of those killed and beaten by soldiers of Mr. Bush's friend Mobutu.

How much blood will have to flow before Washington dares to tell Mobutu that he no longer has our support? The Republican Administration seems oblivious or indifferent to the mounting bitterness toward the United States, expressed more and more openly by the people of Zaire and many in Europe. Questions about the relationship between Bush and Mobutu are being raised more frequently in the foreign press. Why is the administration apparently more frightened of Mobutu than are the thousands of Zairians who have the courage to face his guns?

The senators entered my letter into the Congressional Record. At least we tried.

Chapter 48
Court Jester

YEAR AFTER YEAR, the president sank into the folly of power. Mobutu, like Caligula, came to believe that he was above normal limitations in his behavior. Like the divines of ancient times, he allowed himself rare forms of incest. His psychological metamorphosis provoked great anxiety in his family circle.

In the early 1990s, the late Dr. Apanda, a member of Mobutu's entourage, revealed an episode in Mobutu's personal life:

Some of the oldest members of Mobutu's family on his mother's side traveled to Kawele. At sunset, Mobutu suggested they sit together on the veranda of his magnificent villa. One of the elders spoke.

Ngbandi sword.

"We initiated this family reunion because we are worried about your soul. Some of your behavior, which you seem to have acquired from the Bangala, is in no way compatible with the traditions of the Ngbandi, which we are and which you are. It is bad enough that you make children with the wives of your brothers and cousins. It is also bad enough that you sleep with other women related to your woman. We can understand all that. A goat can only graze next to the tree to which it is tied. But . . . how can you have sexual relations with a woman of your own blood? Mobutu, we think that—"

"Eh," roared Mobutu, "Eh, you there. Don't you know that you are speaking to a marshal?!"

"In Kinshasa and elsewhere," replied an old mama, "you are a marshal. Here you are Mobutu; you are a child of the village, our child."

Mobutu tightened his lips and struck the floor slowly and firmly with his traditional cane. No one spoke. The tension lasted ten seconds, maybe less. Then the marshal stretched his legs and stood. He pretended to brush dust from his sleeves and disappeared into his apartments.

The parents stared at each other for a moment, and then one of them said, "Mobutu is damned. There is nothing more we can do."

In many African societies, the chiefs included among their councillors an individual charged with playing a role similar to that of a jester in European courts. This individual had the right, even the duty, to reveal publicly everything to do with the chief and his assistants, including slander and scandal. The jester's declarations provoked wild laughter, which relieved tension both within and outside the chief's courtyard. Thanks to this special councilor, the chief heard it said regularly, "You may be a supreme chief, but you are not a God: you are still a mortal human being. Never forget it."

This system protected the leaders and their communities from the intoxication of power. However, from time to time, a chief refused to heed these messages of moderation and succumbed to a wicked use of power. In such a case, the community, through the Council of Sages, could lead an unworthy and dangerous chief to retire to the ancestral village. A poison was generally used to effect these voluntary departures to the above and beyond.

Mobutu had no one to act as his court jester after the deaths of his mother and his first wife. The handful of those who told him the truth, including me, were dead or absent.

Chapter 49
Hospital Revisited

"HERE HE IS, DOC. Took me three days to drag him out of the hayfield," said Wilma, stepping into the office ahead of her husband. "Tell him about your headaches, Tuffy."

He laughed. "It's no big deal, Doc. We're haying up at the Fredell place and I got struck by lightning."

Wilma cut in. "I was behind him in the truck. He slumped over the wheel guard and slid off the tractor."

"How long were you unconscious?" I asked.

"Not really unconscious, Doc. Just kinda dingy. You know, dizzy."

"Did it affect the metal valve in your aorta?"

"How?"

"Are you having any heart symptoms like you've had in the past?"

"No. Just a few headaches. It singed the top of my favorite cap."

The top of his head looked normal to me. "You're lucky. What are you taking for your headaches?"

"Nothing."

"I'll give you something that'll help."

"Tuffy" and Wilma, Big Piney, Wyoming, ranchers.

The telephone rang. Roxanna, who ran our answering service, said, "There's a guy holding for you on the line, Doc. I can't understand him. I think he's speaking French or something. I'll put him through."

I signaled Tuffy and Wilma to wait for a moment.

"*Dis, docteur, c'est moi, Kengo.*"

Kengo informed me that he had announced to the press that I was returning to Kinshasa to rebuild the emergency service and nine operating rooms at Mama Yemo Hospital.

I was shocked. "*Tu m'as mis dans la merde*—You put me in shit."

"What?"

"Sorry, *la merde* is a little strong, but I gather the hospital has gone to hell."

"That's why I want you back. We can't renovate the whole place, but we can start on the surgical department. I have allocated $2.5 million in an account over your signature to get the work done."

Prime Minister of Zaire, Kengo wa Dondo, 1994.

"Leon, I appreciate your trust. I have a patient with me. I'll call you back."

I turned to Wilma and Tuffy. "That was the prime minister of Zaire, an old friend and patient. He wants me to rebuild part of the two-thousand-bed hospital I renovated twenty years ago."

"You're not going to leave us, are you?" asked Wilma.

"No way. I did my thing in Africa. I told him I'd call him back."

That evening, Tine and I sat on the porch as the sun set and a light breeze off the mountains gently swept away the day. Kengo's request was a challenge, but we had built our home in a place we loved and I was comfortable in my skin as a rural doc.

"Do you think you'll go?" asked Tine.

"Do you think I should?"

"Do you think you can accomplish something in a

couple of weeks?"

Thirty years ago, in Switzerland, Tine had asked, "How long do you think you'll be away?" "Six weeks," I'd replied. Six weeks became sixteen years.

"I could get things started," I said tentatively. I had kept in touch with Dr. Miatudila, Kengo, and other Congolese friends. With Mobutu and his arch rival, Tshisekedi, facing off like two bulls pawing the ground over an emaciated cow called Zaire, the situation in the country was far worse than it had been at independence, over thirty years ago.

In August of 1994, the protocol officer from the prime minister's office met me at the plane at the Ndjili Airport and ushered me into the VIP lounge while my passport and suitcase were whisked through unique imbroglios of the Zaire customs and immigration services. Kengo and his wife welcomed me warmly to their home. Over breakfast, Leon sketched the dismal picture of his efforts to resurrect the infrastructure of the country so that the government could start to function. The big problem was Mobutu's continued interventions behind his back; he simply would not yield power. Kengo hoped that by investing in the rehabilitation of the hospital, or part of it, people would see that his government was serious about their well-being.

"After breakfast, we'll drive to my office where the press are waiting to interview you," said Kengo.

"I don't want to talk to the press. I haven't even seen the hospital yet or talked to the doctors. I don't have anything to say to them."

"You can say that you're glad to be back in Zaire and you're looking forward to the work."

We drove along tree-lined avenues where the elite had lived in the past. We dodged potholes and garbage. People walked without purpose or leaned against the walls of empty buildings in the gray, flat morning. The flame trees were skeletal, and some of the big mangos needed trimming. The rains would start in three months. Would they wash away the hopelessness brought on by the massacres in the east, massive unemployment, and the pervasive corruption that had become the hallmark of a survival culture?

I shook hands with the journalists and cameramen. I had traveled with some of them on Mobutu's state and private trips. We chatted and passed on memories with laughs. "*En tout cas, on a beaucoup souffert ensemble*—Anyway, say what you want, we suffered much together." Since most of them depended on the government for their jobs, thoughts about the present and the future remained unexpressed. Kengo told them I had accepted his invitation to renew Mama Yemo Hospital's department of surgery, and then invited questions.

An acquaintance, who worked for the national TV, said, "We are glad you've returned to Zaire. How is Madame Close and *les enfants*?"

"They are fine, thank you. But I must clarify a point. I have not returned to Zaire. I am here for a few days at the invitation of the prime minister to help initiate the renovation of the department of surgery at Mama Yemo Hospital."

"But you should stay like before."

"I have a busy practice in my own country. There are good Zairian doctors who can do the work."

They murmured and shook their heads. The reporters wanted details of the project, how long it would take, and how much it would cost.

I replied, "Let me be frank. My job is to *pesa ye ntonga dans le derrière*—give a shot in the behind—to those who will work for the people. I've just arrived. I'm meeting with the chief of surgery and will tour the hospital. Over the next few days we will consider what needs to be done.

Maybe we can meet again before I leave."

Kengo said, "I'm sure Dr. Close wants to get to work. Thank you."

Dr. Miatudila, who was in Zaire on home leave from the World Bank, and the hospital director welcomed me. The office was air conditioned and well appointed with heavy, ornate, ebony furniture and plush carpets. After a brief courtesy call, Miat and I excused ourselves to meet with Dr. Diabeno, the head of surgery, and make rounds with him. The director wanted to be sure that we would keep him up to date on plans and expenditures.

As we walked down the steps of the administration building, Miat said, "He's the last person we'd want to keep appraised of plans and money. He's sucked everything he can out of the hospital." Across the street from the administration building, an impressive display of plastic funeral wreaths were for sale.

As we approached the hospital entrance, Miat said, "You will be shocked when we go inside."

"I'm a big boy, Miat. Unshockable."

Listless, bedraggled people slouched around the open gate. People came and went as they pleased. The plaster ceiling of the walkway that connected the pavilions sagged with rot. We knocked on the door of Diabeno's small office. He unlocked it and welcomed us. He had been trained in urology twenty years before by Dr. Eischelmans, one of our American surgeons.

"I have to keep the door locked or everyone barges in," said Diabeno. He fiddled with the air conditioner, which sounded like a patient with phlegm in the bronchials. We sat on the two metal chairs and he leaned against the desk.

"I understand that everything we built and organized twenty years ago has been destroyed by neglect and corruption," I said.

"You go right to the point," said Diabeno. "We have a few good men who work around the clock."

Miat cut in, "As you taught us, Dr. Close."

"Dr. Eischelmans was like my father in urology," said Diabeno.

Miat added, "We should include Youmans, Johnson, and McPherson in surgery, Beheyt in internal medicine, Pauls in OB/GYN, Drinkaus and Davachi in pediatrics, and McCullough in community heath."

"The problem," said Diabeno, "is that today we have nothing to work with, and salaries average $1.50 a month: the price of two bottles of beer. We have no supplies like syringes, dressings, plaster, sutures; the list is endless. Patients must buy their own operating room supplies, anesthetic agents, and IVs from the local drugstores at inflated prices. One liter of dextrose and water costs 4,000 zaires, which is twice the monthly salary of a doctor. We have no sheets, and only a few beds have mattresses. Most of the surgical instruments have disappeared, so that we have one basket for everything. My cystoscope is missing several components." He paused, "I don't want to discourage you so soon after your arrival."

"You won't, although I may be disgusted."

Miat said, "Don't forget the hospital has received no funding from the government for the past ten years. They are owed huge amounts of money by the army, city hall, and other government services. The theoretical health budget is 2 percent of the theoretical national budget. World Bank studies have shown that, up until now, Zaire is the country in Africa that has done the least for its population."

"What a devastating statistic," I said. "It puts all the money and effort we spent twenty years ago into a pathetic perspective. Now we're supposed to start again?"

"That's right," replied Miat.

"Let's walk around," said Diabeno. "You'll see for

yourself."

We stepped out of his office and he locked the door. I noticed a two-storied concrete block structure with empty windows surrounded by bamboo scaffolding that looked in need of repair.

"What's that?" I asked, pointing to the building.

"That is a sad story. It's a monument to the corruption that rules the country," said Diabeno. "A few years ago an ambassador, a lady from Nigeria, gave $100,000 to build a new emergency facility. The money was entrusted to the director of the hospital and a man from the president's office. The building was started, but the money disappeared and the work was never completed."

We stepped into the orthopedic ward. Patients in metal beds, many with traction frames, filled both sides of the long ward that seemed to stretch to infinity. All the mosquito screens were torn and useless, the ceilings stained with rot. The Zairian habit of personal cleanliness gave way to the sweet, disturbing smell of purulent dressings and the acrid smell of sweaty sheets. The predominant odor came from the toilets, part of a sewage system that had been without emptying or maintenance for over ten years. The patients were polite and resigned. Many had a family member in attendance.

We walked through the "temporary" operating rooms built by Italian contractors hired by Kengo in 1990. The buildings were to cover the six months it would have taken to renovate the operating rooms that we had built twenty-seven years ago. The floor of the unit was destroyed from overuse and no foundations. The worst holes were filled with cement.

"Where's the sterilizer?" I asked.

Diabeno answered, "Part of a sterilizer in the gynecology operating room at the other end of the hospital is the only way anything can be sterilized in the whole hospital."

The emergency room was filthy, hot, and devoid of equipment. Two male nurses in blood-stained gowns showed us the few instruments they had to sew up minor wounds. One of them recognized Miat, wiped his hands on his lab coat and shook hands. "*Tu reviens, patron?*—You are coming back, boss?" he asked, hope written all over his face.

"*On verra*—We'll see," replied Miat. He was the director-general of Mama Yemo Hospital in 1980 and 1981. He had been quickly promoted, primarily to be demoted when his management was making it difficult for various powerful individuals to milk the two-thousand-bed hospital.

Diabeno led us into a bare room that functioned as a holding area for the ER and a post-op room for the temporary operating rooms. "Ten of these patients had intestinal perforations from typhoid. Only three of them have an IV going, and all they're getting is dextrose and water. Their families can't afford more. Over half of them will die from lack of preoperative and postoperative medications and fluids."

"What happened to the hospital pharmacy we supported?" I asked. "It used to produce balanced fluids."

"That was sold off a long time ago," replied Diabeno.

"Another serious problem is self-medication," said Miat. "Since many patients can't afford to see a doctor or come to the hospital, they buy a few pills and dose themselves inadequately, developing resistant strains of organisms. Any medicine can be bought in and outside the pharmacies, without a prescription, and the country is swamped by expired and fake medicines."

Shards of glass, filthy rags, a shattered OR lamp lying on its back, and rat shit by the kilo were all that was left of the operating rooms we had built and equipped with such care and pride in another age. Everything had been pulled out of the walls in central supply and the sterilizer

A statue of Mobutu's mother, Mama Yemo, on the grounds of the hospital.

room. I walked out ahead of the others so they couldn't see my anger.

They joined me at Mama Yemo's statue. There had been a time when she had gazed over a hospital worthy of her name. She must weep now, at night, when no one could see her.

Miat led us into Pavilion 7, which was like walking into a different world. "This pavilion is still for older children. You remember Madame Baudoux, the pediatrician?

"Yes. Her husband ran the X-ray department," I replied.

"With help from the Rotary Club and a mothers' club, she turned the pavilion into a quasi-independent unit with very strict standards of care and cleanliness. She trained Dr. Ndoko to take over when she left in the late seventies."

We walked down the central covered corridor past Pavilion 8 where, in the mid-1980s, Doctors Jonathan Mann, Kapita, Ngali, and others did the original research on the transmission of the AIDS virus into breast milk and through heterosexual intercourse.

In those days, the world considered AIDS to be a disease of the four H's: homosexuals, hemophiliacs, Haitians, and heroin addicts. Governments in and outside Africa were reluctant to deal with a disease that allegedly limited its hold on small and politically insignificant groups of outcasts. In June 1985, as evidence of the heterosexual spread of the disease surfaced, Minister of Health Mushobekwa and Dr. Miatudila, his technical adviser, met with

President Mobutu. Miatudila pleaded for the urgent initiation of public information and communication as essential measures to slow the spread of the disease. Mobutu was skeptical and apprehensive about the negative impact that the publicity would have on his country's reputation. He asked, "If AIDS is spread by normal sex between a man and a woman, why doesn't MBL have the infection?" MBL was one of the members of the party's central committee, and his sexual prowess was legendary.

"Your Excellency," Miat replied, "you may be forcing me to reveal medical information."

Mobutu nodded.

"*Citoyen President,* the fact is that MBL's machinery has ceased to work."

Mobutu laughed, but got the point. A few weeks later, he ordered the removal of all constraints dealing with AIDS. An aggressive multimedia campaign was launched against HIV. The immediate weapons included a song written by one of the top musicians in the country, Luambo Makiadi, nicknamed Franco, and his orchestra, O.K. Jazz. Franco laid out the rugged truth about AIDS, giving all citizens, male and female, warnings about multiple partners, prostitutes, and the need to use condoms. Nobody was exempt from his advice, including clergy, teachers, doctors, and parents. Franco's intervention, which was heard all over the city and most of the country, in all the bars large and small, on radio and television, had an immediate effect of exposing the taboos, making it possible to tackle the disease effectively and energetically. Unfortunately, politicians in the neighboring countries spread the false opinion that AIDS was only a "Congolese problem."

By May 1997, when Mobutu undertook his final trip to Morocco, the Congo was still keeping its HIV prevalence at 5 percent, the same level as in 1985. Mobutu deserves credit for this success, which clearly is unique in a region where prolonged states of denial had resulted in an explosive spread of the lethal infection in most countries. He also deserves credit for backing the findings and efforts of the scientific community and allowing forthright preventative measures in his country.

Word of our visit had spread. The midwives and assistants clapped and shook our hands. One middle-aged midwife stepped forward and took Miat's hand and kissed it. An older midwife recognized me, and with tears rolling down her cheeks, she told us that she walked four hours to come to work every day. She had been part of the team that delivered an average of 120 to 140 babies a day. Now in the labor room, only eleven beds out of thirty-four had mattresses.

For many months, the midwives had not been paid by the state, so the hospital did what it could to pay them, using the revenues that patients contributed as fees-for-services. I was shaken and moved. They remembered the time when they were transported by a hospital bus. These facts had been given to some outfit in the United States whose response was "Let's face it, the country has ceased to exist. The sooner the implosion, the better." As a nation-state, this might be true, but the glimmer of hope remained in some of those who still came to work in a vacuum. I turned to Miat and said, "Their hope must not be betrayed."

We visited the burn ward, which was supported by the Lions Club. Again, with minimal money, these two pavilions stood out from the rest of the hospital. The Zairian doctor in charge of the burn unit built a tile-lined soaking tub with his own hands. The mortality from burns dropped to 30 percent from 75 percent.

Diabeno emphasized, "These two units, within a hospital in the last stages of decay and neglect, demonstrate that with good management, a few outside resources, and tight control of money, people are willing and able to work, and their pavilions provide good medical care." We ended our visit in the building for infants, in the ward devoted to babies with lung abscesses secondary to measles or malaria. The ward was half empty because, even at Mama Yemo, where care was inexpensive, people could not afford the transport to the hospital. Even the doctors thumbed rides to work. One nurse was responsible for the whole ward. Suddenly, a mother shrieked and hugged her infant to her breasts. We followed the nurse to the crib and saw that the child was dead. The father pried the limp body from the woman's arms and glared at us. He strode out of the ward followed by his wife, sobbing uncontrollably. Pain would be added to pain. She would be blamed by her husband's family for the child's death.

Over the next few days, Miat, Diabeno, and I met with the half dozen doctors in the hospital and made plans for what was needed to renew the operating rooms and emergency services. We met over lunch or dinner in open-air restaurants among palm trees and exotic flowers and in a place that used to be a private club for Belgians. Our meetings were pleasant; the doctors ate well for a change.

Other meetings were more frustrating. For two days I waltzed between the minister of plans and the minister of finance to get the signatures necessary to make Kengo's pledge of $2.5 million available for the work he had asked me to do. I asked Kengo to give a lunch for the ministers and the acting governor of the national bank. We ate at the prime minister's official residence, and the papers were signed on direct orders given by Kengo.

That evening, I dined with Kengo and his wife in their beautifully appointed *paillote*. The telephone rang several times. It was Mobutu raising questions. He clearly wanted Kengo to recognize what power he had left.

Kengo's answers were clipped and incisive. On another call, Mobutu said that the suspended governor of the national bank had just been with him to announce that he had been invited to Washington by the World Bank. Kengo denied knowledge of this, but said that he would check on it and reply. I called a senior officer of the World Bank who was a friend of mine and Dr. Miatudila's. The facts were clear. Kengo phoned Mobutu and told him that the suspended governor had written to the World Bank seeking an invitation. The answer had been that he would be invited after certain conditions were met. Kengo hung up without further comment or courtesy. Mobutu needed to let the government proceed with the revisions that were critically necessary without interfering. At that point, Kengo was strong enough to face him down factually and legally. Real support from the West would have strengthened Kengo's hand.

The next morning, one of his men drove me to the airport, and I returned to Wyoming with a briefcase full of work.

Over the next few weeks, the funds were banked in Belgium and could only be disbursed over my signature. A barrier had to be established around the money. A lump sum of $2.5 million was a source of great temptation for the ministry of health, famous for exploiting government hospitals and personnel. I had learned that it was difficult for a local citizen to say no to another local citizen. A foreigner living in the mountains of Wyoming has no difficulty in saying no.

Dedicated people such as Dr. Diabeno and Dr. Nzamushe struggled with huge workloads and no support. These became the professional base of the second renovation of Mama Yemo Hospital. These men and women were doing extraordinary work with nothing and were also under considerable pressure from the minister of health and other government officials. Not only did the money have to be protected, but the staff was also provided with protection from outside influence. Dr. Miatudila and colleagues elaborated a new statute for the hospital that Kengo adopted and enforced.

As the nine major operating rooms and all the ancillary services associated with a huge surgical service were being rebuilt and reequipped, the personnel became increasingly effective and proud of their work. A donation of computers from California was sent to Zaire to help in the details of administration. After Kengo was replaced as prime minister, the ministry of health tried three times to regain control of the hospital. The attempts were resisted and defeated, the last one by an uprising of the hospital staff, which numbered over two thousand members.

Chapter 50
Final Visit,
December 28, 1996

TWO YEARS AND ANOTHER TRIP were needed to complete the work. Kengo and I drove straight to the hospital for the inaugural ceremony before members of the cabinet and a few ambassadors. The prime minister and I addressed the gathering briefly, then led the way on a tour of the new emergency and surgical services. I had hoped to see the president after the work at the hospital was completed, and as luck or fate would have it, he happened to be in Kinshasa for a couple of weeks.

I had phoned Professor Vannotti for news of Mobutu's health. The president had consulted with him and been referred to a specialist in Lausanne, where he had undergone surgery at the end of August for an aggressive cancer of the prostate. His recuperation in his villa, Roquebrune-Cap-Martin, in the south of France, was prolonged.

Mobutu flew back to Zaire on December 18. He walked down the stairs from the plane carefully, holding hands with Madame Bobi. Following the national anthem and welcoming ceremonies, the president stood in an open car for an hour and a half as he was driven through the city communes on the way to his residence. His reception varied from shouting, flag-waving groups to others standing silently. What could this sick man, who had been away so long, do to reunite the country, bankrupt and ravaged by a war in the east involving Rwanda, Burundi, the Hutus and Tutsis, and their local and foreign allies?

Arriving home, Mobutu spoke from the marble terrace where so many private meetings had unfolded over the thirty years of his reign as the man alone, the dictator over his one-party state and country. Those gathered on the lawn were elite loyalists who expected him to produce miracles and whose preoccupation was their own status and safety. Howard French of the *New York Times* stressed, and all present would surely remember, Mobutu's closing statement: "I cannot do everything alone by myself. I need your help and the help of God."

What irony! *L'homme seul,* Machiavelli's man alone, asking for help when he and his country were racing toward self-destruction.

Ten days after Mobutu's return, Kengo and I drove to the residence for lunch on the terrace. After a few minutes, Mobutu shuffled stiffly through the French doors and greeted us. I noticed that there were no people waiting in his living room.

I was shocked by his appearance. He had lost considerable weight. He sat down cautiously at the head of the table and waved us to our chairs. Madame Bobi and her son, Nzanga, walked up the terrace steps to shake hands and welcome us, then took their leave. Antoine, the butler, served a rosé champagne, followed, right away, by a delectable grilled chicken and plantains. Mobutu picked at the food. Kengo told him we had just come from visiting the new facilities at the hospital. The president forced a smile and shifted his weight from side to side in search of less pain. He called for one of his best bottles of wine, a Chateau Lafite from a good year, 1970, according to Kengo. We went through the ceremony of tasting and appreciation, and with a nod from the president, the butler poured this special offering. Everything seemed in slow motion. As in the past, he politely asked for news of Tine and the family and was delighted to hear that Glennie, *l'actrice,* was doing well and that Sandy, Tina, and Jessie were healthy and productive in their lives and work.

Since our meeting two years ago, Mobutu had clung to life as he had tried to cling to power. Kengo told me that any mention of his physical distress or approaching death would not be appreciated. After the meal, Antoine brought each of us blood-red plastic envelopes containing hand wipes. In gold, the national seal and *"République du Zaire—Présidence"* was printed on one side. The bright green flag of Zaire with its red torch was on the back. I admired it, and the president had the butler bring me a dozen.

What had happened to the gold-braided uniforms and the marshal's baton? Were the plastic envelopes adorned with the national emblem all that was left of his years in power? His physical suffering was awful to see. But did he agonize over the millions of his people who had died and the millions more who suffered from festering wounds, broken bodies, and the hollow, deep pain and inanition of hunger, AIDS, and so many other horrors now crushing his people? Or did he feel betrayed by the course of history, betrayed by his people? Like so many, he pointed his finger at others; he would remain blameless, unaccountable. *"Foti ya ngai te*—Not my fault" were the first words I heard from the Congolese in the operating room. If a syringe was broken, an instrument missing, anything wrong, a Congolese had to proclaim his innocence. Personal accountability was not high on the list of must-dos. The decorated plastic envelopes represented lost power; the folded, scented hand wipes washed away responsibility.

I said my adieux with a heavy heart, knowing that we would not meet again.

Chapter 51

Mahele's Assassination and Mobutu's Demise

KENGO'S DRIVER dropped me at the embassy residence. Ambassador Dan Simpson and his wife, Libby, had invited me to stay with them. I lay down in my room to try to sort out all that had happened. I thought of the handful of Zairian surgeons who operate and work under impossible conditions caring for thousands of patients. Miatudila had developed an administrative plan to end corruption in the hospital. Kengo approved the plan, and the new administrator had, as I had been given by Mobutu, full hire-and-fire authority.

I thought of the monumental challenges facing Kengo in his lonely struggle to rebuild the country's shattered infrastructure. Communications within Zaire were at a standstill, and the number of areas isolated from the rest of the country increased steadily. Roads were in gross disrepair, bridges collapsed, deep mud holes entrapped trucks for days on end. Most schools had ceased to function. Hospitals had become repositories for people dying of AIDS and all the killer epidemics like malaria, measles, tuberculosis, dysentery, and sleeping sickness, which had returned with a vengeance. Malnutrition and the wounds of violence had reached pandemic levels. What we were doing at the hospital was a first step in dealing with the catastrophe in health care throughout the country. Sound professionals, backed by accountable financial resources and expenditures, would have to lay aside rivalry and competition and remain focused on the care of the people.

I closed my eyes, and Mobutu's face appeared in pools of darkness. His eyes were infinitely tired, fixed on a void, empty of all emotion except profound sadness. His mouth was closed like a dead man's, with nothing more to say. During our last meeting, he had tried to smile but could only wince from the pain. His face haunted me; even his hair had lost its spring. I could do nothing to relieve his suffering nor the suffering of his people.

He had been the toast of Western capitals. They used him and he used them. Like the heads of many client states during the Cold War, Mobutu's ego had been polished to a high sheen, and the misery of his people mostly disregarded. Extravagant dictatorship provided a burr in the conscience of those who had supported him in the West, but nothing happened. President Bush Sr.'s White House considered it necessary to keep him on to control the army. From being an embarrassment, Mobutu became a pariah, and every howling high priest of righteousness, in the tradition of Margaret Tutwiler, the former voice of the State Department, jumped on the bandwagon with its fluttering banner proclaiming, "We deplore, we deplore, we deplore."

When he and his country's slide to self-destruction became irreversible, he declared to the press, "The people need me more than I need them." Surely bitterness added to his present suffering, knowing, as he did, that the people had little tolerance for weakness. Could the bitterness be fed by the perverse hope that *"après moi, le déluge*—after me, the deluge"?

I dozed as I waited for General Mahele. We had traveled all over the world together when, as a young officer, he'd been head of the president's security detail. On trips, and especially on the president's boat, he'd kept us all in good physical shape by leading us in strenuous exercises every morning. Educated by missionaries and trained in Israel as a paratrooper, Mahele combined professionalism with integrity and loyalty to his country.

A knock on the door brought me to my feet. Mahele had arrived. I hurried down the stairs to meet him. In his camouflage uniform and shining black paratrooper boots, he was a striking figure. I had forgotten how tall he was. We greeted each other warmly.

The president had appointed Mahele chief of staff of the army as well as minister of defense. He was popular with the troops because of his military record in combat and his concern over their living conditions. He was widely considered a soldier's general. At the time of our meeting, the two generals closest to Mobutu were Baramoto and Nzimbi. Mahele was caught between these ruthless men. Both were from the president's Ngbandi ethnic group and both fought exclusively for power and money. Mobutu Sese Seko, the nationalist, the Africanist, had shrunk to an appalling petty *tribaliste*.

We sat in the embassy living room sipping orange juice. He told me frankly that although he had the titles of chief of staff and minister of defense, he did not have the military power to enforce reforms. He would do the best that he could under the circumstances. I briefed him on our work in the hospital and told him that if there was some way I could help with the military part of medicine, he should let me know. Then we reminisced in the way men do with a certain longing for the past when faced with an uncertain future.

I discovered to my surprise, much later, that Mobutu had developed a profound dislike for Mahele. The president had been annoyed by Mahele's popularity with the troops, the population, and foreign chancelleries. After the September 1991 pillaging of the capital, Mahele had severely punished hundreds of soldiers caught in the act of looting. This courageous act had led to his "mutually agreed exile" to Bumba among the Mbuja, his fellow tribesmen. Mahele had been trained in France's military school, Saint-Cyr, and as the situation deteriorated in the army, the French pressured Mobutu to recall Mahele from his internal exile.

Over the next five months, Laurent Kabila led his rebel troops, mostly child soldiers called *kadogo*, officered by Rwandans, from eastern Zaire to the outskirts of Kinshasa. The rebels left in their wake thousands of Hutu refugees massacred and sometimes thrown into mass graves. Mobutu's soldiers were useless against the rebels and, as usual, killed, raped, and looted ordinary civilians fleeing from both sides. During this time, the American embassy established contact between Mahele and Kabila on a satellite telephone. All parties wanted to avoid a massive bloodbath when Kabila's rebels entered the capital. The aim was for a "soft landing," allowing the peaceful turnover of power in Kinshasa. Kabila's troops would enter the city without firing, and Mahele's troops would maintain order in the capital until a peaceful transfer of power could be made. Mahele's army would not resist the invaders. In addition, the one thing that the American Ambassadors Dan Simpson and Bill Richardson, President Clinton's personal envoy to Zaire, wanted to avoid was a "winner take all" situation. The understanding was that Mobutu would leave peacefully for reasons of health. Upon his departure, Monsignor Monsengwo, president of a transitional parliament, and Tshisekedi, who had been elected prime minister at the end of a long-running national conference, together with other senior Zairian politicians, would collaborate and facilitate a political transition. That was the plan. But Mobutu, still hoping that his palace guard, the DSP, would stand with him, refused to leave, and Tshisekedi, for his own reasons, also refused to collaborate with Monsengwo. The soft landing did, in fact, occur, not through collaboration, but simply due to the military and political void that suddenly became a reality. The winner did indeed take all.

Mobutu Sese Seko (president of Zaire), Nelson Mandela (president of South Africa), and Laurent Kabila (rebel chief) at a final meeting called by Mandela. The meeting was held aboard a South African navy ship on May 4, 1997. In spite of Mandela's statesmanship, the effort failed to produce compromise between Mobutu and Kabila.

On the morning of May 15, Mahele drove to Mobutu's house in the paratrooper camp. He told the president he did not have the means to prevent the takeover of the city by Kabila's forces and that the president's troops could not or would not protect him against the insurgents. Mahele delivered this message in the presence of Mobutu's family, including Madame Bobi and her two sons, Kongulu and Nzanga, the latter serving as Mobutu's public relations officer. The family was furious, focusing their anger on Mahele and calling him a traitor. Nzanga pleaded with the family to agree to fly out of Kinshasa to Gbadolite. That same day, in the afternoon, Mobutu, Madame Bobi, and some collaborators left Kinshasa for Gbadolite. The next day, Kabila's troops walked into the city along a railroad track.

An encoded list dated April 5, 1997, had been elaborated by Lieutenant Colonel A. Yangba, a DSP officer intimately linked to the president. On this list were officers and civilians opposed to Mobutu and his regime. Also, in a move worthy of Machiavelli at his worst, those who were pro-Mobutu and might profit from his death were also listed for elimination and had been so informed. The execution of all those on the list, for or against Mobutu, announced the deluge of Mobutu's disappearance.

Mahele drove to the DSP Binza camp to persuade them not to pull that trigger. Mahele, standing by his car, was shot in the head at point-blank range, execution style, probably by an officer in the antiterrorist battalion. Apparently the officer who fired the shot had been trained by the Israelis with technical help from the Americans. He fled across the river to Brazzaville and bragged about what he had done. Kongulu, who reportedly died later of AIDS, was accused of planning and ordering the killing of Mahele.

This killing in cold blood enraged many of the DSP soldiers loyal to Mahele, turning them against Mobutu and his family. The most angry were Mahele's Mbuja brothers, who considered his murder an act of revenge by the DSP Ngbandi troops loyal to Mobutu. Mobutu's house in the paratrooper camp was looted. Kongulu and more than one hundred members of his extended family fled across the river to Brazzaville in small boats. Mobutu sent his presidential jet down from Gbadolite to Brazzaville for Kongulu and the others. When the plane landed in Brazzaville, the crew under Commandant Kuyandila walked off.

With Mobutu in his private palace in Kawele, built on a hill overlooking Gbadolite a few kilometers away, Major Nzali, Mobutu's security officer, learned that a squad of DSP soldiers were on the move from their camp at Katakoli to kill Mobutu in his Kawele residence. Just before dawn, Mobutu and his family left his palace and commandeered a cargo plane that happened to be at the Gbadolite airport unloading arms and ammunition for the Angolan rebel Savimbi and his UNITA party. The pilot, a businessman from East Europe, managed to take off as the soldiers reached the airport and started shooting. The magazine *Jeune Afrique* reported that Mobutu declared, *"Vraiment c'est fini: même les miens tirent sur moi*—It's truly the end: even my own people shoot at me."

On May 17, Mobutu and some of his family landed in Togo, whose dictator, Eyadema, one of Mobutu's oldest friends, refused him sanctuary. In past years I had accompanied Mobutu on several private and official visits to Togo. Eyadema had modeled himself on Mobutu, who must have been crushed by the younger dictator's slap in the face.

Mobutu arrived in Morocco on May 23. A little over a month later, he was admitted to Avicennes Hospital in Rabat for emergency surgery.

On September 7, 1997, Mobutu died in agony —*l'homme seul*. In a published report, South African President Nelson Mandela, another African statesman who has been treated for prostate problems, said Mobutu had suffered incredibly at the end, commenting: "His former friends did not want to assist him. Those who helped him for thirty years and benefited from their association with him, during his last days on earth did not want to know him."

Epilogue

THE TRAGEDY OF MOBUTU, beyond his physical suffering, was the confirmation of his abandonment by all his family except for Madame Bobi and Nzanga. His whole life had been a struggle for acceptance, glorious acceptance. At first, with financial and political support from Washington, his personal ambitions seemed well on the way to fulfillment. Then, buying and selling loyalty, a soul-destroying thirst for power, and his ruthless crushing of any man who smeared his image led him down the road of self-defeat and the destruction of his country. His abandonment toward the end was complete and utterly shattering to him. All paths to acceptance, maybe even from his ancestors, were blocked.

Nelson Mandela of South Africa would have been a better mentor than Napoleon or Machiavelli. Had Mobutu stepped out of the political boxing ring, he could have become a trusted coach for younger, fresher fighters and, not only a true father of the Congolese nation, but also an African statesman.

It is probably easier for a doctor to be accepted if he is trusted and available than for a chief of state whose currency is power and whose survival depends on distrust. Tine and I are fortunate to have made Big Piney, Wyoming, our home in the Rocky Mountains, where I have practiced for the last twenty-nine years. So many of my patients have reminded me in their own undemonstrative ways that a commitment to caring for people and easing their suffering brings satisfaction and humility to the "Doc" and his wife. Tine is a happy expert at grandmothering, and now that this book is done, I will get better at grandfathering. At last, at the age of eighty-two, I can try and throw away the "Workaholic" badge and clip on a new one called "T-Pop" or "Grandpappy."

Before Christmas in 1984, I drove to Pinedale, Wyoming, to see Ira, a ninety-six-year-old resident of the Sublette County Retirement Center. A partial resection of his colon for an obstructive cancer a couple of years ago had gone well. He seemed quite at home at the retirement center and was a friend to most of the people. He had a room in the residential part of the building. He would die if he had to move beyond the metal doors to the nursing home. It seemed that the old folk in the residential area considered the day they moved through those doors "curtains." There was only one way people left the nursing home: when Coroner Bill Meyer arrived and pushed them out feet first.

Ira sat on the edge of his bed, head down, hands clasped on his knees, the oxygen machine purring away next to him. He didn't hear me come in. I sat beside him. The broad smile and twinkle in his bright blue eyes when he saw me were welcome signs. Last night, I'd been told by the head nurse that he rang his bell fourteen times. The aide that pulls night watch in the residential area checked on him each time. He didn't feel well—nothing in particular.

This morning he's not altogether with it. Pressure OK, nothing abnormal to see or feel when I examine him with as little fuss as possible. Maybe he's scared, or lonely, or has some inkling that his time to leave is coming. Who knows? Now he feels better.

"How's your morale, Ira?"

"What's that?"

"Are you happy? How do you feel?"

"OK."

"Ira, is Christmas a hard time for you?"

"Not particularly."

I really think that at ninety-six, things are just winding down for him. "I'm glad you're feeling better than you did last night. I'll keep in touch. You keep in touch too."

"Sure, Doc. Thanks a lot for coming over. I 'preciate it."

December 13, 1984: Around 3 A.M., one of the retirement center nurses called to say that Ira had died. I called Bill Meyer and Ira's son, Bob. Ira must have known that he was going to die. I was glad that I had seen him.

Twenty years later, Bob, now in his seventies, was on his way home from the hospital, dying of lung cancer. I waited with the family. The ambulance crew carried him upstairs to his bed facing a large TV. In the corner, where he could reach it, a small refrigerator held his one-a-day bottle of Bud Light. The crew lowered him gently onto his large soft bed. He saw me and smiled and raised his hand in greeting. I was so glad to be there as a friend and a doc.

"Those who continue to persevere"

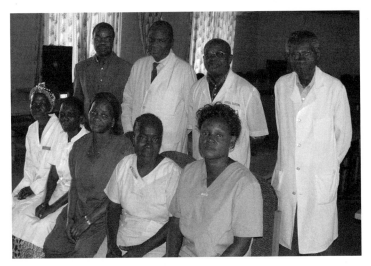

Standing (L-R): Dr. Miatudila, Class of 1971, has a long history of involvement with the Mama Yemo Hospital as a leader and administrative consultant. He retired from the World Bank in Washington, D.C., after fifteen years of service as an expert in medical administration. Dr. Diabeno, Class of 1973, Surgeon and Urologist, is hospital director. Dr. Ndoko, Class of 1972, Pediatrician. Dr. Kapita, Class of 1970, Cardiologist, Internal Medicine, pioneered, with Dr. Jonathan Mann of the World Health Organization, early research at the general hospital on the mother-child transmission of HIV-AIDS.

Sitting (L-R): Midwives Josephine Ntumba, Scholastique Ngungu, Marie-Claire Ipanga, Angele Kawita, and Marie Ikwasa.

(L-R) Dr. Kebana, Class of 2001, and Dr. Ntenda, Class of 2000, are being trained during rotating internships of eighteen months. The program is similar to the internships started by FOMECO in 1971. Dr. Muteba, Class of 1978, General Surgeon. Dr. Nzamushe, Class of 1971, Cardiovascular and General Surgeon. Those who were trained by expatriates in FOMECO are now training their own young colleagues.